Employer's Rights
Your Legal Handbook from Hiring to Termination and Everything in Between

Charles H. Fleischer
Attorney at Law

SPHINX® PUBLISHING
AN IMPRINT OF SOURCEBOOKS, INC.®
NAPERVILLE, ILLINOIS
www.SphinxLegal.com

First Edition, 2004

Published by: **Sphinx® Publishing, An Imprint of Sourcebooks, Inc.®**

<u>Naperville Office</u>
P.O. Box 4410
Naperville, Illinois 60567-4410
630-961-3900
Fax: 630-961-2168
www.sourcebooks.com
www.SphinxLegal.com

This publication is designed to provide accurate and authoritative information in regard to the subject matter covered. It is sold with the understanding that the publisher is not engaged in rendering legal, accounting, or other professional service. If legal advice or other expert assistance is required, the services of a competent professional person should be sought.
From a Declaration of Principles Jointly Adopted by a Committee of the American Bar Association and a Committee of Publishers and Associations

This product is not a substitute for legal advice.
Disclaimer required by Texas statutes.

Library of Congress Cataloging-in-Publication Data
Fleischer, Charles H.
  Employer's rights: your legal handbook from hiring to termination and everything in between / by Charles H. Fleischer.
      p. cm.
  Includes index.
  ISBN 1-57248-365-2 (alk. paper)
  1. Labor laws and legislation--United States. 2. Personnel management--United States. I. Title.

KF3319.8.B84 F58 2003
344.7301--dc22
                              2004022487

Printed and bound in the United States of America.

BG Paperback — 10 9 8 7 6 5 4 3 2 1

ACKNOWLEDGEMENTS

This book is an outgrowth of a series of lectures on employment law topics I had the pleasure of giving to the Greater Bethesda-Chevy Chase (Maryland) Chamber of Commerce. Once the basic lecture materials were prepared, I thought it would be easy to add a few chapters and pull together a book. It wasn't.

Many months later a book finally did emerge—thanks to invaluable assistance from my friends and colleagues at Oppenheimer, Fleischer & Quiggle. I am particularly indebted to Jim Quiggle for his patience in teaching me some of the intricacies of deferred compensation plans and federal pension law. Joe Oppenheimer not only guided me through the federal tax labyrinth, he exhibited more patience than Job while my book writing took the place of practicing law. Susan Leiter updated the tax calendar. Special thanks go to my agent, Susan Hall of Integrity Ink, LLC, who read the entire manuscript and helped greatly in making it readable. Without them, the book would have been woefully deficient.

But the real inspiration came from my wife Barbara. The publication of her first book on geriatric social work offered just the competitive challenge I needed to complete the project.

CONTENTS

State Requirements
Smoking
Ergonomics
Violence in the Workplace
Disaster Planning

Title VII of the Civil Rights Act
Protected Employers
Religious Discrimination under Title VII
Other Anti-Discrimination Laws
State and Local Prohibitions
Professional Codes of Ethics
Discrimination Based on Genetics
Contingent Workers
Former Employees
Record Keeping
Foreign Workers

Equal Pay Act
Pregnancy
Harassment, in General
Employer Liability for Harassment
Sexual Orientation
Other Issues

Exceptions
Benefit Plans
Proving Age Discrimination
Releases of ADEA Claims

ADA in Employment
Medical Examinations
Duty of Reasonable Accommodation
Reasonableness of Requested Accommodation
Effect of Remedial Measures
Accommodation and Seniority
Other Prohibited Conduct
Direct-Threat Defense

CHAPTER 23: EMPLOYER LIABILITY TO THIRD PARTIES 321

Vicarious Liability
Intentional Misconduct
Alcohol-Related Liability
Negligent Employment
References
Tortious Interference
Racketeer Influenced and Corrupt Organizations Act
Indemnity and Subrogation
Insider Trading

Conclusion

INTRODUCTION

EMPLOYERS BEWARE! Not too many years ago, managing employer-employee relations was relatively simple. Little more was required than meeting payroll and remembering to deposit withholding taxes on time. Since then, life has gotten infinitely more complicated and uncertain. Employment practices that easily passed muster yesterday now expose employers to substantial risk and expense. At the same time, employees have become more knowledgeable about their rights and much less bashful about exercising them.

It is easy to cite examples of practices that may once have been common, but now, depending on the circumstances, could give rise to civil lawsuits and even criminal prosecutions. Do any of these sound like good ideas?

- *I'll just call my staff independent contractors and avoid the hassles that come with employees.*
- *Bob worked overtime all day Saturday copying and stapling the proposal, so I'll give him a day off next week.*
- *Nancy quit on me in the middle of her project. There's no way I'm going to pay her for the two weeks' vacation she had coming.*
- *If I hire through a temp agency, I can tell them to send me men for the sales positions and women for the secretaries without having to worry about sex discrimination.*
- *Becky in Accounting has been dating her assistant. I hear they're having problems, but they're just going to have to work things out.*

• *The next person who gets his salary garnished is out of here!*

If any of these do strike a familiar chord, this book is for you!

Employment is, fundamentally, an *economic relationship*. The employer seeks an employee who will work competently and dependably in furtherance of the employer's business. The employee seeks regular work at reasonable compensation.

At the same time, the employment relationship is awash in powerful, psychodynamic currents. Employers, having risked their personal capital to keep their businesses afloat, may have unreasonable expectations of loyalty and devotion from their workforce. Employees, on the other hand, may feel at sea when subjected to seemingly arbitrary and unexplained decisions by their bosses. Both sides often define themselves and derive their sense of self-worth from the employment relationship—so stormy encounters can be devastating.

Employment is also a highly regulated relationship. Since employers have historically held far greater economic power than individual employees, federal and state governments have felt it necessary to intervene. As a result, employers do not have freedom to dictate (or even negotiate) many terms and conditions of employment. They must pay minimum wages and time-and-a-half for overtime. They must comply with detailed workplace safety standards. They must conform their employee benefit plans to complicated legal requirements. And they are forbidden from making employment decisions based on a whole host of prohibited criteria.

Employers are also easy targets for the imposition of requirements that otherwise have little to do with the employment relationship. In the income tax area, for example, employers enforce their employees' obligations to the IRS and to state taxing authorities by withholding an array of items from employee paychecks. Employers also finance government social policy embodied in workers' compensation and unemployment compensation laws. They even assist the government in tracking down welfare cheaters and parents who ignore their child support obligations.

This book is aimed at employers who are proving themselves successful at what they do, but who find themselves a bit bewildered by the employment problems that seem to arise with increasing frequency. The first few chapters explore the employment relationship primarily as it is affected by the common-law (the law we inherited from England) and by subsequent judicial decisions in this country. Most of the other chapters deal with federal and state statutes that bear directly on the employment relationship or that impose obligations on employers. The goal in each case is to present general principles, to highlight the hot issues, and to offer specific examples and suggestions to make the employer-employee relationship run more smoothly.

For readability, statutory and case citations have been omitted, no footnotes have been used, and wherever possible, technical legal terms have been avoided. Employment issues are often technical, however, so an extensive glossary has been included. Also included as an appendix is a table of federal employment-related statutes and regulations, along with a brief summary of their major provisions.

The employment relationship involves a wide range of complex issues, and is also subject to frequent change. Congress, state legislatures, federal and state regulatory agencies, and courts, at all levels, have a say in the relationship. Any one of those bodies can make illegal tomorrow what was thought to be perfectly legal today. It would be impossible, therefore, to write a fully comprehensive, *this-is-all-you'll-ever-need-to-know* treatise.

Reading this book will not make you an employment lawyer or a tax expert. You will not be competent to respond to an Equal Employment Opportunity Commission charge, to set up a pension plan, or to deal with a union organizing campaign. But you will gain a broad understanding of employer-employee relations, know where most of the dangers lurk, and be alert to situations where professional advice is needed.

While there is no substitute for familiarity with the intricacies of the employment relationship, we dare to offer, at the outset, three rules of conduct for employers. Adopt them now, follow them faithfully, and you will avoid many of the pitfalls discussed here.

ONE: *Treat your employees reasonably.* They are not indentured servants, nor are they part of your extended family. They usually respond best when treated like reasonable adults, and they may quit or (worse) sue, if they feel unfairly treated.

TWO: *Focus your personnel policies and decisions directly on accomplishing your business mission.* Leave your biases, prejudices, and social agendas at home.

THREE: *Keep detailed, current, written records of all personnel actions.* If it is not in writing, it didn't happen.

● ● ● ● ● ●

While every attempt has been made to provide accurate, authoritative, and current information regarding the subject matter covered, this book is for general information only and is not intended as legal or other professional advice. The reader should consult an attorney, accountant, or other appropriate professional regarding specific questions or problems. Neither the author nor the publisher is liable for any errors or omissions.

This book contains links to third-party websites. Website addresses are subject to frequent change and over time may no longer work as intended. Neither the author nor the publisher is responsible for the functioning or content of any third-party website.

–1–
THE EMPLOYMENT RELATIONSHIP

The employment relationship is a mutual, voluntary arrangement between two parties. The *employer*—which may be a corporation, some other form of entity, or an individual—voluntarily agrees to pay the employee in exchange for the employee's work. The employee—who is always an individual—voluntarily agrees to work for the employee in exchange for pay. The relationship is *voluntary* in the sense that the law will not force anyone to work for a particular employer.

Since the implementation of the *Thirteenth Amendment*, forced labor through use of physical restraints, threats of physical harm, or threats of legal action, is a federal crime. The prohibitions against forced labor also protect persons from compulsory work to pay off a debt—sometimes called *peonage* or *indentured servitude*.

In general, the employment relationship is voluntary from the employer's viewpoint as well, in that the employer usually has no obligation to employ anyone in particular, or anyone at all, for that matter. In limited circumstances, however, an employer can be forced to hire a particular individual where, for example, the employer rejected the individual's employment application for *discriminatory* or *anti-union reasons*. In addition, once an employment relationship is established, an employer can be forced to retain or re-hire a particular individual as a remedy for violating anti-discrimination or labor laws or if the employee has been in a *protected leave status*.

The employment relationship is often thought of as a *contract* between employer and employee. However, it usually does not take the form of a typical *mutual contract*, where each party makes a promise to the other, such as, *I promise to deliver goods to you next week if you promise to pay me $1,000 in 30 days*. Instead, the employment relationship is sometimes described as a *unilateral contract*, where only one party (the employer) makes a promise. *If you come work for me, I will pay you $10 per hour*. The employee usually does not promise to work. He or she just shows up, works, and becomes entitled to the promised pay. Circumstances where employer and employee enter into a mutual employment contract are discussed in more detail below.

EMPLOYEES, INDEPENDENT CONTRACTORS, AND AGENTS

The workforce an employer can retain to further his or her business can be broken down into three catagories—employees, independent contractors, and agents.

Employees

An *employee* is someone whose manner of work the employer has a *right to control*, even if the employer does not actually exercise that control. An entry-level file clerk will likely be subject to close, daily, or even hour-by-hour supervision and is therefore an employee. So, too, is the president of a large corporation, not because he or she is closely supervised, but because the corporation's board of directors has the *right* to control his or her work. This right to control is illustrated by the legal terms *master* and *servant* traditionally used to describe the employment relationship.

True employees (as distinguished from independent contractors) are sometimes known as *W-2 employees*, referring to the W-2 form issued to them for federal income tax purposes.

Other types of work relationships include *independent contractor* and *agent*. These relationships can overlap somewhat. Although the distinctions may seem technical, they are important because employers have *obligations* relating to their employees that they do not have for independent contractors. In addition, employees and agents can, through their actions, impose *legal liabilities* on the employer that mere independent contractors generally cannot.

Independent Contractors

An *independent contractor*, in contrast to an employee, is someone you engage to perform a certain task but whose manner of work you do *not* have a right to control. Good examples are professionals such as doctors, lawyers, or financial consultants, and trades persons such as electricians and plumbers. In each of these examples, the independent contractor's work is governed by professional standards, state and county codes, and the like, with which you are probably not familiar. Your lack of familiarity is precisely why you engage an independent contractor instead of doing the work yourself or having one of your employees do it.

> ## EMPLOYER TIP
>
> Whenever a worker's status as an independent contractor could reasonably be questioned, the safest course is to treat that worker as an employee.

Certainly you can tell your independent contractor what it is you want done, and you remain free to dismiss him or her if you do not like the work. But it is the *result* you are interested in. The manner in which that result is accomplished is up to the independent contractor and is not subject to your control.

Independent contractors are issued *1099 Forms* to report income for federal tax purposes, as opposed to *W-2 Forms* issued to employees.

Employers sometimes try to classify their workforce as independent contractors, rather than employees, in an effort to avoid being subject to some of the laws and regulations that apply to employees. In response, the various regulatory agencies, such as the *Internal Revenue Service (IRS)*, the *Department of Labor*, the *Equal Employment Opportunity Commission (EEOC)*, the *Occupational Safety and Health Administration (OSHA)*, state wage-and-hour

EMPLOYER TIP

Some workers are required by law to work under another's supervision. This is true, for example, in various health care professions. Even though the worker may otherwise qualify as an independent contractor, the duty to be supervised may convert the worker into an employee.

departments, workers' compensation and unemployment insurance administrators, have adopted complex tests to distinguish employees from independent contractors. These tests tend to be biased in favor of an employer-employee relationship—that is, in favor of finding that the person is covered by the particular law or regulation the agency is charged with enforcing. (Tax issues relating to independent contractors are discussed in Chapter 7.)

Agents

An *agent* is someone you authorize to make contracts for you and to bind you to those contracts. Employees can be agents, but employees do not automatically become agents—it depends on what, if any, additional authority you give them. For example, if you told your employee to take a computer to the shop and make arrangements to have it repaired, you have given your employee authority to act as your agent. When he or she signs a work order in your name, you as the principal, not the employee, will have to pay the repair bill.

Similarly, an independent contractor can be, but is not necessarily, an agent. When you engage a landscape architect to prepare a design for the grounds around your new office building, the architect is an independent contractor but not an agent. However, when you then authorize the architect to actually buy plantings, he or she becomes your agent as well, and has the power to obligate you to the nursery.

The consequences of misclassifying an employee or a group of employees as independent contractors can be expensive. For example, the employer might be held liable for income taxes that should have been withheld but were not, for wage-and-hour violations, for retroactive coverage under employee benefit plans, and for backpay, penalties, statutory damages, and interest.

STATUTORY EMPLOYEES AND NONEMPLOYEES

Some laws classify workers as employees or independent contractors regardless of the employer's right of control or lack of control over the manner in which the work is done.

The Internal Revenue Code has four categories of statutory employees:

- a delivery driver (other than one who delivers milk);
- a full-time life insurance agent;
- an individual who works at home on materials or goods supplied by the employer; and,
- a full-time salesperson who sells merchandise for resale or for use in the buyer's business operation.

The Internal Revenue Code also has two categories of statutory *nonemployees*:

- direct sellers of consumer products in the home or a place of business other than a permanent retail establishment and
- licensed real estate agents.

Workers' compensation statutes, unemployment insurance statutes, and other laws also state who does or does not qualify as an employee for purposes of the statute.

THE EMPLOYMENT *AT-WILL* DOCTRINE

Most employment is *at will*. That means there is no fixed period of time that the employment relationship is to last and either party is free to terminate the relationship at any time, with or without cause. In other words, the employer may fire, or the employee may quit, for any reason or for no reason at all.

In most states, there is a presumption that any particular employment relationship is at will. The presumption applies unless it is shown that employment for a specific period of time, such as two years, was intended. The fact that the employer and the employee intended the relationship to last a long time, or for an indefinite period, does not overcome the presumption of at-will employment, since in almost all cases the parties hope (at least at the outset) that the relationship will last a long time or indefinitely. An employer's promise of work *for as long as the job exists and for as long as you want it* is nothing more than indefinite, at-will employment. Even so-called *permanent employment* is still employment at will (although employers should not use the term *permanent* when intending only an at-will relationship).

An important corollary of the at-will doctrine has to do with the *implied covenant of good faith and fair dealing.* In most states, every contract is presumed to contain that implied covenant. Parties to the contract must act reasonably toward each other. However, the covenant is not implied in the normal at-will employment arrangement, since the covenant depends on the existence of an *employment contract with a definite term.* It follows, at least in theory, that an employer may treat at-will employees unreasonably and may fire them without cause. (Of course, it is seldom good practice to do so.)

A decision by the U.S. Court of Appeals for the Fourth Circuit involved the question whether an at-will employment relationship is *contractual* at all. The case was a *Section 1981* discrimination action, based on a Reconstruction-era federal statute that extends to all citizens the same right to *make and enforce contracts* as was previously enjoyed by *white citizens.* (See Chapter 14 for more on Section 1981.) The employer argued that since he had no contract with his at-will employee, he could discriminate against the employee without violating Section 1981. The court disagreed, ruling that an employment at will relationship is contractual, even though it is not a contract for a definite term.

Three very significant exceptions exist to the at-will doctrine:

◆ the contract exception (discussed in the next section);

◆ the abusive discharge exception (discussed in Chapter 4); and,

◆ the discrimination exception (covered in Chapters 14 through 17.

When one of these exceptions applies, discharging an at-will employee may result in a lawsuit, an award of money damages against the employer, or an order that the employer reinstate the employee.

EMPLOYMENT CONTRACTS

An *employment contract* is an agreement between the employer and the employee that the employment relationship will last for a fixed, definite period of time, or that the relationship can be terminated only for cause or under specified conditions. Employment contracts should be in writing, since *oral contracts* that cannot be performed within one year are generally unenforceable according to the *Statute of Frauds*. Even if an oral contract of employment is enforceable, it can give rise to misunderstandings and its provisions are difficult to prove.

In most cases, the employer will want to preserve an at-will employment relationship and avoid being bound by an employment contract or by any implied covenant of good faith and fair dealing. This would be true, for example, in the case of lower-level employees who can be replaced fairly easily. However, in a tight labor market where qualified employees are difficult to find, the employer may want the protection of an employment contract. The employer might also want contract protection for employees in whom costly training is being invested, for employees who have access to closely guarded company secrets, or for employees who have unusual or complicated compensation arrangements. Often these contracts will contain additional provisions for the employer's benefit, such as *noncompete* and *nonsolicitation* clauses. (see Chapter 19.)

An employee may want the security of a contract when, for example, the employee is resigning from a stable position to take a job with a start-up company, or when needing to make a costly move to the new employer's headquarters. Whether the employer gives a contract in those circumstances depends on the employee's bargaining power and worth to the new employer.

Overview of Contract Content

The contents of any particular employment contract will depend on the circumstances. A typical contract might include provisions dealing with:

- ◆ job description, including employee duties and authority;
- ◆ whether the position is exempt or nonexempt;
- ◆ beginning date and term of the contract and extensions;
- ◆ compensation arrangements;
- ◆ bonuses and stock options;
- ◆ health and other benefit plans;
- ◆ other fringe benefits—company car, expense account, etc.;
- ◆ exclusivity—no moonlighting, no conflicts-of-interest during term;
- ◆ vacation and sick leave arrangements;
- ◆ grounds for early termination—death, disability, etc;
- ◆ confidentiality and trade secrets;
- ◆ ownership of intellectual property—copyrightable and patentable works or inventions;
- ◆ noncompetition and nonsolicitation of customers and fellow employees after termination;
- ◆ liquidated damages for breach by employee;
- ◆ arbitration of disputes; and,
- ◆ indemnification.

Fill-in-the-blank contract forms are available from commercial publishers. Electronic forms can even be purchased or downloaded from the Internet. But if the employment relationship is important enough to justify a contract in the first place, it should be important enough to justify a consultation with employment counsel to be sure the contract fits the particular circumstances and conforms with local law.

ARBITRATION AGREEMENTS

Arbitration of disputes is often viewed as preferable to litigation. Arbitration is generally faster and cheaper, it involves only limited pretrial discovery, the proceedings take place in private, and the results are usually final and unappealable. Since arbitration means no jury trial, an employer who fears a runaway jury and a runaway damage award may view arbitration as a highly desirable alternative to litigation.

Both the *Federal Arbitration Act* (FAA) and its state counterparts say that a contract provision for resolution of future disputes by arbitration is valid and enforceable. The courts have gone so far as to rule that the law favors arbitration and that when a contract contains an arbitration clause, a presumption arises that all disputes relating to the contract must be arbitrated. These principles have been applied to labor disputes under *collective bargaining agreements* and to employment disputes in the securities industry, where arbitration clauses have been common for years.

For some time, there was a question whether an employee could be forced to submit *federal statutory* claims to arbitration. Suppose an employer routinely requires employees, as a condition of employment, to sign an agreement that subjects all future employment-related disputes to binding arbitration, including discrimination claims based on the various federal anti-discrimination statutes. Under the principle that statutory rights cannot be waived in advance, some federal courts initially ruled that an employee will not be bound by this agreement, made in advance of any dispute, to arbitrate claims based on federal anti-discrimination statutes.

The Supreme Court, which is the ultimate authority on questions of federal law, resolved the question in March 2001. In a decision involving an employee of an electronics store in California, the Court ruled that an agreement to arbitrate discrimination claims was valid and enforceable under the FAA. The Court went on to

> ## EMPLOYER TIP
>
> A pre-dispute arbitration agreement—that is, an agreement to arbitrate made at the outset of employment or at some other time before a dispute has arisen—should be distinguished from an agreement to arbitrate made after a dispute has arisen. Courts will almost always enforce a post-dispute arbitration agreement that is entered into knowingly and voluntarily.

praise arbitration agreements in employment, saying, *Arbitration agreements allow parties to avoid the costs of litigation, a benefit that may be of particular importance in employment litigation, which often involves smaller sums of money than disputes concerning commercial contracts.* In other words, even though resolving disputes is the very function of the courts, the process can be so expensive that everyone benefits by avoiding the courts and opting for arbitration instead.

The *Equal Employment Opportunity Commission (EEOC)*, which opposes binding arbitration of discrimination claims, will not stay its own hand in investigating or attempting to reconcile a discrimination charge just because the parties have entered into an arbitration agreement. In a recent case, an employee of a chain restaurant was fired from his short-order cook job when the restaurant learned he suffered from seizures. In response to the EEOC's suit for violations of the Americans with Disabilities Act, the restaurant argued that the employee had signed a pre-dispute arbitration agreement that barred the EEOC's suit. The Supreme Court upheld the EEOC's suit, saying the EEOC has an independent statutory right to pursue whatever remedies it feels appropriate that included not only injunctions against future violations, but also *victim-specific* relief such as reinstatement and backpay.

Arbitration may not always be cheaper than litigation. There are substantial filing fees just to initiate arbitration. Unless the arbitration agreement says otherwise, each party normally pays its own attorney's fees without any right to reimbursement.

Some employers have tried to shift the burden of arbitration costs to the employee, so that the employee ends up paying far more to arbitrate than he or she would to sue in court. Other employers have drafted arbitration agreements that are so one-sided in favor of the employer as to be fundamentally unfair to the employee. Decisions by a number of federal appellate courts have refused to enforce such agreements, ruling that any attempt to burden an employee with excessive costs or to give employers unfair procedural advantages is a denial of the employee's statutory rights.

The *American Arbitration Association*, which has its own set of rules for resolving employment disputes, will not arbitrate a dispute if the underlying agreement does not assure minimal standards of fairness to the employee. The AAA's procedural rules and guidelines for the various types of disputes it handles may be found at **www.adr.org.**

Another private organization, known as *JAMS* (formerly, Judicial Arbitration and Mediation Service), also handles employment matters. Its employment rules and procedures may be viewed at **www.jamsadr.com/employment_guide-2003.asp**.

Despite the Supreme Court's blessing, legal issues involved in pre-dispute arbitration agreements continue to develop, particularly in the area of fairness and cost-shifting. Following these steps should help to assure the validity of such agreements, but there can be no guarantees.

- The agreement should contain a *clear and unmistakable waiver* of the employee's right to go to court and should specify that arbitration is *final and binding.*
- The agreement should specifically identify the types of potential claims that the employer intends to submit to arbitration—claims under *Title VII*, the *ADA*, the *ADEA*, state human rights and fair employment practices acts, county and local non-discrimination laws, claims for abusive discharge, pay disputes, etc.
- The agreement should not burden the employee with costs significantly in excess of the costs he or she would incur in court.
- The agreement should be balanced, fair to both sides, and should not attempt to give the employer any procedural advantages.
- Finally, the agreement should not attempt to take away any of the employee's substantive statutory rights or to limit an employee's statutory remedies.

For companies that require employees to sign *noncompetition* or *nonsolicitation clauses*, an arbitration agreement should have an exception allowing the employer to go to court for an injunction to bar an employee's or former employee's violation of the clause.

Arbitration provisions should not be placed in the employee handbook, since the employee handbook is not intended to be a contract of employment. (The fact that an employer *has* an arbitration-of-disputes policy may be *mentioned* in the handbook.) For those employees with whom the employer has a formal contract of employment, the arbitration provision would be included there. For at-will employees, the employer should use a separate written document, dated and signed by the employee, that contains both the desired arbitration provision and a disclaimer to the effect that the arbitration provision is not a contract of employment and does not change the at-will status of the employee.

Breach of Contract

When employer and employee have agreed that the employment will last a fixed period of time, the courts will generally enforce such an agreement by awarding money damages for its breach. If the *employer* breaches, he or she may be liable not only for the compensation the employee would have earned, but also for fringe benefits such as health insurance, pension plan contributions, stock options, etc.

If the *employee* breaches, damages are more difficult to measure, since it is difficult to quantify just how a particular employee's performance would have affected future profitability. Absent a *liquidated damages* provision (a provision that specifies in advance the amount of damages to be recovered), the employer's claim might be limited to employment agency fees, employee relocation costs covered by the employer, and any license or similar fees paid by the employer on the employee's behalf.

EMPLOYER TIP

Even if no actual contract is found, the employer may be held liable for fraud or deceit when an employee is induced to accept work based on false or incomplete representations as to the conditions of employment.

Remember that a court will not order the employee back to work since such an order would violate the Constitution's involuntary servitude rule.

Even where no contract is intended, the employer's actions can inadvertently bind the employer to the same extent as if there were a signed, written agreement. Some courts have found, for example, that the provisions of an *employee handbook* amount to an employment contract, even though no contract was actually intended. Even the wording of a simple employment letter can create a contract if it implies that a specific time period is contemplated. Consider this letter:

> *We are pleased to offer you the position of Sales Manager beginning January 1. Your base salary will be $35,000 per year, increasing to $40,000 your second year and $45,000 your third year. You will also earn an override commission of 2½% on all sales.*
>
> *We have already made definite plans to expand our market into the southeastern states over the next three years. By the end of the third year, sales should reach $1.5 million, which translates to a commission to you of $37,500. We are counting on you to take the lead in these expansion plans and we have every confidence that, with you at the helm of our sales department, we will reach our goal.*

While the letter does not exactly promise a three-year arrangement, it certainly implies that the Sales Manager should expect to stay that long. Couple that with the Sales Manager's own testimony that he was indeed promised three years and the employer might find himself bound to such a contract.

BUSINESS OWNERS' EMPLOYMENT STATUS

Business can be conducted in a variety of forms, from the sole proprietorship to the publicly-held, multi-national *corporation*. In between are general partnerships; small or close corporations that have elected S status for federal income tax purposes (S corps); *lim-*

ited liability partnerships (LLPs); limited liability companies (LLCs); and *professional corporations (PCs).*

The right choice of business entity goes well beyond the scope of this book. This section is concerned with the status of business owners who also work for the entity they own. Are they considered employees of the entity? What liability do they have for entity obligations or the negligence of other employees? Can they participate in benefits available to employees? The answers depend on the specific type of entity involved and on certain tax elections available to those entities.

Sole Proprietorships

A *sole proprietorship* is a business owned by a single individual in his or her individual name. While a sole proprietor can *have* employees, he or she is considered *self-employed* and can never *be* an employee of the business. Sole proprietors report their business income and expenses on Schedule C of *Form 1040* for federal income tax purposes.

Sole proprietors are personally liable for their own negligence and, as employers, they are *vicariously liable* for the work-related negligence of their employees. They are also *personally liable* for the business' obligations, such as wages, lease payments, business loans, and vendor invoices. (For liability reasons, a sole proprietorship is usually not a recommended form for doing business.)

General Partnerships

A *general partnership* is a group of individuals who share profits and losses of the partnership's business. Partnerships are treated as separate entities for some purposes and as *pass-through* entities for other purposes. For example, a partnership can have employees (other than the partners themselves) and file its own income tax returns. However, partnerships generally do not pay any income tax. Instead, any net income or loss shown on the partnership return is allocated to the partners according to the partnership agreement. The partners pay tax on their allocated share (as shown on *Form K-1* that the partnership issues to them), whether or not net income has actually been distributed to them in cash. The partners themselves are considered to be self-employed.

Partners are personally liable for partnership obligations, just like sole proprietors. Worse, each partner is considered the *agent* of each other partner and is personally liable for the negligence and contractual obligations of each partner. (Think of a partner as a sole proprietor with multiple personalities.) This is the main reason for the popularity of S corps and, more recently, LLPs and LLCs.

S Corporations

An *S corp* is just like any other corporation formed under state law, but it has elected S status for federal income tax purposes. (The S refers to the Internal Revenue Code subchapter that permits the election.) As a result, it is treated much like a partnership for federal income tax purposes, yet it retains the limited liability features of a corporation. An owner of an S corp is considered self-employed and gets a K-1, just like a partner in a partnership. However, there is no personal liability for corporate obligations or for the negligence of other employees or co-owners. Because they have characteristics of both corporations and partnerships, S corps (along with LLPs and LLCs) are sometimes called *hybrids*.

S corp status is available only to small business corporations with one class of stock and with fewer than 75 shareholders. Only individuals, decedent's estates, and some types of trusts can be shareholders. Partnerships and other corporations cannot own stock in an S corp.

Limited Liability Partnerships and
Limited Liability Companies

Owners of LLPs (who are called *partners*) and owners of LLCs (who are called *members*) are the equivalent of partners in a general partnership for tax purposes. Therefore, they are normally considered self-employed and they get year-end K-1 forms, showing their taxable shares of LLP or LLC profits. However, LLPs and LLCs (or any other entity treated as a partnership under state law) may take advantage of the IRS's *check-the-box* rule and elect to be taxed as corporations. Worker-owners would then be treated as employees, just as with any other corporation.

Regardless of an LLP's or LLC's status for tax purposes, its partners or members have no personal liability for obligations of the LLP or LLC or for the negligence of other partners, members, or employees.

Professional Corporations

Traditionally, professionals like doctors, lawyers, accountants, etc., were only permitted to practice as sole proprietors or as partnerships. The fear was that if they practiced in corporate form their professional judgment would be compromised by being subjected to the wishes of a corporate board of directors. At the same time, however, federal income tax law (particularly regarding pension plans) strongly favored corporations over partnerships. So professionals brought pressure on state legislators and licensing boards to allow them to incorporate. The result was the *professional corporation* (PC).

PCs are in every respect true corporations under state law. An owner who works for the PC is usually classified as an employee and receives a *W-2* at year-end, just like employees of other corporations. (PCs can elect S corp status, in which case owners are treated as self-employed for federal tax purposes.) However, only licensed members of the particular profession for which the PC was organized can be shareholders, directors, and officers.

> **EMPLOYER TIP**
>
> Depending on a variety of factors, owners of a professional corporation may or may not be counted as employees for federal anti-discrimination law purposes.

Professionals who work for a PC are *personally liable* to their clients for *professional negligence*, regardless of their status as employees for other purposes. But the good news is that they are not personally liable for the negligence of their fellow professionals—a liability they would have if they had organized in partnership form.

C Corporations

Large businesses have little choice in their type of entity. To participate effectively in capital markets they must organize in corporate form. And because they have a broad shareholder base, and perhaps several classes of stock, they cannot qualify as S corps under the Internal Revenue Code. C corp shareholders may work for the corporation but they have no special status as shareholder-employees. Both the president who owns 10,000 shares and the janitor who owns ten shares get *W-2* forms, and neither is liable for *corporate obligations* or the negligence of fellow employees.

> ## EMPLOYER TIP
>
> Although sole proprietors and partners are considered self-employed, many workers' compensation statutes allow them to *opt in* and obtain coverage. Conversely, while members of LLCs and corporate officers are covered by workers' comp statutes, they are often permitted to opt out of coverage. (Workers' compensation insurance is discussed in Chapter 11.)

EMPLOYMENT PRACTICES LIABILITY INSURANCE

Most standard premises liability insurance policies or *comprehensive general liability (CGL) insurance* policies have exclusion for claims arising out of employment matters. That means that if you are sued for abusive discharge, for race or sex discrimination, or for employment-related defamation, your insurance carrier will not provide a defense attorney and it will not pay any judgment against you. Unless, that is, you have *Employment Practices Liability (EPL)* insurance.

A number of companies offer coverage that picks up where the usual exclusion leaves off. However, the coverage is likely to be expensive. It may also be difficult to get.

As with other forms of non-mandatory insurance, whether you should have EPL insurance really depends on how *risk adverse* you are (how much risk you are willing to carry yourself) and what you can afford. It is probably a good idea at least to discuss EPL insurance with your insurance broker to find out whether it is available and at what cost. Even if you eventually decide not to buy coverage, the process of looking into it may highlight shortcomings in your employment practices.

If you do decide to buy EPL insurance, make certain you understand and comply with the policy's notice requirements. A policy issued to one unfortunate Missouri company required *immediate* notice of a claim or lawsuit. When the company was sued for sexual harassment, it decided to handle the matter itself. It lost at trial; took an appeal; and, settled the case while the appeal was pending. Only then did it notify its insurance carrier. The carrier denied coverage and the Eighth Circuit Court of Appeals agreed, ruling that late notice barred any right of recovery under the policy.

–2–

THE HIRING PROCESS

Employers and employees have numerous interactions during the employment relationship. While any of these interactions can give rise to liability, three stand out as particularly critical:

1. hiring;
2. evaluating; and,
3. terminating.

This chapter explores hiring, Chapter 3 discusses evaluation performance, and Chapter 4 discusses terminations.

STEPS IN THE HIRING PROCESS

The hiring process has one purpose—to exchange enough information so that the parties can make an informed decision about whether to enter into an employment relationship. Good hiring practice involves the collection of appropriate information untainted by information that should not be the basis for a hiring decision. (Discrimination is discussed in Chapters 14, 15, 16, and 17.) The hiring procedure usually involves the following steps.

Job Description

In order to focus on job qualifications, the employer should first prepare a clear, written description of the job being offered. The description should include at least the following:

- *essential functions* of the job (the critical functions that go to the heart of the job and that the person holding the job must, unquestionably, be able to do);

- *less critical functions* that the employee may be called upon to perform from time to time or that could be done by others if necessary;
- *special skills required*, such as ability to operate complex equipment;
- *special education, licenses* or *certificates* required;
- *title* or *position* of the person to whom the employee reports;
- *number and classification of persons who report* to the employee;
- whether the employee is *exempt* or *non-exempt* under the Fair Labor Standards Act; and,
- *date the description was prepared* or most recently revised.

The job description should be prepared *before* the job is advertised and *before* any candidates are considered.

EMPLOYER TIP

Use of only a single method for recruiting unduly restricts the candidate pool and discourages workplace diversity. Word-of-mouth recruiting, for example, has been attacked by the EEOC as discriminatory.

Advertising the Opening

Any want ads you run or notices you post should describe the job being offered, not the person you think you are looking for. Expressions such as *recent graduate* or even *energetic person* could provide evidence of age discrimination if the position is filled by a younger candidate after an older candidate has been turned down. Expressions that indicate a gender preference such as *gal Friday* or *waitress*, for example, should also be avoided.

Internet Recruiting

Advertising job openings via the Internet is a convenient, relatively inexpensive way to attract resumés—and that's just the problem. An employer can be overwhelmed with the number of responses and lack sufficient staff time to screen them effectively. Screening software, while effective, may inadvertently discriminate if the wrong key words are used to do the screening. Employers who limit their recruitment to this medium should also be alert to possible disability discrimination claims if their website lacks accessibility features.

Application

A written application form should be developed for initial screening purposes. The application form should obviously not ask for information that the employer is prohibited from considering as part of the hiring process. Some seemingly innocuous inquiries can also cause trouble. For example, the applicant should not be asked to attach a photograph. Age and/or birthdate questions should be saved until after the applicant has been hired (although for child labor purposes, the employer should ask whether the applicant is at least 18). Similarly, immigration status questions should be saved for later and the application should be limited to the question, *Are you legally eligible to work in the United States?* Even a question about who to contact in an emergency should be avoided in the initial application, since it could reveal marital status or family information not pertinent to the hiring process.

Interview

Interviews should be conducted by experienced personnel using a standard written interview form. The interview form should be limited to questions or topics directly relevant to job performance and the interviewer should stick to the form, noting the applicant's responses on the form itself. By having and following a standard written form, the employer can more easily show that no inquires about prohibited matters were made, and that no particular applicant was singled out for special questioning.

It is difficult to get a feel for an applicant's personality and communications skills if all that is asked are yes/no questions, so interviewers naturally like to ask open-ended questions such as *Why do you want to work here?* or *Tell me what you like and don't like about your current job*. There are risks to open-ended questions, however, particularly when they are not strictly job-related.

Another common pitfall in the hiring process is *family status.* Suppose an interviewer asks, *Do you have any family responsibilities that could keep you from getting to the office?* The applicant responds, *I'm a single parent and my son has special needs, but I have day care arrangements that work pretty well.* Later, on checking with the applicant's previous employer, the interviewer learns of serious attendance and tardiness problems. If the applicant is rejected, the employer is open to charges of violating the Americans with Disabilities Act or other anti-discrimination laws, as it is not the employer's right to guess that, for family reasons, a particular candidate may be unable to get to work on time each day.

An employer may not ask, *Are you disabled?* or, *Do you have any medical conditions that could interfere with your performance?* However, an employer may say, *Can you do this job?*—provided the question is asked of every applicant and not just those who may appear to have disabilities.

Background Checks

Once you have a short list of candidates, or have tentatively chosen a single candidate, it is time for background checking. This could include, as appropriate, calls to references and prior employers, ordering a consumer report, ordering a criminal convictions check, and obtaining a copy of the candidate's driving record. It may even include a drug test. Background checking will *not* include a lie detector test, and until you have actually made a conditional offer to the candidate, it will not include a medical exam.

> **EMPLOYER TIP**
>
> Special notice and disclosure requirements apply to credit reports and background checks.

Offer

When you have finally identified a single candidate and background checks have been completed and are satisfactory, the next step is to make an offer. A *written* offer is recommended to avoid any misunderstandings and reduce the possibility of disputes down the road.

For at-will employees, the offer will usually be in the form of a simple letter. The following is an example of a written offer letter:

We are pleased to offer you the position of Senior Programmer at a starting salary of $62,000 per year, beginning March 1, 2004. This offer is subject to your furnishing sufficient evidence that you are eligible to work in the United States, and to a satisfactory medical exam at the company's expense [if applicable].

Vacation and sick leave policies, benefit plans and other Company rules and policies are explained in our Employee Handbook, a copy of which will be given to you on your start date. You are expected to read and be familiar with the Employee Handbook.

This letter is not intended to be a contract of employment. You will be an at-will employee of the Company, meaning that either you or the Company can terminate the employment relationship at any time for any reason, with or without good cause.

If you accept this offer, please sign and return the enclosed copy of this letter no later than _____.

You should report to _____ at 8:30 a.m. on your first day of work to complete the hiring process.

Very truly yours,
ABC COMPANY
By _____
President

> *I accept this offer of employment:*
> *Signature:* _____
> *Date:* _____

NEW EMPLOYEE REGULATIONS

The following steps should be taken when the employee actually starts to work:

◆ obtain evidence of the employee's eligibility to work in the U.S. and complete *Form I-9;*

- administer a medical exam if desired (requirements for medical exams are covered in Chapter 17);
- have the employee complete IRS *Form W-4* and the appropriate state counterpart (see Chapter 7);
- obtain any additional personal information not given on the application, such as birthdate, emergency contact, etc.;
- collect information as to the employee's race, sex, and national origin if required to file *Form EEO-1* (see Chapter 14);
- deliver copies of the employee handbook and other applicable work rules, policies, etc. and obtain a signed receipt;
- deliver a copy of the employee's job description and obtain a signed receipt;
- have the employee sign an arbitration agreement if appropriate (covered later in this chapter);
- have the employee sign confidentiality, noncompete, and non-solicitation agreements if appropriate (discussed in Chapter 19);
- obtain a certificate of creditable coverage from the employee or his or her previous employer if you offer group health insurance;
- have the employee enroll in any benefit plans for which he or she is then eligible; and,
- within twenty days after the employee begins employment, notify the appropriate state agency of the new hire.

I-9 Requirements

It is illegal to knowingly hire, recruit, refer for a fee, or continue to employ persons who are not eligible to work in the United States. The *knowingly* qualification is not satisfied by staying ignorant. For these purposes, a *don't-ask-don't-tell* policy will not work.

Employers must check documents to establish the eligibility of *every* new employee (including U.S. citizens) to work in the U.S. You must establish his or her eligibility to work here by completely filling out *Form I-9* in accordance with its accompanying instructions—both of which are available from the *Bureau of Citizenship and Immigration Services* (BCIS) of the Department of Homeland Security at:

www.immigration.gov/graphics/formsfee/forms/index.htm

The I-9 verification process must be completed within three working days after the employee begins work. (For employees who are hired for three days or less, the entire verification process must be completed on the first day of employment.) For employees whose eligibility to work in the United States is only temporary, the employer must either re-verify eligibility or terminate the employee upon expiration of the initial eligibility period.

> ## EMPLOYER TIP
>
> It is good practice, though not required, to make a photocopy of any documents exhibited by the employee to establish eligibility to work. Note, however, that attaching a photocopy of an exhibited document is not a substitute completing Form I-9 completely.

In addition to criminal exposure, employers who fail to comply with I-9 requirements face civil liability. Several courts have ruled that an employer who uses illegal aliens can be sued by competitors of the employer under the federal *Racketeer Influenced and Corrupt Organizations Act* (RICO). Government contractors are also subject to debarment.

Directory of New Hires Database

Federal law requires each state to establish a *Directory of New Hires database*, that is then shared with other states to track persons who have child-support obligations. (see Chapter 6.) The information is also used to detect fraud or abuse in welfare and unemployment programs. The states, in turn, have passed laws to establish the *Directory* and to require in-state employers to report new hires within twenty days after hiring. The one-page form can be mailed or faxed. Forms can be obtained, and in some cases completed, online.

Multistate employers (employers with employees in more than one state) have two reporting options:

- they may report each newly hired employee to the state where the employee is working, following the new hire reporting regulations of that particular state or

◆ they may select one state where they have employees working and report all new hires to that state electronically.

Employers must choose between the two options. They cannot use both. Employers who choose the second option must register with the U.S. Department of Health and Human Services as a multistate employer. More information on multistate reporting and the multistate registration form are available from:

Department of Health and Human Services
Administration for Children and Families
Office of Child Support Enforcement
Multistate Employer Notification
P.O. Box 509
Randallstown, MD 21133
202-401-9267
www.acf.dhhs.gov/programs/cse/newhire/employ/emult.htm

Employee Resumé Fraud

Prospective employees sometimes lie on their job applications. When the position being applied for involves risk to the public, the employer should take reasonable steps to verify the information. Even when no obvious risk is involved, the employer may wish to verify education or past experience that bears on the applicant's qualifications for the job.

But suppose a falsified resumé slips past the employer and is not discovered until months or years down the road. What rights and remedies does the employer then have?

At-will employees may, of course, be discharged for any reason (except a prohibited reason) or for no reason. As for those employees with employment contracts, if the resumé contains a false statement about some *material matter* (that is, about a matter that a reasonable person would find significant) and the employer actually relied on the statement in offering employment, then the employment contract is the product of the employee's *fraud*. The employer may treat the contract as void and discharge the employee so long as the employer acts promptly after discovering the fraud. However, if the false statement is an obvious typographical error (say, inversion of two digits in the date for previous employment), it is trivial, or it is so inherently improbable that the employer could not reasonably have relied on it, then the contract of employment remains enforceable.

Example: If an employee has filed a discrimination claim, and the employer discovered resumé fraud after a more thorough background investigation than was done at time of hiring, the after-acquired evidence of resumé fraud may be used, in part, as a defense to a discrimination complaint.

After acquired evidence—even evidence of a serious nature that would have been grounds for firing had it been discovered earlier—is not a complete defense to a discrimination claim. But it does limit the remedies that are available to the aggrieved employee. As the Supreme Court said in just such a case, it makes no sense to compel

EMPLOYER TIP

For both contract and at-will positions, it is a good idea to include in the employment application a certification by the applicant that the application is truthful and that all supporting items such as transcripts, reference letters, etc., are genuine.

an employer who fired an employee for discriminatory reasons, to re-hire the employee and then turn around and fire the employee again based on resumé fraud. But it does make sense to award the employee backpay, at least for the period between the wrongful firing and the time the resumé fraud was discovered.

Misrepresentation by the Employer During the Hiring Process

Suppose an employer makes an offer of at-will employment and, in the process, makes certain statements to the prospective employee about the nature of the job, working conditions, etc. The applicant relies on those statements, accepts the job, turns down other offers, and begins work. Then, for the first time, the employee learns that the employer's pre-hiring statements were untrue and that actual job conditions are much less favorable than as represented. It could be argued that the employee has no basis to complain about the employer's false pre-hiring statements, since in an at-will relationship, the employer has the absolute right to change working conditions at any time and to fire an employee whenever the employer feels like doing so.

However, several court decisions have ruled that an at-will employee who, in reliance on an employer's false statements, resigns from another job can sue the employer for fraud, deceit, and negligent misrepresentation. One case, for example, involved an applicant for a physical therapist position at a hospital. During the interview process, the hospital's CEO represented that the hospital's contract with an outside therapy provider would be ending and that the hospital would be bringing physical therapy services in-house. However, the CEO lacked authority to make those changes on his own. He also lacked authority to hire without approval by certain other officials. Nevertheless, the CEO made a firm offer to the therapist.

The therapist accepted the offer and turned down another opportunity. Only then did he learn that the offer had not been authorized and that, in fact, the offered position was not available. In the therapist's suit against the hospital for negligent misrepresentation, the hospital argued that, since the offer was only for at-will employment, the hospital could have gone through with the hiring, then fired the therapist the next day. The court answered that argument by saying that while the at-will nature of the offer would affect the amount of damages that could be awarded, that factor had no bearing on whether the therapist could bring suit for negligent misrepresentation in the first place.

Avoiding Misrepresentation. An employer can protect itself from negligent misrepresentation suits brought by disappointed applicants by being careful what is said. In the application process, the employer should:

- describe the job accurately by furnishing a written job description that is complete and up-to-date;
- give accurate estimates of job features that are likely to be of interest or concern to an employee, such as overtime requirements, travel, etc.;
- allow the applicant an opportunity to review the employee handbook and other important policy statements with which the applicant will be expected to comply if hired;
- furnish copies of all agreements the applicant will be required to sign upon hiring, such as agreements dealing with non-competition, non-solicitation, work-for-hire, arbitration, etc.;
- describe the hiring process, including who makes the decision to offer a job and what further approvals, if any, are necessary;
- state clearly and explicitly that the offer is conditional on approval by the company's board of directors or by some other official, if that is the case;
- disclose facts such as if the company is about to move its facilities; is considering a possible bankruptcy; or, is facing the loss of an important contract or some other event that could significantly affect the applicant's job;
- give the applicant a firm date by which the company will make a decision and, if the company has not made a decision by that deadline, contact the applicant, inform him or her that the decision is still pending, and ask if the applicant wishes to continue being considered;
- inform the applicant promptly once a decision is made; and,
- send a note confirming the rejection and thanking the applicant for his or her interest—(do not encourage the applicant to think he or she is still under consideration when in fact he or she is not)—if the applicant is being rejected.

EMPLOYEE HANDBOOKS

While there is no obligation for an employer to have a written employee handbook, many employers find them to be a valuable management tool.

Advantages. Handbooks promote uniformity in treatment of employees, particularly for larger employers with several layers of management. That in turn improves morale and frees the employer from a stream of requests for special treatment.

Handbooks are also a convenient source of information for job applicants and new hires, as well as existing employees. They promote efficiency and they help to establish an institutional culture. They set out rules of workplace behavior which, if willfully violated and result in termination, provide the employer with a defense to an unemployment insurance claim or an abusive discharge suit. Finally, they provide evidence of employer compliance with law in areas such as workers' compensation, equal employment, and sexual harassment.

Employers who choose to have an employee handbook should not overlook the requirements below.

- ◆ If the handbook describes leave policies and the employer is covered by the *Family and Medical Leave Act*, the handbook *must* include a description of extended leave benefits under FMLA. (see Chapter 8.)
- ◆ An employer *must* have a written sexual harassment policy to be able to defend against sexual harassment charges. (see Chapter 15.)

When distributing employee handbooks to employees, have each employee sign an *acknowledgment* that he or she has received the handbook and will read it. Such acknowledgments are helpful in meeting an employee's claim that he or she was unaware of a particular policy or procedure contained in the handbook.

Disadvantages. The down side is that an employee handbook or similar statement of policy might be considered a *unilateral contract*—that is, a one-sided *offer* by the employer to abide by the provisions of the handbook, which the employee *accepts* simply by working for the employer. In other words, courts may treat a poorly worded handbook as converting an at-will employment relationship to a contractual relationship that limits an employer's right to fire.

An employer who wishes to adopt an employee handbook but who does not want to be contractually bound by its provisions can

take steps to reduce, if not eliminate, the risk of contractual liability.
Consider:

- ◆ including prominent disclaimers that the handbook is not a
  contract of employment and is not intended to change the at-
  will status of any employee;
- ◆ stating that the handbook is intended only as a convenient
  source of information about the company and its current practices and procedures, that are subject to change at any time
  without prior notice;
- ◆ stating that employees are free to resign at any time and that
  the company is free to discharge an employee at any time, with
  or without cause;
- ◆ stating that the company is not bound to follow any particular
  disciplinary procedures and that the company need not be consistent in imposing discipline;
- ◆ avoiding statements such as the company *promises* or *guarantees* or *will* take specified action in certain circumstances; and,
- ◆ avoiding any requirement that employees sign an agreement to
  comply with or be bound by the handbook.

In addition to an employee handbook, some companies have a
managers-only manual, distributed only to managers, setting out
required procedures for them to follow for discrimination complaints, discipline, termination, etc. involving their subordinates.
Placing procedural requirements in a managers-only manual, rather
than the employee handbook, makes it more difficult for rank-and-
file employees to claim that the company is contractually obligated
to follow the procedures.

Dress Codes

An employer may generally impose a dress code or grooming code
on employees, so long as doing so has a legitimate business reason
and so long as the code is not discriminatory on the basis or gender,
race, religion, or other protected criteria. (Dress codes as a form of
sex discrimination are discussed in Chapter 15. See also Chapter 14
regarding religious discrimination.)

EMPLOYER TIP

Relaxing dress code standards may be a reasonable accommodation required of an employer for an employee suffering from a medical condition covered by the *Americans with Disabilities Act.*

Dress codes are nothing new. For example, safety considerations may warrant banning long sleeves or flowing skirts. Companies often require their delivery personnel to wear identifying uniforms sporting the corporate colors. Physicians wear white lab coats. Lawyers wear conservative suits and carry briefcases. In office settings, jackets and ties for men and dresses or skirts with hose for women have long been the *official uniforms*. The only exceptions might be casual, summertime Fridays, or special allowances for persons with medical conditions or temporary injuries.

Casual, summertime Fridays are giving way to casual everyday all year. *Casual* can mean anything from a comfortable old sports jacket with leather elbow patches to a beer-stained T-shirt and torn jeans; from a blouse and slacks to a bare midriff.

If you decide to go casual, keep the following points in mind.

◆ Your dress policy should be in writing (the employee handbook is a good place) and well publicized.

◆ The policy should contain a clear definition of *business casual*. For example, *Dress and grooming should be neat and consistent with a professional office atmosphere. Clothing should be clean and without rips or excessive wear. Women may wear dresses, blouses, sweaters, slacks, skirts, blazers, and dress sandals; men may wear shirts with collars, polo shirts, sweaters, chino slacks, jackets, and dress sandals.*

◆ The policy should also contain a clear statement of what is *not permitted.* For example: *the following are examples of items that do not qualify as 'business casual' and are not permitted at any time: T-shirts; tank tops; halters; jeans; shorts; sweats or similar athletic clothing; see-through clothing; clothing that exposes areas normally covered by business attire; clothing that exposes under-*

wear; work boots; beach sandals; and sneakers.

◆ Managers should have the authority to determine that casual dress for their immediate staff is inappropriate on particular days, such as when customers or visitors are expected.

◆ Since not everyone is comfortable wearing casual clothes to work, those who would prefer to dress more formally should feel free to do so.

◆ The consequences of inappropriate dress should be spelled out. For example: *employees who report to work unacceptably dressed may be required to return home to change and will be charged with leave during their absence.*

◆ The policy should be consistently and even-handedly enforced.

PERSONNEL FILES

The employment relationship generates a vast array of documents. Some of them are required by law and must be retained for specified time periods. A good example is *Form I-9*, and wage-and-hour records. (see Chapter 5.) Other documents, though perhaps not legally required to be retained, provide evidence of legal compliance. A copy of the *New Hire Report* form submitted to the state Directory of New Hires (discussed earlier) falls in this category. Finally, there are documents that management needs, like job descriptions, evaluations, and disciplinary actions to make sound employment decisions.

Employers should maintain a separate *personnel file* for each employee. The file should not be a waste basket containing everything related to the employee. Instead, management should determine in advance what documents are, and are not, to be kept in the file. In addition, the file should be organized into sections so that particular items can be located easily. A checklist placed on top of each section avoids misfiling and enables management to see, at a glance, whether it is complete and current. Files should be reviewed periodically to assure compliance with established requirements and procedures.

The contents of a typical personnel file might include:

♦ employment application, along with supporting materials such as resumé, transcripts, and interview notes;

♦ recommendation letters and reference checks;

♦ copies of restrictive covenants with employee's prior employers;

♦ offer letter and any contractual documents, such as restrictive covenants, arbitration agreements, etc.;

♦ *Form I-9*;

♦ copy of New Hire Report form;

♦ tax withholding forms (*W-4*, *W-5*, and state equivalents);

♦ job description, including statement as to whether position is exempt or nonexempt;

♦ copies of any required licenses or certificates required for the position;

♦ receipt for employee handbook;

♦ testing materials, if the employee was required to take any tests as part of the application process;

♦ training records relating to job competency, safety, sexual harassment policies, etc.;

♦ evaluations;

♦ commendations and disciplinary actions;

♦ pay records;

♦ personal information—home address, home telephone, name of spouse, etc.—and emergency contact (see Chapter 18);

♦ benefit plan participation records (application, beneficiary designation, etc.);

♦ exit interview notes; and,

♦ recommendation letters and notes of references given prospective employers.

Employers should also establish a *records retention policy*. When particular documents are required by law, the law usually specifies how long they need to be retained. In the absence of a specific requirement, the applicable *Statute of Limitations* should, at a minimum, be the guide. (A Statute of Limitations says that a claim may be barred unless suit on the claim is filed within a specified time period, such as three years.) Convenience also plays a role. For example, if the employer commonly receives reference inquiries up to two years after an employee leaves, then the employer may want to retain relevant records at least that long in order to respond.

Employers also need to establish rules for who has access to personnel files and who may add, remove, or change file contents. Access restrictions also need to be in place for files that are maintained electronically. Also, backup information needs to be kept off-site to protect against disasters and sabotage.

EMPLOYER TIP

A variety of federal laws and regulations, including the *ADA* and *HIPAA*, require that medical records and information be kept separate from general personnel files, that access be further restricted to a need-to-know basis, and that all persons with access be trained in handling such records.

Employee Access

A number of states have a statute affording an employee the right to see his or her personnel file, copy it, and/or rebut any negative evaluations or comments contained in the file. However, absent a statute affording such rights or a contract or collective bargaining agreement in which the employer has agreed to grant access, the employer does not have to allow an employee access to the file.

Even in the absence of a statute or agreement, it is probably a good idea to allow employees access to their personnel files. One approach, which California has made state law, is to allow an employee to inspect the file generally, but to only get copies of documents he or she has signed. So if an employee wants a copy of a disciplinary notice, for example, he or she first has to sign it, which places the employer in the desirable position of having a receipted copy of the notice.

Another advantage of a policy allowing an employee access to his or her other personnel files is that it promotes open communication and a healthier, less secretive work environment. Yet another advantage is that if an employee has access but fails to dispute unfavorable information, he or she is in a poor position to complain about subsequent personnel actions or references that are based on the information. Perhaps most important, under an open access policy, managers and supervisors are likely to be more disciplined in how they keep personnel files and what they put in them.

–3–
EVALUATING PERFORMANCE

Evaluating an employee is a whole lot easier if there is a history of open communication and regular feedback. In short, the situation should not be full of surprises.

Some employers have their employees fill out a self-evaluation form that the evaluator then reviews and comments on. While that approach may ease the manager's burden, it seems less direct. The employee may end up feeling not only that his or her work habits need improvement, but also that his or her character, honesty, and self-insight are under attack as well.

Some organizations use what are known as *360-degree evaluations* (also called *360-degree assessments* or multirater feedback systems). These involve evaluations not only by an employee's supervisor, but also by peers, direct reports, and, in some cases, internal or outside customers and clients. 360-degree evaluation programs need to be planned with particular care and the procedures and objectives need to be clearly understood and communicated to employees. Follow-up is also critical, otherwise substantial time will have been wasted collecting useless or unused data.

EMPLOYER TIP

Since evaluations themselves are not usually considered adverse actions, a bad evaluation will normally not justify a claim of discrimination or retaliation. However, imposing discipline or terminating an employee based on a discriminatory evaluation can give rise to a claim.

GOOD REASONS FOR EVALUATION

Regardless of the type, if done properly, there are some good reasons to do evaluations.

- ◆ They provide a rational basis on which to promote, discipline, and terminate.
- ◆ They provide powerful evidence to meet a claim that adverse action was taken for discriminatory or other improper reasons.
- ◆ Employees—particularly newer employees who may be uncertain of their performance—like them.

If not done properly, however, they do more harm than good.

LEGAL CONSIDERATIONS

Below are a few suggestions for evaluating employees.

- ◆ If you have an evaluation policy, follow it. Nothing looks more suspicious than a negative evaluation, done just before taking adverse action, especially where the employer's past evaluation procedures have been haphazard and intermittent.
- ◆ Use a written form containing a standard set of objective criteria.
- ◆ Avoid vague, subjective comments like, *unprofessional, bad attitude, poor work habits.* Such comments offer little guidance.
- ◆ Avoid comments that could be construed as discriminatory, such as, *Your approach to the job is stale* (age discrimination), *You need a softer, less aggressive demeanor with clients* (sex discrimination when directed to a female employee), *I know your wife's health has been a distraction for you* (disability discrimination).
- ◆ Keep job descriptions up-to-date. Employees will feel unfairly treated if they are criticized on aspects of their jobs for which they did not know they were responsible.
- ◆ Tie comments on job performance—whether positive or negative—to the job description.
- ◆ Tie comments on behavioral problems to the employee handbook or other written policy statement.

◆ Give specific examples to support all comments—*John's report last May on production problems in the York, PA plant was prompt, thorough, and contained many good suggestions. This is typical of the high quality of his work.*

◆ If you evaluate annually, be sure the evaluation considers the entire past year and not just the last few months.

◆ Discuss your evaluation with the employee and offer him or her an opportunity to comment in a private, confidential setting. Reduce the employee's comments to writing and include them in the employee's personnel file.

◆ Follow up on any specific deficiencies noted in the evaluation, and make a record of your follow-up in the employee's personnel file.

◆ Provide regular feedback—particularly, positive feedback—between evaluations.

An evaluation that is misleadingly *favorable* might convince an employee that he or she has long-term prospects with the company, when in fact that is not true. Therefore, any evaluation that is shared with the affected employee should contain the following disclaimer:

This evaluation is solely for the Company's benefit. Nothing in this evaluation is intended to change or affect in any way the at-will employment relationship between the Company and the employee or to limit or affect the Company's or the employee's right to terminate the employment relationship at any time for any reason.

DISCIPLINARY ACTIONS

Assuming you have made the decision to issue an *employee handbook*, to what extent should you spell out in the handbook the substantive reasons that will trigger discipline? If your handbook says that employment will only be terminated for cause, or for specified reasons, then, regardless of the number and prominence of disclaimers in the handbook, you will have converted at-will relationships into employment contracts that can only be terminated for cause. Similarly, if your handbook describes procedures for discipline or termination–for example, *employees will be counseled on their shortcomings before more severe discipline is imposed*— failure to follow those procedures will subject you to a lawsuit that you will lose.

Larger organizations may find it helpful to develop internal guidelines, distributed only to management (a *managers-only manual*), covering termination and disciplinary matters. Guidelines might specify who has authority to fire or discipline; what types of discipline may be imposed; how notices of adverse actions are to be communicated to employees; and, what opportunity (if any) employees will be given to contest adverse actions. However, those guidelines should not be published in a general distribution employee handbook. In short, employers should act reasonably, but, unless they intend to create employment contracts, they should not make commitments to their employees as to the specifics of how discipline will be imposed.

Progressive Discipline

Most authorities recommend *progressive discipline*. For less serious offenses, the steps typically include:

- oral warning, done in private;
- written warning;
- suspension without pay;
- demotion; and then,
- termination.

EMPLOYER TIP

In suspending without pay, the employee must be paid for all past work. Loss of pay can only occur for the period the employee is suspended.

Each of these steps should be accompanied by a current, written, signed, and dated entry in the employee's personnel file describing the offense and the action taken.

Last Chance Contract

Depending on the seriousness of the offense, some employers use a *last chance contract* in which the employee agrees, in writing, that he or she is being given one final opportunity to correct the problem and will be terminated if it is not corrected.

Offenses meriting a multi-step approach might include:

- tardiness;
- excessive absenteeism;
- minor neglect of work;
- violation of company parking regulations;
- violation of smoking regulations; or,
- frequent personal phone calls.

More serious offenses justifying immediate suspension, demotion, or termination might include:

- insubordination;
- theft or unauthorized use of company property or property of fellow employees;
- use or possession of illegal substances or weapons;
- other illegal activity such as gambling on company premises or use of company facilities to transmit obscene material;

> ## EMPLOYER TIP
>
> Although currently illegal drug use is not protected by the *Americans with Disabilities Act (ADA)*, drug addiction and alcoholism are disabilities that can trigger company obligations under the ADA.

- violence or threats of violence against supervisors;
- racial or sexual harassment;
- other forms of intentional discrimination;
- falsifying records or reports; and,
- willful disregard of important company policies such as workplace safety procedures.

This list of offenses is not, of course, complete. Discipline needs to be tailored to each employer's circumstances. A restaurant, for example, will be far more concerned about the failure of its kitchen staff to report communicable diseases than will a computer software company whose programmers work at home.

−4−
TERMINATION

Adverse action against an employee, whether some form of discipline short of termination or termination itself, should bear a reasonable relationship to the employer's legitimate business needs. Say that an employee has an off-beat lifestyle or holds views on social issues that are personally offensive to the employer. If the employment relationship is at will, it may be terminated for these very reasons. But if the employee's lifestyle or social views do not interfere with his or her work and are not otherwise disruptive to the workplace, a termination may be unwise.

Consider the effect on morale of a termination where the reason bears no relation to the company's business. Consider also the risk of a lawsuit. While a suit in these circumstances would probably be unfounded, it is always possible that the court will find a violation of some previously unrecognized public policy, and that it will rule the termination to be abusive. Even a successful defense costs money and time and it creates turmoil in the workplace. (If you have never had to answer written interrogatories propounded by your former employee's attorney, or produce box loads of personnel records, or suffer through depositions of half your workforce, you are in for an unpleasant surprise.) Consider, finally, the effect of such a termination on your unemployment insurance rate.

EXIT INTERVIEWS
When an employee quits or is terminated, the employee should normally be interviewed by a senior member of management just prior to departure. If the termination is not completely voluntary (for

example, the employee was fired or the employee quit after being offered the opportunity to do so in lieu of being fired), two members of management should conduct the interview together.

If the termination is voluntary, the employee may be asked about the reasons for quitting. Often the employer can gain valuable insight at this juncture into morale or other problems such as a hostile sexual or racial environment. However, the employee should not be pushed to respond if reluctant. If the termination is involuntary, the reasons for termination have probably already been stated to the employee. If not, they may be simply (and truthfully) stated at this point, but an extended discussion serves no purpose and it could rile tempers unnecessarily and compromise the employer's legal position.

EMPLOYER TIP

Giving a false or ambiguous reason for termination may seem less painful, but it can make defending an unemployment insurance claim or a suit for abusive discharge or discrimination, more difficult.

Exit interviews should be conducted in private and in a closed office. If the employee has been fired or is leaving under unfavorable circumstances, the departure should be accomplished with as little commotion and embarrassment as possible. Security guard escorts and other forms of intimidation should be avoided unless absolutely necessary. Failure to observe these rules can provoke claims of defamation. (This liability is discussed later in this chapter.).

Points of Discussion

The following matters, as applicable, should be accomplished during the exit interview:

- ◆ collect keys, security passcards, ID badges, and other property belonging to the employer;
- ◆ confirm the employee's current address and phone number;
- ◆ instruct the employee to remove all personal belongings;

- inform the employee as to when a final paycheck will be available and determine the employee's wishes as to whether the check should be mailed or held for pickup;
- inform the employee of *COBRA* or other continuation benefits under any medical expense insurance plan maintained by the employer;
- inform the employee of any conversion privileges available under any health, life, disability or other insurance plans maintained by the employer;
- inform the employee of any rights or obligations regarding retirement plan participation and benefits;
- remind the employee of any continuing confidentiality, non-compete, and nonsolicitation obligations;
- remind the employee of the employer's policy on references;
- inform the employee that he or she is prohibited from returning to the employer's premises and will be considered a trespasser if he or she returns, depending on the circumstances of the termination; and,
- obtain a signed release of liability from the employee in exchange for a severance package or other consideration, depending on the circumstances of the termination.

EMPLOYER TIP

A release will be unenforceable if the employee gets no additional benefit beyond what he or she is already entitled to. To validate a release, offer the employee a severance payment as consideration. (see Chapter 19.)

The employee should be asked to sign a written acknowledgment that all the above points have been discussed. If the employee refuses to sign, the points should be covered in a letter to the employee, with a copy placed in the employee's personnel file.

EMPLOYER TIP

Releases of claims under the *Age Discrimination in Employment Act* must comply with detailed statutory requirements to be effective. (see Chapter 16.)

Upon Completion of Exit Interview

Immediately after the exit interview, the interviewers should prepare a file memo summarizing the interview, including any reasons given by the employee for a voluntary quit.

Promptly after the interview, the employer should (as applicable):

- ◆ notify human resources and payroll of the employee's status change and request a final paycheck;
- ◆ arrange for issuance of a final *W-2*;
- ◆ arrange for issuance of a certificate of creditable coverage per the *Health Insurance Portability and Accountability Act*;
- ◆ terminate any signature authority the employee has over employer bank accounts or other financial accounts;
- ◆ notify insurers and retirement plan managers of the employee's status change;
- ◆ notify affected employees of the termination (without discussing the reason);
- ◆ notify others of the termination, such as security personnel, customers, vendors, financial institutions, etc., with whom the employee had contact (again, without discussing the reason); and,
- ◆ notify persons receiving garnishment or withholding order payments from the employee's wages of the employee's status change.

Final Pay

A departing employee is entitled to be paid at the agreed rate for all work actually performed up to the time of termination. The employer cannot withhold wages on the ground that the employee failed to give two weeks' or some other specified notice before quitting. Nor can the employer dock the wages of a fired employee on the theory that the employee's work quality was unacceptable.

State law also specifies *when* a departing employee must be paid. In some states, the final paycheck need not be issued until the next regular payday. In others, the departing employee must be paid immediately or within a few days of termination, depending on the circumstances of termination.

The employer may deduct from the employee's paycheck any claims the employer has against the employee, so long as the employee has agreed to the deduction. Suppose, for example, that the employee borrowed money from the company, to be repaid out of future paychecks. Or suppose the employer advanced unearned leave on the understanding that, in the event of an early termination, the employee would make reimbursement out of the final wages. In these examples, an appropriate setoff against the employee's paycheck is permitted. However, the employer should not deduct the amount of a disputed claim or any other amount not agreed to by the employee, since doing so may violate wage and hour laws.

TERMINATION FOR CAUSE

Sometimes an employer is willing to give up the right to terminate an employee at will and offer job security in the form of an employment contract. For example, the labor market may be tight and the employer may be having trouble attracting qualified candidates, or a particular position may just be difficult to fill, or a highly desirable candidate may also be of interest to the competition.

One way to promise job security is to offer employment for a specified period of time as long as the employee's performance remains satisfactory or to agree that employment can be terminated only for *cause* or *good cause*. When an employer makes such an offer to a prospective employee, and the employee accepts the offer and begins work, the employer is bound by the arrangement, the employee is no longer at will, and he or she cannot be dismissed except for cause.

> **EMPLOYER TIP**
>
> The employer may unintentionally be limited to terminating only for cause as a result of statements inadvertently made in the employee handbook.

What does *cause* or *good cause* mean in this context? The parties to a contractual arrangement are free to spell out in their contract exactly what they mean by the term. For example, if the employee needs a particular license in order to work (such as a plumbing license), suspension or revocation of the license might be listed as a cause for termination. Convictions for certain types of crimes, repeated insubordination, drunkenness, and physical assaults on customers or fellow employees might also be on the list. There may also be explicit do's and don'ts set out in a employee handbook or job description.

The employment relationship itself implies certain duties on the part of the employee, including a duty to show up for work in reasonably fit condition, a duty to have and exercise reasonable skill in performing the job, a duty of loyalty and honesty, and a duty to refrain from insubordinate and threatening behavior. A substantial breach of any of these implied duties is cause for termination.

In the absence of a definition or clear indication of the meaning of *cause* in a contract of employment or an employee handbook, the courts have defined the term along the following lines:

> *fair and honest reasons, regulated by good faith on the part of the employer, that are not trivial, arbitrary, or capricious, unrelated to business needs, goals, or pretextual. A reasoned conclusion, in short, supported by substantial evidence gathered through an adequate investigation that includes notice of the claimed misconduct and a chance for the employee to respond.*

In a recent Wyoming case, the court adopted a definition similar to the above. The court went on to say that, in determining whether an employer had cause for termination, the question is not, *Did the employee in fact commit the act leading to termination?* Rather, the question is, *Was the factual basis on which the employer concluded a dischargeable act had been committed reached honestly, after an appropriate investigation and for reasons that are not arbitrary or pretextual?* In other words, the courts are not going to second-guess an employer's *business judgment,* so long as the decision to terminate is reached honestly and fairly.

Changed Economic Conditions
No definitive answer exists whether an employer who is permitted to discharge a particular employee only for cause can eliminate a position based on changes in economic condition. In the case of an *express employment contract,* one that promises employment for a specific period of time, it would seem that unless the contract permits termination under that circumstance, the employer intended to assume the risk of an adverse economic change and cannot cut the contract short for that reason. On the other hand, an employer who is inadvertently held to a for-cause-only termination through provisions in the employee handbook can hardly have intended to assume any risk. In the latter circumstance, an adverse economic change should constitute good cause for termination. But again, the answer is not clear.

CONSTRUCTIVE DISCHARGE
When the law looks behind the form of a transaction to discover its true substance, it uses the strange term *constructive.* In a *constructive discharge,* it may appear on the surface that the employee quit, but because of the underlying circumstances, the law concludes that he or she was fired.

Take, for example, the employee who is told that unless he quits he will be fired. It is easy to see why the law would view that as an involuntary termination. An employer's request for a resignation will be treated the same way.

But the concept of constructive discharge goes beyond the *quit-or-be-fired scenario.* When an employer permits working conditions to become so intolerable that a reasonable person would quit, an employee who actually does quit rather than suffer the conditions will be deemed to have been fired. Suppose, for example, that serious safety hazards exist at the workplace that the employer knows about but refuses to fix. Or suppose that a minority employee is subjected to regular and pervasive racial harassment by supervisors and fellow employees.

The point of a constructive discharge is that an employer will be held liable to precisely the same extent as if it had directly fired the employee. If there was a contract of employment and insufficient grounds for termination, the employer will be answerable for breach of that contract. And in the racial harassment example given above, the employer can be charged with illegal racial discrimination.

> ## EMPLOYER TIP
>
> Employer liability for harassment is not dependent on the employee actually quitting. Merely subjecting an employee to severe and pervasive harassment can constitute illegal discrimination. (see Chapter 15.)

RETALIATION

Federal and state laws that grant statutory rights to employees often go on to prohibit employers from *retaliating* against their employees for *exercising* those rights. Examples include:

- ◆ federal and state anti-discrimination laws;
- ◆ federal and state wage and hour laws;
- ◆ federal labor laws;
- ◆ federal and state workplace safety laws;
- ◆ state workers' compensation laws;
- ◆ whistleblower laws, such as the federal *False Claims Act*, that encourage employees to report government fraud; and,
- ◆ federal corporate ethics laws.

These statutes effectively modify the at-will employment relationship by prohibiting an employer from terminating or otherwise retaliating against an employee, despite the employee's at-will statutes.

Ironically, retaliation claims sometimes become the tail wagging the dog. In the discrimination arena, for example, an employee may have a weak or improbable claim of race or sex discrimination. When the employee complains, however, the employer responds by firing the employee. In effect, the employer has converted a weak discrimination claim, that the employee would probably have lost, into a strong claim of retaliation that the employee will likely win.

In a recent federal appeals court case, a father and son were both employed by the same organization. When the *father* complained of discrimination, the employer retaliated by firing the *son*. The court said that form of retaliation is also illegal under federal anti-discrimination laws. As the court pointed out, t*o retaliate against a man by hurting a member of his family is an ancient method of revenge and is not unknown in the field of labor relations.*

Another example of statutory protection is a Reconstruction-era civil rights law that prohibits persons from conspiring to force, intimidate, or threaten witnesses in federal court proceedings. In a case involving a grand jury investigation of a company accused of Medicare fraud, the Supreme Court held that an employee of the company, who was fired for cooperating with the grand jury, could sue for damages under the statute even though he was an at-will employee.

WHISTLEBLOWER REGULATIONS

Persons who go public with violations of law by their employers, particularly violations involving fraud against the government, are known as *whistleblowers*. In the absence of specific statutory protections, whistleblowers may find themselves out of a job, with little right to complain. A number of jurisdictions have decided, however, that whistleblowers should receive some limited protection.

A pre-Civil War federal statute known as the *False Claims Act* permits anyone who learns about fraud against the U.S. Government to file a lawsuit in the name of the Government. For example, suppose a computer company that has a contract to provide programming services to the Treasury Department overbills for time spent in writing a software program. If a disgruntled company employee learns of the overbilling and files suit against the company under the False Claims Act, a provision of the Act prohibits the company from firing or otherwise retaliating against the employee. The Act provides the employee with an incentive to sue by allowing him or her to collect a percentage of any recovery from the suit.

Some states have enacted their own whistleblower laws protecting employees who disclose government fraud at the state level.

ABUSIVE DISCHARGE

An important variation on the retaliation theme can arise when there is no statute expressly prohibiting retaliation, but when some significant, well-established, *public policy* is involved. When a firing tends to undercut such a policy, courts may characterize the discharge as *abusive* or *wrongful* and allow the employee to recover damages against the employer despite an at-will employment relationship.

There are no clear answers as to what public policies will override the at-will employment doctrine. The doctrine of *abusive discharge* has been developed (and is still developing) on a case-by-case basis as suits come before the courts. In addition, judges' views of what is and what is not important and well-established public policy differ from state to state and vary over time.

One consistent theme has emerged from the cases—firing an employee for *refusing to commit an illegal act* or for *fulfilling a duty required by law*, is abusive and will provide grounds for a wrongful discharge suit. Another theme involves an employee's exercise of rights granted or protected by law. For example, employees covered by workers' compensation statutes have a right to file claims for work-related injuries and cannot be fired (or otherwise disciplined) for doing so. Refusal to take a lie detector test when administering the test would be illegal, is also not grounds for firing.

Things become less clear when the employee is engaged in conduct that is permitted by law or is even seen as socially desirable, but is not necessarily protected by law. To illustrate, suppose a dispute arises between employer and employee, and when the employee threatens to contact a lawyer for advice regarding the dispute, she's

fired. In other words, is the right to consult with counsel so fundamental that termination for exercising that right violates public
policy?

A 1994 federal case applying Iowa law concluded that termination under those circumstances did violate Iowa public policy. That
same year an intermediate appellate court in Ohio reached the same
conclusion. But a decision by Maryland's highest court in 2003 ruled
otherwise, saying that while access to counsel may be *favored*, there
is no violation of any clear mandate of Maryland public policy in firing an employee for involving counsel in an employment dispute.

Knowing how to proceed in the face of uncertain and changing
rules can be difficult for an employer. At the least, a prudent
employer should hesitate to fire an at-will employee for:

- ◆ engaging in an activity that is protected or encouraged by the
  law or that is usually considered of value to society or
- ◆ refusing to engage in illegal conduct or conduct that is usually
  considered immoral or otherwise improper.

DEFAMATION AND LIABILITY

It may be surprising to learn that one of the more significant liabilities an employer faces is *defamation*. In fact, many, if not most,
abusive discharge cases include claims of defamation.

To defame someone is to make a false statement of fact that
injures the person's reputation. A *written* defamatory statement is
libelous; a *spoken* defamatory statement is known as slander. In
order for a person to have a good claim of defamation, the false
statement must be *published*—communicated either in writing or
orally to some third person. Generally, to be defamatory the statement must be one of fact, for example, *John stole office supplies for
his personal use.* Mere statements of opinion such as *John does not use
office supplies efficiently*, are not usually defamatory.

Conduct can also amount to defamation. Suppose that after
being informed of a termination, an employee is escorted off the
employer's premises by senior management. Even though the
employee may feel embarrassed, that conduct alone, without more,
does not constitute a defamatory publication. But suppose that

instead of being escorted by management, the company uses its security guards who, in the process, search the employee and question him or her at length about suspected stealing, all in front of his or her coworkers. That conduct could give rise to a good defamation claim.

Privileged Statements

A statement that might otherwise be defamatory can sometimes be *privileged*, protected by law from a claim of defamation, even though the statement is false, it is published to a third person, and it is injurious to reputation. Privileges come in two types: *absolute* and *conditional* (sometimes called *qualified*). When a member of Congress makes a speech on the House floor, for example, the statements are *absolutely* privileged, meaning that he or she can never be sued for defamation, no matter how offensive the words might be. In contrast, employers who give references for former employees, who issue warnings and termination letters, and who offer candid employee evaluations, are entitled only to a *conditional* privilege.

The employer's privilege is *conditional* because it can be lost if the communication is made:

◆ without any *legitimate business purpose*;

◆ with knowledge of its *falsity* or with a *reckless disregard* for its truth or falsity;

◆ with *malice, spite,* or *ill will* toward the employee; or,

◆ if the employer disseminates the statement *beyond* those who have a business need to know.

To illustrate, suppose an employee is terminated, finds a new position, and *after* starting work at the new job, the old employer contacts the new employer and, without being asked, relates derogatory information about the new employee. This *blacklisting* of a former employee will be compelling evidence of malice and will also void any privilege defense.

Unfortunately for the employer, issues of legitimate business purpose, malice, spite, ill will, and excessive dissemination usually turn on the specific facts of each case. As a result, even weak defamation claims may result in protracted and expensive court proceedings.

Job References

Job references present a special problem. On the one hand, if the employer provides highly detailed information about a former employee, including factual statements and opinions that go beyond what the prospective new employer specifically asked, the employer runs a substantial risk of a defamation or invasion of privacy claim. On the other hand, if the employer undertakes to provide a reference, but then provides a skimpy or inaccurate one, leaving out favorable information, a defamation claim may loom as well.

Rather than run these risks, some employers have adopted a *neutral reference or no comment* policy under which they do no more than confirm dates of employment and perhaps title and salary. While such a policy may be the safest for individual employers, it has a social cost in restricting the amount of pertinent information available to prospective employers. Less qualified workers may get jobs that more qualified applicants would have received had full information been available. Worse, persons who would otherwise be rejected because of the danger they pose to the public may not be weeded out in the application process.

> **EMPLOYER TIP**
>
> Giving a bad reference for a former employee in retaliation for the employee's filing a discrimination claim is itself illegal discrimination under Title VII. (see Chapter 14.)

A middle ground is to adopt a *no comment* policy but to make an exception where the employee or former employee approves in writing the content of a proposed reference letter, authorizes its issuance, and releases the employer from liability for issuing the letter.

Whatever policy you adopt, be sure it is communicated to all employees and that it is faithfully followed. The policy should also identify those persons within the company who are authorized to give out reference information and it should prohibit everyone else within the company from doing so.

Some states offer a measure of protection for employers who provide information to prospective employers about an employee's or former employee's job performance or reason for termination. In these states, mere negligence in providing an erroneous reference is not sufficient to support a defamation suit. Instead, the unhappy employee must show that the employer acted maliciously or intentionally in disclosing false reference information.

Compelled Self-Publication

A bizarre twist on the law of defamation deserves mention. Suppose an employer terminates an unsatisfactory employee and tells the employee the reason for the termination. Further, suppose the employer tells no one else about the reason and, consistent with the employer's *no comment* policy, confirms only the dates of employment, job title, and salary to a prospective new employer. No defamation claim could possibly be brought, right?

Unfortunately, no. Some courts have adopted a doctrine known as *compelled self-publication*, which holds that since the employee must honestly tell a prospective employer about the reason given for the termination, the employee has no choice but to defame him or herself and may therefore sue the former employer. Fortunately, the doctrine of compelled self-publication is not widely recognized.

> ### EMPLOYER TIP
>
> Giving an inaccurate reference may expose an employer to third-party liability. For example, if a former employer is asked for a reference by a subsequent employer but fails to mention the employee's dangerous propensities, and the employee later causes injury or damage, the former employer may be liable. (see Chapter 23.)

INTENTIONAL INFLICTION OF EMOTIONAL STRESS LIABILITY

Another ground on which an employer can be held liable is intentional infliction of emotional distress. In general, if an employer (or anyone else, for that matter) acts in an extreme or outrageous way, and, either intentionally or recklessly, causes someone else to suffer severe emotional distress, the victim of such conduct can recover damages in court. Claims for intentional infliction of emotional distress are sometimes coupled with charges of harassment based on sex, race, etc.

In a strange case involving Georgetown University in Washington, D.C., an employee of the University claimed that her supervisor placed two electrically-operated noisemakers outside the supervisor's door aimed at the employee's workplace. According to the employee, the devices emitted an unbearably loud, static-sounding, piercing, humming, and droning noise every hour of the workday for some nine months, causing the employee extreme emotional distress. Despite her complaints, the University did nothing. The District of Columbia Court of Appeals ruled that the employee stated a good claim for intentional infliction of emotional distress and that the case should not have been summarily dismissed by the trial judge.

CORPORATE ETHICS AND THE SARBANES-OXLEY ACT

The rash of recent corporate scandals by publicly traded companies has prompted Congress to pass tough new legislation. Although the *Sarbanes-Oxley Act of 2002* focuses primarily on accounting oversight and corporate governance, the Act contains a number of provisions that directly affect high-level, and in some cases lower-echelon, employees of publicly-traded companies. Highlights of the Act include the following:

◆ *Certification of financial statements.* The Act requires the *Securities and Exchange Commission (SEC)* to issue rules requiring a company's principal executive and financial officers to certify the company's financial statements as true and complete.

In the event of any failure to comply with reporting requirements such that financial statements have to be restated, those same officers must forfeit their bonuses and incentive compensation for a 12-month period.

◆ *Blackouts.* Whenever a company imposes a blackout by prohibiting pension plan participants from trading in company stock, company directors and executive officers are also prohibited from selling any stock they may have acquired through their employment with the company. Plan administrators must give advance notice of the blackout to plan participants and beneficiaries, including a statement of the reason for the blackout.

◆ *Loans.* Subject to certain narrow exceptions, companies are now prohibited from making personal loans or extending credit to their directors and executive officers.

◆ *Code of Ethics.* Companies must report to the SEC whether they have adopted a code of ethics for their senior financial officers and, if they have not, why they have not.

◆ *Document retention.* Pursuant to the Act, the SEC will adopt rules governing companies' retention of documents relating to financial audits and reviews. Knowing and willful violation of the rules will be a criminal offense.

◆ *Fitness to serve.* The SEC is authorized by the Act to prohibit persons who are deemed unfit from serving as officers or directors if they have violated rules governing deception or fraud.

◆ *Whistleblowing.* It is also now criminal for a company to retaliate against an employee who assists in any investigation by federal regulators, Congress, or company supervisors, or who provides information to federal law enforcement officers. Any person who suffers unlawful retaliation may also initiate a civil proceeding for reinstatement, backpay, and other damages.

Prohibited Activities

Even if your company is not publicly traded and subject to the *Sarbanes-Oxley Act*, it is a good idea to have a corporate code of ethics for employees, covering the president on down. Prohibited activities, many of which are illegal as well as unethical, might include:

- hiring relatives;
- carrying phantom employees;
- borrowing money from subordinate employees, vendors, or customers;
- accepting bribes, kickbacks, expensive gifts, or lavish entertainment from vendors or customers;
- accepting discounts on purchases from vendors or customers that are not offered to the general public;
- falsifying business records, tax returns, or reports to government agencies;
- carrying *off the books* accounts or funds;
- performing paid services for customers on a personal basis outside normal company channels;
- blacklisting employees, customers, or vendors;
- fixing bids or sharing pricing or cost information with competitors; and,
- requiring customers to buy unwanted products in order to get products they do want.

EMPLOYEE DUE PROCESS

We so often hear terms like *due process, freedom of speech, freedom of the press, freedom of information,* etc., that we may be tempted to think those rights apply in all our relationships. Not so. The constitutional right of *due process* limits the ways in which the *government* can deal with us. Our free speech right only prevents *government* censorship. And federal and state Freedom of Information Acts and sunshine laws only guarantee us access to certain *government* information and proceedings. In a recent Fourth Circuit Court of Appeals case, for example, an employee was fired from private employment for displaying confederate flags on his toolbox, which the employer felt violated the company's anti-harassment policy. The employee's subsequent First Amendment claim was dismissed because the First Amendment protects citizens only from government interference with their rights to free speech.

In general, the employment relationship does not include employee due process rights. An at-will employee can be arbitrarily disciplined or fired without any right to a hearing, without any opportunity to explain or justify the supposedly offending conduct, and without any opportunity to confront the person who supposedly reported the offending conduct. Of course, arbitrariness is seldom the best way to manage employees.

There are a few, limited exceptions to an employer's ability to act out of sheer arbitrariness. An employer cannot discriminate on the basis of race, ethnicity, gender, or other irrelevant characteristics. The employer cannot discharge an employee in violation of public policy; and the employer cannot act contrary to his or her contractual obligations.

When an employee does have an employment contract, or when an employee is a member of a union that has a collective bargaining agreement, an employer's right to discipline or discharge the employee is typically limited by the contract to *for cause* terminations. The contract may also provide a grievance procedure, leading to binding arbitration, should an employee dispute the employer's personnel action. Even absent an employment contract, statements in an employee handbook dealing with disciplinary procedures may rise to the level of a contractual obligation.

The Fifth Amendment

The Fifth Amendment to the U.S. Constitution protects a variety of personal rights. Among them are that no person *shall be compelled in any criminal case to be a witness against himself.* In other words, no one may be compelled, under threat of being held in contempt of court, to answer questions under oath when it is reasonable to assume that the answers could help convict the person of a crime. Although on its face the Amendment is limited to compelled testimony in criminal cases, the Supreme Court has held that the protection applies in a range of situations in which testimony is coerced, including civil cases, grand jury proceedings, and appearances before Congress.

The privilege is limited to *testimony* and does not extend to compelled production of physical evidence such as handwriting exemplars, blood specimens, etc. Nor does the privilege protect documents from compelled disclosure, unless by the very act of producing the document, the person is admitting the existence of the document and thereby incriminating himself.

Corporations and other organizations have no Fifth Amendment privilege. So if a corporation is served with a subpoena for records, it has no basis, at least under the Fifth Amendment, to resist the subpoena and refuse to produce the records. While corporate officials can claim the privilege in order to protect *themselves* from incrimination, they cannot claim privilege to protect their corporate employer.

> ## EMPLOYER TIP
>
> In jurisdictions where the abusive discharge exception to the at-will employment doctrine is unsettled, employers should be cautious in firing an employee for claiming the privilege. It is certainly conceivable that a court will find a public policy protecting an employees' Fifth Amendment rights.

If employees are invited or required to testify, an employer *cannot* in any way encourage employees to claim the privilege, threaten them should they fail to do so, or promise rewards for doing so. This type of conduct could amount to an *obstruction of justice*—a serious crime that will likely get the prosecutor's attention. Employers also need to avoid indirect encouragement. This can arise, for example, when the employer urges employees to be represented by the same attorney who represents the company, and the attorney, in turn, advises the employees to claim the privilege.

Employers are generally free, however, to require their employees to testify, and to discipline them if they refuse and claim the privilege. Remember that the Fifth Amendment is designed to protect against *government* coercion, not private coercion.

The rules are different for public-sector employers, because they *are* the government. In that situation, two competing principles are at stake. On the one hand, the Fifth Amendment protects public employees from coercion by their employers. On the other hand, the public has an interest in knowing whether public employees have properly discharged their public trust. In balancing these principles, the courts have held the following.

- A public employer may *request* its employees to answer questions about matters that may tend to incriminate them. If the employee responds to the request and answers the questions, any resultant information may be used in a later criminal prosecution against the employee.

- A public employer may *demand* that its employees answer questions about matters that may tend to incriminate them, and it may fire any employee who refuses to answer. However, when a public employee is faced with a choice between answering questions and being fired, and the employee chooses to answer, the resultant information may not be used in a later criminal proceeding against the employee. In other words, a coerced answer effectively immunizes the employee from future prosecution based on that testimony.

- A public employee *cannot* be forced, under threat of being disciplined, both to answer questions that may incriminate him or her *and* to waive immunity from prosecution based on the answers.

The rules applicable to public employment spill over to the government contracting arena. In a 1973 case, the Supreme Court considered the constitutionality of a New York statute that required any person who had a contract with the state to testify concerning the contract and to waive immunity from subsequent prosecution based on his or her testimony. Under the law, if a contractor refused, the existing contract would be canceled and the contractor would be debarred from doing business with the state for five years.

When an architect who did business with New York State refused to testify in a grand jury corruption investigation, he was threatened with loss of his state contract. The architect then challenged the constitutionality of the law. The Supreme Court ruled that loss of state contracts amounted to a sufficient economic sanction that the architect's testimony should be deemed coerced. Therefore, said the Court, New York could insist upon the testimony, but it could not at the same time require a waiver of immunity from prosecution.

DOWNSIZING AND MASS LAYOFFS

Terminating an employee is among the most difficult tasks facing any employer. When a decision is made to lay off a significant portion of the workforce, the difficulty and the legal risks are multiplied. Particularly in tough economic times, laid-off employees will have a more difficult time finding new employment, so their incentive to sue is even greater.

While the legal risks associated with a mass layoff can never be entirely eliminated, employers can take steps to reduce their exposure by:

> **EMPLOYER TIP**
>
> When an exit incentive program is made available to a class or group of employees, coupled with a severance agreement and release, the *Older Workers Benefit Protection Act* requirements may be triggered. (see Chapter 16.)

- considering other cost-saving alternatives to a layoff, such as offering wage rate or hour reductions to employees;
- developing and documenting the business reasons for the layoff;
- focusing on *positions*, not *people*, to be eliminated;
- hiring an outside expert to help decide what positions to eliminate;
- making sure that layoff decisions are not influenced in any way by discriminatory factors, such as race, gender, or age;
- using an outside expert to review the unintended impact along race, gender, and age lines once tentative layoff decisions have

been made, and assuming the decisions have not been intentionally influenced by discriminatory factors;

◆ offering severance packages, early retirement packages, or other exit incentives in exchange for a release of all claims; and,

◆ following customary exit interviews and procedures for each individual being laid off.

Worker Adjustment and Retraining Notification

The federal *Worker Adjustment and Retraining Notification (WARN) Act* requires an employer with 100 or more employees to provide notification 60 days in advance of a planned plant closing or mass layoff. In determining whether an employer meets the 100-employee floor, only full-time employees are counted, unless part-timers in the aggregate work at least 4,000 hours per week, in which case part-timers are counted, too.

A *mass layoff* for *WARN* purposes is a layoff of at least 50 employees at a single site, which amounts to at least 33% of the employees at that site. So if an employer has 1,000 employees at a given site and lays off 100, that would not be a mass layoff.

The 60-day notice must be given to the affected employees, to the state dislocated worker unit, and to the chief elected official of the local government where the plant closing or layoff is to occur.

The *WARN Act* recognizes that in some circumstances it may not be possible for employers to give the requisite notice. The Act's so-called *unforeseeable business circumstances exception* is applicable when a similarly situated employer, exercising commercially reasonable business judgment, would not have foreseen the closing. So long as an employer is exercising reasonable business judgment, the employer will not be held liable under WARN for failing to predict economic conditions that may affect demand for the organization's products or services.

–5–
WAGE-AND-HOUR REQUIREMENTS

Wage and hour requirements are a mix of federal and state law. The principal federal law is the *Fair Labor Standards Act* (FLSA), enacted in 1938.

In general, and subject to the exemptions discussed later in this chapter, the FLSA applies to all employees of an enterprise engaged in interstate commerce or in the production of goods for interstate commerce if the enterprise is of the following type and/or meets the following minimum annual sales volume:

- ◆ retail and service establishments—$250,000;
- ◆ construction companies—*no minimum*;
- ◆ laundries, cleaners and tailors—*no minimum*;
- ◆ hospitals, nursing homes, schools and other institutions—*no minimum*; or,
- ◆ all other enterprises—$250,000.

MINIMUM WAGES
The FLSA requires every employer to pay each employee the minimum wage. ($5.15 per hour at this writing, but subject to change by Congress.) The minimum rate for newly hired employees who are under twenty years of age is currently $4.25 per hour, but that rate is applicable only during the first 90 days of employment. Although an employee need not receive the minimum wage for every hour worked, the employer must average the minimum wage over a 40-hour week.

There is a long list of occupations that are exempt from minimum wage requirements. The exceptions are narrowly drawn, however, and in some cases apply only in very limited circumstances. Employers should assume that they owe the minimum wage to each of their employees unless they have obtained competent advice to the contrary.

Volunteer Employees

Among the potential pitfalls for an employer is the *volunteer employee*. Although the FLSA and Department of Labor regulations permit the use of volunteers by government agencies and they permit student workers to participate in college-sponsored programs, they generally do not allow use of volunteers in private business.

Example: Suppose an architectural firm receives an inquiry for summer employment from a third-year architecture major at the state university. She says that job opportunities are extremely tight and, in order to gain experience, she is willing to work for free. Since the proposed arrangement would likely be of direct benefit to the employer and the student would, most likely, be performing for free work that the employer normally has to pay for, the FLSA's minimum wage requirement probably applies.

Tips

Special rules apply to employees who receive tips. Tips may be counted against the minimum wage, but only up to $2.77 per hour at this writing. (Some state minimum wage laws do not count tips or count tips only up to a lesser dollar amount.)

EMPLOYER TIP

Tips are subject to withholding and other tax requirements just like regular compensation. (see Chapter 7.)

State and Local Laws

The states are free to adopt higher minimum wages and some have done so. Some local governments have decided to get involved in minimum wage issues by adopting so-called *living wage* laws that require government contractors doing business with those jurisdictions to pay

EMPLOYER TIP

Pay differentials based on gender or on any other prohibited consideration such as race, national origin, etc., are illegal under anti-discrimination laws. (see Chapter 15.)

their employees a minimum wage substantially in excess of the federal and state floor. Instead of living wages, some states have laws that require government contractors to pay their employees at *prevailing* wage rates.

Penalties

In general, the FLSA and state wage and hour requirements cannot be waived by the employee and any private agreement that purports to modify those requirements is void. Penalties for violating the FLSA and state laws are substantial, including liquidated damages, attorneys' fees payable to the employee involved, criminal fines, and even prison sentences.

OVERTIME

Overtime requirements give rise to issues of how much to pay and when to pay. The basic rules for nonexempt, private sector employees are:

- the maximum number of hours an employee may work in any workweek without receiving overtime compensation is 40;
- overtime compensation is 1½ times the employee's regular rate of pay-per-hour; and,
- overtime compensation must be paid on the regular payday for the period in which the overtime workweek ends (or as soon thereafter as practical if the amount due cannot be computed by that payday).

Calculating Work Time

The workweek is a period of 168 hours (7 x 24). It is up to the employer to establish when the workweek begins and ends and it need not coincide with pay periods. Where the two do not coincide (for example, where the employer's pay period is semi-monthly— 24 paydays per year) each paycheck includes regular pay for 13, 14, 15, or 16 days and includes overtime pay for one, two, or three workweeks, depending on how many workweeks end during the particular pay period involved. The workweek cannot be repeatedly changed in order to manipulate overtime obligations.

Overtime must be paid at 1½ times the employee's *regular hourly rate*. In general, the regular hourly rate is the hourly rate actually paid the employee for the normal, non-overtime workweek for which the employee is employed. Employers are not required to compensate their employees on an hourly rate basis. They may, for example, compensate on piece-rate, salary, commission, or other basis, but in such cases a regular hourly rate must be computed to determine what the overtime rate should be. In computing the regular hourly rate, all remuneration for employment must be included, such as commissions and production bonuses. However, the FLSA specifies that the following items are *not* included in computing the regular hourly rate:

- ◆ Christmas or other gifts, so long as they are not measured by or dependent on hours worked, production, or efficiency;
- ◆ payments made while the employee is on leave;
- ◆ expense reimbursements;
- ◆ bonuses paid in the sole discretion of the employer and not pursuant to any prior contract or promise;
- ◆ profit-sharing payments;
- ◆ employer contributions to employee benefit plans; and,
- ◆ premium payments for work on weekends and holidays, so long as the premium rate is at least 1½ times the rate for regular work.

Example: Suppose a company's normal workday is 9:00 a.m. to 5:30 p.m. with an hour for lunch. That equates to 37½ hours of work per workweek. If an hourly employee works 39½ hours in a particular week, at what rate should he be paid for the extra two hours? The company is free to adopt a policy of paying overtime at 1½ times the normal rate after 37½ hours, but it is not required to do so. The company is in full compliance with wage and hour laws if it pays only straight time for the two hours, since overtime obligations only kick in after 40 hours.

Employers should not overlook the effect of holidays, vacations, and other time off on their overtime obligations. In order for time to be counted toward overtime, the employee must actually be at work. Even though an employee may be on paid leave, if he or she is not actually working, the time is not included in computing overtime. For that reason, overtime is usually not a problem during periods such as the Christmas week when many employees take time off.

Pitfalls

Wage-and-hour violations can occur unintentionally. Employers should be alert to pitfalls illustrated by the following situations.

♦ *Would you mind running an errand for me on your lunch hour? I'd appreciate it if you'd take the late mail to the post office when you leave today. Could you drop off this package on your way in tomorrow?* If these favors take more than a few minutes of an employee's time, they need to be counted for overtime computation purposes.

♦ *Company policy prohibits overtime unless explicitly approved by your supervisor.* If the time actually required to complete the assigned job is more than the standard workday, an official policy limiting overtime will not excuse the employer from paying time-and-a-half.

♦ *I need you to carry a beeper. In your job, you're on call 24 hours-a-day. You can't drink on your off hours, since I may need you in on short notice. I want you at home where I can reach you.* Restrictions on off hours can trigger overtime obligations if they substantially limit the employee's freedom. The *you're on call 24 hours-a-day* dictate, without more, is probably not a substantial restriction, nor is the alcohol prohibition. But the beeper requirement could be if the beeper's range is very limited. The stay at home requirement definitely would need to be counted as work time.

♦ *For next week's project I'm going to consider you an executive.* Even if the employee does, in fact, perform executive-level duties, a week isn't sufficient to convert him from non-exempt to exempt. Exempt functions must account for more than 50% of the employee's total job requirements, and they must be part of his regular duties, not just part of a temporary assignment.

Portal-to-Portal Act

Another area of risk involves activities immediately prior to and immediately after regular work periods. The *Portal-to-Portal Act* (an amendment to the FLSA) makes clear that an employee's *commuting time*—time walking, riding, or traveling to and from the actual place of performance of the principal activity or activities that such employee is employed to perform—is not compensable for minimum wage or overtime purposes. Similarly, activities that are *preliminary* or *postliminary* to principal activities are not compensable.

On the other hand, an activity *is* compensable if it is primarily for the employer's benefit; if there is an express written or oral contract that the employer will pay for the activity; or, if it is compensable by custom or practice. Examples of activities which may or may not be compensable, depending on the circumstances, include: changing into or out of a work uniform; punching a time clock, waiting in line to punch a time clock; settling up a cash register drawer at the end of a shift; cleaning or repairing tools; showering after working with hazardous or toxic materials; and, inspecting a motor vehicle prior to driving a delivery route.

ALTERNATIVES TO OVERTIME

Overtime obligations significantly increase an employer's payroll costs. In addition to time-and-one-half, other costs such as payroll taxes, workers' compensation premiums, and retirement plan contributions may increase as well. So it is usually in an employer's interest to avoid overtime when possible. The following alternatives to overtime may be available, depending on the employer's specific circumstances.

Comp Time

If an employee who normally works an eight-hour day happens to work nine or ten hours on a particular day, he or she may be offered the opportunity (or may even be required) to work fewer hours on another day, so long as it is in the same *168-hour workweek*. However, with few exceptions overtime may not be taken as *compensatory time (comp time)* in another workweek. If overtime is not offset by time off within the same 168-hour workweek, wages at the overtime rate must be paid. This rule applies regardless of the pay periods established by the employer. For example, even though the pay period may be every two weeks, 45 hours of work in week #1 cannot be offset by 35 hours in week #2.

The rule also applies even if the employee is perfectly willing to waive overtime pay and take comp time the following week. Suppose, for example, that an employee wants to take an extended vacation later in the year and offers to build up comp time so that regular paychecks will continue during the vacation. The request cannot be honored, since neither the employer nor the employee can agree to an arrangement different from the overtime requirements of federal and state law.

On a number of occasions, Congress has considered amending the FLSA to permit comp time in the private sector. (Comp time has long been allowed for federal government employees.) Organized labor has generally been opposed to any such change, however, and the proposed amendments have all died without passage.

Time Off Plan

There is one exception to the rule that comp time in workweek #2 does not satisfy the employer's obligation for overtime in workweek #1—the so-called *time off plan*. Suppose an employer pays every other week. If a nonexempt salaried employee works overtime in workweek #1, the employer can give the employee time off in workweek #2 at the rate of one and one-half hours for each hour of overtime worked in workweek #1. By paying the employee the regular salary for both workweeks, the employer fully satisfies the overtime obligation.

Example: Say the employee normally works 40 hours per workweek and is paid a bi-weekly salary of $800 ($400 per week). If the employee works 50 hours in workweek #1, the employee can take (or be ordered to take) 15 hours off in workweek #2, since 1.5 times the 10 hours of overtime worked in workweek #1 equals 15. In this example, the employee has worked a total of 75 hours over both workweeks, but will be paid his or her regular bi-weekly salary of $800. In effect, the employer satisfies its overtime obligation by paying *comp time* at a premium rate instead of paying a *cash* premium.

A time off plan only works if the employer's pay period is longer than one workweek and if overtime occurs in the first workweek. In the above example, if the overtime occurred in workweek #2, the employer would have to pay the overtime premium in cash.

Belo Plan

Belo plans (from a Supreme Court case of that name), are available only for employees whose duties necessitate irregular hours because of the nature of the work. Examples might include on-call service workers and emergency repair crews. Under a Belo plan, the employer enters into a contract with the employee that guarantees the employee a fixed salary regardless of the number of hours worked. The contract specifies a regular hourly rate for the normal

40 hours and one and one-half times that regular hourly rate for guaranteed overtime (so long as total time covered by the plan is no more than 60 hours per workweek).

Example: Suppose a power company employee's job is to restore electrical service following outages caused by storms, traffic accidents, construction mishaps, etc. The amount of work needed is unpredictable, typically varying anywhere from 30 to 50 hours per workweek, so the employer enters into a contract guaranteeing the employee a fixed weekly salary of $550, representing 40 hours at $10 per hour and 10 hours at a $15 overtime rate. In other words, the contract guarantees the employee 10 hours of overtime each week. Then, regardless of the number of hours worked (up to the agreed total of 50 hours in this example), the employer has no additional overtime obligation. Of course, if the employee works less than 50 hours, he or she still gets paid his $550.

In the above example, any time worked in excess of 50 hours would have to be compensated at $15 per hour. While the parties could have agreed to guarantee more than 10 hours of overtime, their agreement could not go beyond 20 hours of overtime under a Belo plan.

Half-time Plan

Belo plans are only available when the inherent nature of the work necessitates irregular hours and when the number of hours per workweek vary both above and below a normal 40-hour workweek. In contrast, under a *half-time plan* (sometimes called a *fluctuating workweek plan*), the fluctuation can be subject to the employer's control and hours worked can routinely exceed 40.

Under a fluctuating workweek plan, the employer and employee agree that the employee will be paid a fixed salary covering all time worked in the workweek. This should be a written agreement by which the employee clearly acknowledges that the fixed salary covers the straight-time component of all hours worked, even if they exceed 40. For any given workweek, the employee's regular hourly rate is computed by dividing the fixed salary by the number of hours actually worked in that workweek. If the number of hours worked exceeds 40, the employer pays the employee one-half (not one and one-half) of his or her regular hourly rate for the hours exceeding 40. The reason the employer pays only half-time for the overtime is that the straight-time component is already covered by the fixed salary.

Example :   Suppose the employer and employee agree to a fixed salary of $400 per week. If, in a particular workweek, the employee works 50 hours, then the employee's regular hourly rate for that workweek is $8 ($400 / 50). Therefore, the employer's overtime obligation for that workweek is $40 (1/2 of $8 x 10 hours) and total compensation due the employee for that workweek is $440. Now suppose the employee works 55 hours. His regular hourly rate would then be approximately $7.27 ($400 / 55) and the total compensation due would be $454.53 ($400 + 1/2 of $7.27 x 15 hours).

As this example shows, as overtime increases, both the regular hourly rate and the overtime rate decrease. If the employee worked 80 hours in a particular workweek, his or her regular hourly rate would then drop to $5.00 per hour, which is below the minimum wage of $5.15 and which would therefore violate federal law. The fixed salary under a half-time plan must be high enough to guaranty at least the minimum wage.

EXEMPTIONS FROM OVERTIME REQUIREMENTS

Overtime requirements are subject to a long list of exemptions. An employee (or position) covered by one of these exemptions is referred to as *exempt* and is not entitled to time-and-a-half for overtime. In contrast, an employee (or position) not covered by any exemption is referred to as *nonexempt* and is entitled to overtime.

White Collar Exemptions

Probably the most significant exemptions for most businesses are salaried employees employed in a bona fide *executive, administrative, or professional* capacity. These exemptions, together with the exemption for *outside salespersons*, are sometimes called the *white collar exemptions*.

The terms *executive, administrative, or professional* are defined at great length in both federal and state regulations. At this writing, federal regulations provide both a *short test* and a *long test*, depending on the employee's weekly salary, for determining executive, administrative, and professional status (but see proposed new DOL regulations, discussed below). Specifically, if an executive, administrator, or professional is paid at least $250 per week, then he or she need only satisfy the short test to be covered by the exemption. On the other hand, if he or she is paid at least $155 per week ($170 per week for professionals) but less than $250, he or she must satisfy the more difficult long test. Current short test definitions are summarized below.

An *executive* is an employee whose primary duty consists of the management of the enterprise in which he or she is employed (or a customarily recognized department or subdivision thereof) and includes the customary and regular direction of the work of two or more other employees.

An *administrator* is an employee whose primary duty consists of the performance of office or nonmanual work directly related to management policies or general business operations of the employer or employer's customers, and includes work requiring the exercise of discretion and independent judgment.

> ## EMPLOYER TIP
>
> Even though an employee may be exempt from minimum wage and overtime requirements, the employer must still comply with the FLSA's equal pay provisions, which prohibit gender-based wage discrimination. (see Chapter 15.)

A *professional* is an employee whose primary duty consists of (1) work requiring knowledge of an advance type in a field of science or learning customarily acquired by a prolonged course of specialized intellectual instruction and study or (2) work that is original and creative in character in a recognized field or artistic endeavor that depends primarily on the invention, imagination, or talent of the employee. Computer programmers and others with highly specialized knowledge of computers qualify as professionals even if they are compensated on an hourly basis, so long as their hourly rate is at least 6½ times the minimum wage (approximately $33.48 per hour).

Executives, administrators, and professionals who satisfy the short test will not lose their exemption by being temporarily reassigned to nonexempt work, even for reassignments lasting several weeks, so long as their primary duties satisfy the short test definition of exempt. On the other hand, the exempt/nonexempt status of employees who are subject to the long test is determined on a workweek-by-workweek basis.

Proposed Regulations. In March 2003, the Department of Labor issued proposed new regulations that would substantially rewrite the white collar exemptions. The new regulations would eliminate the long and short test for executives, administrators, and professionals and substitute a *standard test*. The salary component of each test would be raised to $425 per week. (Neither the current test nor the new proposal contains a salary test for outside sales employees.) The job descriptions would also be clarified and simplified.

The new regulations would contain a special exemption for highly compensated employees—employees who earn more than $65,000 per year in base salary, commissions, and non-discretionary bonuses—so long as they have an identifiable executive, administrative, or professional function.

The comment period for the new regulations expired on June 30, 2003, but at this writing, no further action has been taken. (To see a copy of the proposed regulations and learn their current status, go to **www.dol.gov/esa/whd**.)

Salary Basis. For an executive, administrator, or professional to be exempt, he or she must be paid on a *salary basis*. DOL regulations provide that an employee will be considered as paid on a salary basis if, under the employment agreement, the employee *regularly receives each pay period on a weekly, or less frequent basis, a predetermined amount constituting all, or part, of his or her compensation, which amount is not subject to reduction because of variations in the quality or quantity of the work performed.*

Under this definition, an employee must generally be paid a full week's compensation for any week in which he or she performs any work, without regard to the number of days or hours worked. In other words, so long as the employee is ready, willing, and able to work a full week, the employer cannot reduce the compensation for the week just because the employer does not have any work available.

An employee will not qualify as salaried under DOL regulations if the employer docks wages for jury duty, temporary military leave, or attendance as a witness in court. However, the employer may *reduce* an employee's salary by the amount the employee is paid as a juror or witness or for military service.

> ## EMPLOYER TIP
>
> Many employers mistakenly think that all salaried employees are automatically exempt. To the contrary, while being salaried is one of the requirements for exemption, the employee must also qualify as an executive, administrator, or professional as defined in DOL regulations.

If an employee fails to report to work for a day or more for personal reasons (other than sickness or accident), the employer may dock his or her salary for the days the employee is absent without affecting the employee's exempt status. (Deductions for absences of a day or more relating to sickness or accident are also permitted if the employer has a plan, policy, or practice of providing alternative compensation under those circumstances.) But if the employee is absent for *less than a day*, no deduction is allowed. In short, if an

EMPLOYER TIP

Federal law protects the jobs of employees on military leave. Many states offer similar job protection to employees called to jury duty or to testify as a witness. (see Chapter 8.)

employer treats exempt employees as if they were hourly instead of salaried, they will cease being exempt.

The Department of Labor's definition of *salary basis* says that *all or part of* an employee's compensation must be *predetermined*. This means that an employee will be considered salaried even if some portion of his or her compensation is paid in the form of commissions or bonuses that vary depending on productivity or other factors. However, the predetermined amount must satisfy the minimum salary requirements for either the short test or the long test, whichever is applicable.

Improper Deductions
Improper deductions from an otherwise exempt employee's salary will convert that employee to nonexempt status. Any overtime the employee worked while in a nonexempt status will then have to be paid at time-and-a-half.

If an employer inadvertently makes improper deductions for reasons other than lack of work, the employer may avoid penalties by reimbursing the employee for the deductions and promising to comply in the future. A recent case illustrates how this so-called *window of correction* works. A restaurant chain had a policy of deducting recurrent cash register shortages from its (exempt) managers' monthly bonuses. Deductions from *bonuses* did not affect their exempt status because the managers qualified as exempt on their base salaries. (As mentioned above, it is permissible to vary a portion of an exempt employee's pay to reflect quality or quantity or work, so long as the employee's compensation includes a fixed component which does not vary based on hours worked, productivity, etc.) In an effort to reduce cash register shortages, the employer changed its policy and began deducting shortages from its managers' *base salaries.* The new policy *did* affect the managers' exempt status because it amounted to treating them as hourly workers, not salaried employees.

Other Exemptions
Other exemptions may be significant for some employers. Unlike executives, administrators, and professionals, there are a few exemptions that do not require payment of a fixed salary. These include:

- *lawyers and physicians* who are licensed in their respective professions and who are actually practicing their professions;
- *outside salespersons* who are customarily and regularly employed in making sales away from the employer's place of business; and,
- *drivers, drivers' helpers, loaders,* and *mechanics* for motor carriers, whose duties affect safe operation of motor vehicles in interstate commerce and who are subject to regulation by the U.S. Department of Transportation.

Even if an employer is not subject to federal overtime requirements under the FLSA, it may be subject to state overtime requirements. State law is similar to the FLSA, but states often have different exemptions from overtime.

SETTLING FLSA WAGE DISPUTES
When an employer underpays an employee in violation of the FLSA, the employee may recover not only the balance of wages owed, but also additional liquidated damages equal to the unpaid amount and the attorneys' fees incurred in pursuing the claim. In cases of underpayment, the employer and employee generally cannot enter a binding settlement agreement in which the employer agrees to pay something less than the full amount due.

In a 1945 decision, the Supreme Court invalidated a settlement agreement between an employer and an employee which did not include a provision for payment of liquidated damages to the employee. The Court reasoned that the FLSA affords statutory rights that simply cannot be waived. A year later the Court ruled that even where there was a bona fide dispute between the parties as to the employer's overtime obligation, a settlement agreement would not be enforceable. However, in that case the dispute involved a *legal issue* of whether the employer was engaged in interstate commerce and, therefore, whether the FLSA applied. The Court left open the question whether a bona fide dispute over a *factual issue*, such as how many hours of overtime the employee worked, might support a settlement agreement in which an employee agrees to compromise his of her FLSA claim.

The question left open by the Court in 1946 remains unanswered today. So to resolve disputes where an employer does not want to roll over and pay whatever the employee claims due nor fight it out in court, the employer should request the Department of Labor to participate in and supervise a settlement. Prudent employers will want to involve the Department of Labor in just this way, particularly if substantial amounts are in dispute or a whole class of employees claim to have been underpaid.

OTHER WAGE REGULATIONS

The states regulate many other aspects of wage-and-hour requirements. Typical requirements are that employers:

- ◆ establish regular pay periods;
- ◆ pay hourly workers at least twice a month and pay salaried employees at least monthly;
- ◆ pay in U.S. currency; and,
- ◆ pay terminated employees within a specified time period after termination.

If bonuses and commissions are part of an employee's regular compensation package, they must be paid just like other wages.

Although direct deposit of employee paychecks is a great convenience to employer and employee alike, employers may be barred under state wage regulations from *insisting* that employees participate in a direct deposit program.

All employers are *required* to deduct taxes and related items from employee paychecks and amounts subject to garnishment. (see Chapter 6.) Employers *may* deduct other amounts agreed to by the employee, such as voluntary contributions to a retirement plan, the employee's contributory portion of health insurance premiums, etc. Employers are generally *prohibited* from deducting amounts on account of workers' compensation benefits or unemployment insurance, or from deducting other amounts claimed due from the employee like reimbursement for breakage or for mistakes on customer accounts.

State laws also impose certain record-keeping requirements. In general, employers must keep records for at least three years showing the name, address, social security number, and occupation of each employee, the employee's rate of pay, the amount actually paid each pay period, and the hours worked each day and each workweek. The records are subject to onsite inspection by wage and hour officials.

CHILD LABOR

Both federal and state laws regulate child labor. On the federal side, the Fair Labor Standards Act (FLSA) prohibits *oppressive child labor*, which is defined as:

- ◆ employment of any child who is under the age of 16, regardless of the occupation and
- ◆ employment of a child who is between the ages of 16 and 18 in mining, manufacturing, or any other industry the Secretary of Labor finds particularly hazardous.

Excluded from the definition is:

- ◆ employment in a family business, so long as the employment is not in mining, manufacturing, or other particularly hazardous industry;
- ◆ agricultural employment (with parental consent if the child is under 14 and only when school is not in session if the child is under 16);
- ◆ employment as an actor or performer in movies, the theater, and radio and television productions;
- ◆ delivering newspapers to consumers; and,
- ◆ making wreaths at home and harvesting forest products to be used in wreath-making.

Separate federal legislation prohibits the employment of children in the production of child pornography for distribution in interstate commerce.

State regulation of child labor differs from jurisdiction to jurisdiction. The definition of *minor* may vary, for example. And each state also has its own list of exclusions, reflective of prominent local industries or regional customs.

EMPLOYER TIP

Specific work, such as serving alcoholic beverages or driving commercial vehicles, may be subject to additional age restrictions.

Minors need a *work permit*, typically issued through the school system, before being able to work. Employers must keep permits on file and available for inspection. Even when a minor is properly permitted to work, additional restrictions may apply, such as when and how many hours a minor may work. These time restrictions vary depending on whether school is or is not in session.

The illegal employment of minors exposes the employer to substantial criminal and civil penalties.

PRIORITY OF WAGES AND BENEFITS IN BANKRUPTCY

At any given time, an employer usually owes wages to employees. Depending on the frequency of pay periods and the lag between the end of a pay period and the date checks are issued, nonexempt employees could be owed as little as a few days' pay or as much as a few weeks' pay. Exempt employees and employees who are due commissions may be owed substantially more. Similarly, at any particular time employers with pension or other benefit plans usually have an unfunded obligation to those plans.

When an employer's assets are being administered in bankruptcy court, the U.S. Bankruptcy Code specifies an order of priority for payment of claims against the employer. High on the priority list are amounts due to employees and to employee benefit plans.

Under the Bankruptcy Code, the items that come before claims of the employer's other unsecured creditors include:

- wages, salaries, and commissions (including vacation, severance, and sick leave pay) earned during the 90-day period prior to the filing of the bankruptcy petition, capped at $4,650 per employee and
- contributions due to employee benefit plans arising from services rendered during the 180-day period prior to the filing of the bankruptcy petition, also capped at $4,650 per employee.

ANTITRUST CONSIDERATIONS

Federal antitrust laws generally prohibit contracts, combinations, and conspiracies in restraint of trade. It would be illegal, for example, for a group of service station operators in a particular region to fix prices by reaching an agreement among themselves that none of them will sell gasoline below, say, $1.80 a gallon.

Likewise, employers may not engage in *wage-fixing* agreements. Suppose a particular industry faces a labor shortage so that employers in that industry are unable to attract all the employees they need. Rather than engage in a bidding war (that the employers perceive as just running up everyone's labor costs without solving the problem), they decide to impose a cap on wages by mutual agreement. *This is illegal.*

However, it is perfectly legal for *employees* to conspire among themselves for wage increases or other benefits. Employees and labor unions, while engaged in efforts to better the wages and working conditions, may conspire to increase wages and other benefits. However, labor unions lose this ability when they conspire with employers outside the scope of legitimate union objectives. The Supreme Court ruled, for example, that an agreement between a coal miner's union and one set of mine owners, that the union would insist on specified wage standards in its negotiations with other mine owners, violated the antitrust laws.

EMPLOYER TIP

If the targeted employer has protected itself with noncompete agreements, the employer doing the targeting may also be liable for tortious interference with contract. (see Chapter 23.)

Predatory Hiring

One other issue deserves mention—*predatory hiring*. Wholly apart from contracts, combinations, and conspiracies, an employer might well have liability under the antitrust laws if, without regard to its own business needs, it targets a competitor's employees in order to harm the competitor's business. The risks here can be reduced if the new employer can demonstrate a genuine business need for the employees and if it can be shown that a particular competitor was not just targeted, but that qualified employees were sought from a range of sources.

–6–

WAGE ATTACHMENTS AND ASSIGNMENTS

The obligations an employer owes its employees under wage-and-hour laws (discussed in Chapter 5) are trumped by a variety of court-ordered garnishments and wage attachments. When an employee's wages are garnished or attached, the employer satisfies its wage-payment obligations by paying a portion of the employee's wages to a third party to whom the employee is indebted.

GARNISHMENTS

When an employee's creditor sues your employee on an unpaid debt and obtains a court judgment, the creditor is authorized to *execute* on the judgment, meaning that the creditor can try to collect the judgment out of assets belonging to the employee. One of those assets is the stream of wage payments the employee becomes entitled to as he or she works for you. Collecting a judgment out of an employee's wages is known as a *garnishment*. The cast of characters in that arrangement is the judgment *debtor* (your employee), the judgment *creditor* or *garnisher*, and you, the *garnishee*.

NOTE: *Wages are* garnished *not* garnisheed.

> ## EMPLOYER TIP
>
> Some employers may be tempted to help their employees evade garnishments and withholding orders by falsifying information about compensation or paying employees off the books. Doing so exposes the employer to criminal prosecution.

An employer usually first finds out about a garnishment when served with a court *writ* (or order). (When the garnishment relates to family support obligations in a domestic relations case, it is called a *withholding order*.) The employer must respond by filing an answer in court within the time limit specified in the writ, stating whether the judgment debtor is in fact an employee and, if so, what the wages are. The employer may assert any defenses to the garnishment and any defenses the employee could assert. If the employer states that the judgment debtor is not an employee, that usually ends the matter, unless the judgment creditor requests a hearing to explore the issue further.

Attachable Wages

Assuming the judgment debtor is an employee, the employer will then be required to withhold the *attachable wages* of the employee and remit them periodically to the *garnisher* (the judgment creditor) until the judgment is paid or the employment ends. The garnishment applies to any wages that are unpaid at the time of the attachment, as well as wages that become due in the future. The attachable wages are limited by the federal *Consumer Credit Protection Act* to the *lesser* of (a) 25% of the employee's disposable earnings (after deducting tax and similar withholdings and after deducting the employee's portion of any medical insurance premiums) or (b) the amount by which the weekly disposable earnings exceed thirty times the federal minimum hourly wage. The writ of attachment will say exactly how to compute the amount to be withheld.

> **EMPLOYER TIP**
>
> Even though an employer is making payments to a garnisher, the employer must treat the payments as part of the employee's compensation for purposes of computing income tax withholding, FICA, etc.
> (see Chapter 17.)

Penalties

Penalties for ignoring a garnishment can be substantial. In some circumstances, the employer might be held in contempt or might be required to cover the costs and attorneys' fees incurred by the garnisher to enforce the garnishment. The employer might even have to pay double wages—once to the employee and again to the garnisher. In other words, it's a good idea to take garnishments seriously.

If the employee quits or is fired while the garnishment is in effect, the employer's obligation to remit attachable wages ends. (In some states, rehiring an employee within a short time period automatically revives the garnishment.) If several garnishments for the same employee are received, the employer must honor the garnishments in the order they are served, paying off the first one completely before starting payments on the next one.

Federal law prohibits an employer from firing an employee because the employee's wages are subjected to attachment for any one indebtedness within a calendar year. Many states have similar laws protecting the jobs of garnished employees. One federal district court ruled that an employer was not free to fire a employee for a second garnishment, since the employer was obligated to satisfy only one garnishment at a time.

Wages Subject to Garnishment

State law defines what constitutes *wages* for garnishment purposes. The definition generally covers bonuses and commissions, as well as regular compensation. In some states, employee tips may also have to be included.

Contributions to a pension plan that is subject to the *Employee Retirement Income Security Act* (ERISA) are exempt from garnishment, even where state law seems to provide otherwise. ERISA requires plan documents to contain a provision protecting benefits from an employee's creditors and ERISA preempts (supersedes) state law relating to pension plans. (ERISA is covered in Chapter 9.)

WITHHOLDING ORDERS

A withholding order is a special kind of wage attachment issued in a domestic relations case in connection with spousal or child support.

Alimony and child support used to be the exclusive concerns of state courts. With enactment of the *Child Support Enforcement Act* in 1975, the federal government got involved in a big way. Under the Act, each state must establish a formal program, which is subject to approval by the Secretary of Health and Human Services, for locating noncustodial parents and obtaining child support and support for the spouse (or former spouse) with whom the noncustodial parent's child is living. *Child support* must include health care coverage whenever it is available to the noncustodial parent at a reasonable cost, without regard to enrollment or open season restrictions. In accordance with these requirements, each state now has a Directory of New Hires (discussed in Chapter 2) and the states have support guidelines and collection procedures.

When an *existing* employee who is obligated to make support payments becomes more than thirty days delinquent, the delinquency will usually result in issuance of a withholding order directing the employer to withhold the support payments from the employee's wages. Within twenty days after an employer hires a new employee, the employer must submit the employee's name, social security number, and other identifying information for inclusion in the state's Directory of New Hires. If that information matches with an outstanding withholding order, then the state sends a notice directing the employer to withhold the required amount from the employee's wages.

As with garnishments, the federal *Consumer Credit Protection Act* also sets limits on the amount of wages that may be withheld pursuant to a withholding order. However, the limit may be as high as 65% of disposable earnings if the employee is in arrears in support payments and has no new spouse or dependent children to support.

Pursuant to the *Child Support Enforcement Act*, withholding orders will direct the employer to remit withheld payments not to the employee's child or to the parent who has custody of the child, but instead to the state agency or court that monitors enforcement of such orders.

Employers are prohibited from retaliating in any way, such as by firing or disciplining an employee who is the subject of a withholding order. States may, however, permit employers to charge a fee for processing withholding orders.

(Also related to family support obligations are *Qualified Medical Child Support Orders* (QMCSOs), discussed in Chapter 10.)

TAX LEVIES

When your employee fails to pay his or her federal income taxes, the IRS can collect the unpaid taxes from you, the employer, by serving you with a *levy*. Levies, like garnishments, require the employer to pay to a third party (in this case, the U.S. Treasury) some portion of the wages otherwise due the employee in order to extinguish the employee's debt to that party. Corporate officials who are responsible for payroll matters can have *personal liability* for disregarding a tax levy.

State law also provides means for collecting delinquent taxes through garnishment of salary or wages, although the procedures and exemptions differ from state to state.

If your employee disputes the validity of the levy and sues you for unpaid wages, you are discharged from any obligation or liability to the employee because you made payments in accordance with an IRS levy.

DEBTORS IN BANKRUPTCY

Chapter 13 of the federal *Bankruptcy Act* is entitled *Adjustment of Debts of an Individual with a Regular Income*. Under Chapter 13, a debtor with a regular income may ask a bankruptcy court to prohibit creditors from suing him or her or otherwise attempting to collect debts. In exchange, the debtor must propose a plan to pay down the debts out of ongoing disposable income (generally defined as income not reasonably necessary for the support of the debtor). The plan can last no more than three years and it must be designed so that the creditors receive at least as much under the plan as they would

> **EMPLOYER TIP**
>
> Federal law prohibits discrimination against persons who have filed for bankruptcy.

have received had the debtor simply brought all assets into court in a Chapter 7 liquidation.

If the bankruptcy court approves (confirms) the plan, then the court will issue an order directing the debtor's employer to pay specified amounts to a Chapter 13 *trustee*. The trustee, in turn, makes periodic payments to the creditors. Bankruptcy orders are exempt from the limitations imposed by the *Consumer Credit Protection Act*.

DEPARTMENT OF EDUCATION GARNISHMENTS

Under the federal *Higher Education Act*, the U.S. Department of Education may garnish the *disposable pay* of individuals who are delinquent in repaying *student loans* made, insured, or guaranteed by the federal government. Under the garnishment procedure, the Department issues a withholding order to the employer. If the employer fails to withhold in accordance with the order, the employer can be sued not only for the amount that was not withheld, but also for attorneys' fees and punitive damages. The term *disposable pay* is defined as compensation remaining after deduction of any amounts required by law to be withheld.

Employers may not retaliate by discharging or disciplining an employee whose pay is subject to a Department of Education withholding order. Employers are also prohibited from refusing to hire a prospective employee because he or she is the subject of a Department of Education withholding order.

WAGE ASSIGNMENTS

An *assignment* of wages is different from a garnishment. Garnishments are government orders with which the employer must comply. Assignments, on the other hand, are private agreements between an employee and a third person—usually a creditor to whom the employee owes money—that may or may not be valid, depending on whether they comply with state law.

State law often restricts the ability of an employee to make a voluntary assignment of wage. It may also impose specific requirements and procedures in order to make a valid assignment. The safest practice is for an employer to adopt a uniform policy and distribute it to all employees, such as through the employee handbook, that the employer will not honor any wage assignments and that, except as otherwise required by law, all wages will be paid directly to the employee (or direct-deposited in the employee's account) without regard to any assignment.

$-7-$
TAX CONSIDERATIONS

Tax considerations drive, or at least help shape, any number of transactions in the business world. The same is true for the employer-employee relationship. With combined federal and state income tax rates at or above 40%, the deductibility of employer expenditures becomes a critical factor in a business' survival. At the same time, employees look to limit or defer tax on their employment-related benefits. The result is a complex web of employer opportunities and requirements.

DEDUCTIBILITY OF WAGES AND BENEFITS
Wages and benefits paid to employees are deductible from the employer's gross income for purposes of computing the employer's federal and state income tax, so long as the amounts are reasonable, ordinary, and necessary. This means, for example, that for a corporate employer who is in the 39% marginal federal tax bracket and the 7% state tax bracket, 46 cents of each additional dollar in wages and benefits is effectively paid by federal and state governments in the form of reduced tax liabilities.

As a general rule, whenever the employer takes a deduction for a wage or benefit payment, the employee who receives the payment must include it in his or her own gross income for federal and state tax purposes. The IRS keeps track of these shifting tax burdens by requiring employers to report employee payments on *Form W-2* and payments to independent contractors on *Form 1099*.

There are, however, important exceptions to the general rule. One exception is for items of *deferred compensation*—compensation that the employee cannot immediately enjoy, such as qualified retirement plan contributions. It may make little difference to an employer whether compensation to employees is in the form of wages, or partly in wages and partly in the form of a qualified retirement plan contribution, since both are fully deductible if they are within the limits imposed by law. But it can make a big difference to the employee because of the time value of money.

> **EMPLOYER TIP**
>
> When employer-sponsored group health insurance covers an employee's domestic partner, the premium is taxable income to the employee. (see Chapter 10.)

Take, for example, an employee whose marginal tax bracket for federal and state tax purposes is 46%. For each additional dollar received in wages, 46 cents is paid to the government and only 54 cents is left to invest. (The employee's portion of FICA and Medicare reduce this even more.) Worse, any income earned on that 54 cents is also subject to current taxation.

In contrast, a dollar of deferred compensation is not subject to immediate tax, so the full dollar can be invested without reduction for taxes. In addition, earnings on that dollar—called *inside build-up*—are not subject to immediate tax either. In the end, the employee should have a much greater nest egg than if he or she had received and invested taxable wages. Of course, that nest egg is subject to income tax as it is withdrawn during retirement, but in most cases, the employee is still better off, particularly since the tax bracket in retirement is probably lower than when actively working.

There are other important exceptions to the general rule that whatever the employer deducts, the employee must report. For example, employer contributions to group health insurance, medical savings plans, and group term life insurance up to $50,000 in coverage (discussed in Chapter 10) are generally deductible by the employer, but not includible in the employee's income.

Some noncash *fringe benefits* may be deductible for the employer but (subject to specified limits and conditions) not includible in the employee's gross income. For example:

- *no-additional-cost service*—a service to an employee that the employer normally provides to its customers, so long as doing so is without substantial additional cost to the employer;
- *employee discounts* on goods (so long as the discount does not exceed the employer's profit margin) and on services (so long as the discount does not exceed 20% of the retail price);
- *working condition benefits*, such as upscale office appointments and use of a company car for business purposes;
- *de minimis benefits*, such as use of the copying machine or office supplies for personal purposes, and such as eating facilities at or near the employer's premises (so long as the facility is operated on at least a break-even basis and so long as the employer does not discriminate in favor of highly compensated employees); and,
- *transportation benefits*, including a transit pass, parking, or cash reimbursements for those items.

Federal tax law allows companies to deduct all *ordinary and necessary expenses* of carrying on a trade or business. This includes reimbursements to employees who have incurred expenses on behalf of their employers. But special rules apply to transportation and travel expenses. For example, while companies can reimburse their employees for, and then deduct, *actual expenses* incurred in operating an automobile for business, IRS regulations have long allowed use of *standard mileage rates* in lieu of providing substantiation for actual expenses. (At this writing, the standard rate for business use of an automobile is 36.5 cents per mile.)

The IRS takes a similar approach to *per diem* business travel expenses (meals, lodging, and incidental expenses), allowing standard reimbursement/deduction rates instead of requiring substantiation of actual expenses. Employers may use one of two methods to reimburse employees, either of which will satisfy the substantiation requirement:

◆ the federal per diem rates method, based on location-specific rates established by the federal government for cities within the continental U.S. (the CONUS rates) and outside the continental U.S. (the OCONUS rates). A complete listing of those rates is available at **www.policyworks.gov/perdiem** or

◆ the high-low method, available only for travel within the continental U.S., which allows a deduction of $204 per day for specified high-cost areas and $125 per day for all other areas within the continental U.S.

(A full listing of high-cost areas is located in IRS Publication 1542 available at **www.irs.gov**.)

The deduction for food, beverages, and entertainment (but not lodging) is limited to 50% of the otherwise deductible amount, subject to a number of exceptions. Amounts paid to employees in excess of deductible amounts constitute income to the employees and are subject to withholding requirements and payroll taxes.

LIMITATIONS ON DEDUCTIBILITY

Most business corporations are classified as C *corporations* for federal income tax purposes. C corps are separate taxable entities, whose taxable income is determined by starting with the corporation's gross revenue and deducting the cost of goods sold, salaries, rent, and other expenses. After paying tax on the resulting net income, the corporation may choose to distribute some or all of what is left to its shareholders in the form of a *dividend*. Dividends represent taxable income to the shareholders.

Because a C corp is a taxable entity, income is taxed twice on its way through the corporation to its shareholders. One tax is paid at the corporate level and a second tax is paid at the individual shareholder level. Particularly in the case of small, closely-held corporations, where the shareholder-owners are also the directors, officers, and employees, this *double taxation* burden is problematic.

One way to avoid double taxation is to accumulate income inside the corporation and not pay dividends. But depending on the amounts involved, the corporation may end up owing an *accumulated earnings tax* that is designed to stop that very practice.

Another way to avoid double taxation is to elect *S corporation status*. (see Chapter 1.) Although S corps are generally not subject to tax as separate entities, there are restrictions on who may elect S status. There may also be undesirable tax consequences to S corp owners.

> **EMPLOYER TIP**
>
> Although nonprofit, tax-exempt organizations do not have to worry about the deductibility of their compensation payments, they do need to be concerned about paying excess benefits to their board members, officers and high-level managers.
> (see Chapter 20.)

Yet another way is to pay year-end bonuses to owner-employees. Through careful calculation, the bonuses can be set so that the corporation has virtually zero taxable income and it pays almost no tax. (It is usually not possible to reach *exactly* zero, since some cash expenditures during the year, such as equipment purchases, may not be deductible, but they reduce the amount of cash available to pay bonuses.) The owner-employees, of course, will owe tax on the bonuses along with whatever other compensation they receive, but that is still just one tax—not two.

The taxpayer corporation has the burden of proving that its compensation payments are reasonable under Internal Revenue Code (I.R.C.) Section 162. And particularly where the taxpayer corporation is controlled by the employees receiving the compensation, the payments are subject to careful scrutiny by the IRS to be sure that they truly represent (deductible) compensation for services rendered, rather than disguised (nondeductible) dividends. In determining whether compensation is reasonable, the courts look at a number of factors, including:

- the employee's qualifications;
- the nature, extent, and scope of the employee's work;
- the size and complexity of the employer's business;
- a comparison of salaries paid with the employer's income;

◆ prevailing rates of compensation for comparable positions in comparable companies;

◆ the amount of compensation paid to the employee in prior years; and,

◆ whether the employer offers pension and profit-sharing plans to its employees.

These factors are applied on an individual employee basis, rather than in the aggregate to a group of employees. In other words, it does not matter that the company's overall deduction for compensation is reasonable. Each individual employee's compensation must be reasonable as well.

Under I.R.C. Sec. 162(m), publicly-held corporations also face limits on the amount they can deduct. In general, the Code places a $1 million per year cap on deductions for remuneration paid to *covered employees*—defined as the chief executive officer and the four highest paid officers other than the CEO.

> **EMPLOYER TIP**
>
> Payments to partners in a partnership, to shareholders of S corps, and to members of limited liability companies, where the partners, shareholders, or members work for the company they own, are generally treated as nondeductible distributions rather than as deductible wages and salaries.

INDEPENDENT CONTRACTORS

Recent news articles illustrate the hazard of misclassifying employees as independent contractors. *Microsoft*, for example, agreed to pay almost $100 million to a group of so-called *temporary* workers who should have been, but were not, classified as regular employees entitled to participate in Microsoft's benefit plans. Time-Warner faced similar problems, although the amount at stake was only a few million dollars.

In addition to benefit plan participation, employees (but not independent contractors) are subject to federal and state income tax withholding. They are entitled to have employer FICA contributions made on their behalf and they are covered by workers' compensation and unemployment insurance for which the employer must pay premiums. So if an employer wrongly treats a group of employees as independent contractors over a period of years, the total cost of remedying the error can be staggering.

Traditionally, the question whether a worker is an employee or an independent contractor turns on whether the employer has a *right to control* the manner in which the worker does his or her job. (see Chapter 7.) This is sometimes known as the *common-law test*. In order to determine whether there is or is not a right of control, a number of subsidiary factors are considered, such as who sets the worker's hours, whether the worker works for one or several employers, whether the worker or the employer provides necessary tools and workspace, whether the worker has specialized knowledge or requires a license or a professional degree to do the job, etc. The problem with the common-law test is its lack of certainty. If the employer guesses wrong, disaster can strike.

In an effort to resolve this uncertainty, Congress enacted legislation to provide a *safe harbor* for employers. Under these safe harbor provisions, an employer's treatment of a worker as an independent contractor is relatively safe from IRS challenge if:

♦ the employer has never treated the worker as an employee;
♦ the employer filed all required tax reports and returns relating to the worker on a timely and consistent basis; and,
♦ the employer had a reasonable basis for treating the worker as an independent contractor.

The employer will be considered to have a reasonable basis for treating the worker as an independent contractor if the employer relied on a court decision involving facts similar to the employer's own or if the employer relied on rulings or technical advice from the IRS. The employer can also demonstrate a reasonable basis if a *significant segment of the industry* in which the worker is engaged has a *long-standing recognized practice* of treating such workers as independent contractors. A *significant segment* of the industry is 25%. However, the employer will *not* have a reasonable basis for treating a particular worker as an independent contractor if the employer has other workers doing similar jobs who are treated as employees.

While the IRS can still challenge a safe harbor classification, the burden of proving that the classification is wrong falls on the IRS. In order to ensure that the safe harbor provisions are fully effective, the IRS must provide the employer with a written notice of the provisions when it audits an employer in connection with a worker classification issue. The IRS is also prohibited from issuing regulations or rulings dealing with the safe harbor provisions.

A recent case decided by the federal district court in Maryland illustrates how the safe harbor provisions work. A company licensed as a residential service agency provided nonskilled, home health aids for the elderly. Before opening for business, the company conducted a survey of some 20 to 30 competitors in the Washington, D.C. metropolitan area. It found that approximately 80% of the agencies surveyed treated their workers as independent contractors, while only 10% treated them as employees. The other 10% did not respond. When the company decided to open additional offices in Baltimore and Richmond, it conducted similar surveys in those areas and obtained similar results. Based on these surveys, the company classified its workers as independent contractors. The court ruled that the company's reliance on its surveys was reasonable and that the company's classification of its aids was correct.

Another approach to resolving the employee/independent contractor issue for federal tax and withholding purposes is to ask the IRS to decide. Upon filing *Form SS-8* (either by the employer or by the worker whose status is in doubt), the IRS will determine whether the worker is an employee or an independent contractor. The determination can then be relied on for safe harbor purposes. It is probably fair to assume that the IRS resolves close questions by concluding that the worker is an employee, not an independent contractor. So as a practical matter, the SS-8 route may not be very helpful to employers.

Example: Suppose an employer incorrectly classifies a worker as an independent contractor when, in reality, the worker should have been treated as an employee. As an independent contractor, the worker pays a self-employment tax equal to 100% of the FICA tax ($10,788 as of this writing, assuming earnings of at least $87,000). Had the worker been properly classified as an employee, however, the employer would have paid only half the FICA amount, or $5,394 and the employer would have paid the other half. So the question arises whether, as a result of misclassification, the worker has a claim against the employer for the $5,394 that the employer should have matched but did not.

In a recent case, the Eleventh Circuit Court of Appeals ruled that FICA is a tax statute that only the federal government can enforce and that it does not create a private right of action. In other words, so far as FICA is concerned, an employer may be liable to the government for misclassification, but the employer is not liable to the misclassified employee himself.

FEDERAL WITHHOLDING REQUIREMENTS

We are all used to seeing a long list of deductions and withholdings on our pay stubs. Some of them are voluntary, like the employee portions of retirement plan contributions and health insurance premiums. Others are required by law.

How does the employer know how much to withhold? And what is done with the money? The first step in the process is for the employer to obtain an *Employer Identification Number* (EIN). The number has nine digits, as do social security numbers, but instead of being in the format 123-45-6789, an EIN is formatted 12-3456789. EINs are obtained by filing *Form SS-4* with the IRS, and may also be obtained by phone or facsimile. An electronic fill-in-the-blank SS-4 is available at **www.irs.gov/pub/irs-fill/fss4.pdf**.

The next step is for the employee to submit IRS *Form W-4* and the applicable state equivalent to the employer. This must be done at hiring time and whenever the employee's tax withholdings need to be changed. *Form W-4* calls for basic information—the employee's name, address, social security number, marital status, etc. It also contains a worksheet for figuring the number of exemptions to be claimed on the employee's tax return and various other factors that affect the employee's tax liability. These factors, known as *allowances*, are then totaled and entered on the form. Finally, *Form W-4* permits the employee to claim a complete exemption from federal income tax withholding under certain conditions.

When a *Form W-4* claims more than ten withholding allowances, or claims an exemption from withholding that would otherwise amount to more than $200 per week, a copy must be submitted to the IRS. The IRS may then direct the employer to withhold on some different basis.

The employer has four basic federal tax obligations relating to employees. These are:

1. federal income tax;
2. social security tax (FICA);
3. Medicare tax; and,
4. unemployment insurance contributions.

(The first three are discussed below. Unemployment insurance is covered in Chapter 12.)

Federal Income Tax

With *Form W-4* in hand, the employer turns to a set of tables issued by the IRS in *Circular E, Employer's Tax Guide* (also known as Publication 15), to determine how much to withhold from each paycheck. The tables are based on four variables:

1. the frequency of paydays (weekly, bi-weekly, etc.);
2. the employee's marital status as shown on *Form W-4*;
3. the amount of the wage payment; and,
4. the number of allowances claimed by the employee.

Circular E is really the employer's Bible when it comes to federal employment tax matters. It can be downloaded from the IRS's website by searching for Publication 15 at **www.irs.gov**.

Social Security (FICA) Tax

At this writing, the tax rate for the employee is 6.2% on a maximum wage base of $87,000, which translates to a maximum withholding of $5,394.00. The employer must match whatever amount is withheld from the employee. So for an employee whose annual salary is at least $87,000, the total payment on account of social security is $10,788.00, half of which is withheld from the employee and half of which is the employer's own *matching contribution*. The amount to be withheld from each paycheck is simply 6.2% of the gross payment until the maximum amount ($5,394.00) has been withheld. These rates and the wage base are subject to periodic change.

Medicare Tax

The Medicare tax rate is 1.45% of all wages for the employee and a matching amount of 1.45% for the employer. There is no wage base cap—the Medicare tax applies to all wages. The amount to be withheld from each paycheck is 1.45% of the gross payment.

Many dealings with the Social Security Administration can be accomplished online. For more information, see the *Business Services Online Handbook* at **www.ssa.gov/employer/bsohbnew.htm**.

Exceptions

In general, all employees who are U.S. citizens or resident aliens are subject to withholding for federal income tax and to FICA and Medicare withholding. Circular E contains a list of situations where special rules apply, including:
- ◆ nonresident aliens;
- ◆ household employees;
- ◆ clergy; and,
- ◆ disabled and deceased workers.

Independent contractors are also exempt from withholding requirements. However, a few, limited types of workers, called *statutory employees*, are required by law to be treated as employees even though they would otherwise qualify as independent contractors. (see Chapter 1.)

Nonregular Pay

Questions sometimes arise regarding withholding on back wages paid to an employee for some earlier year. Suppose, for example, that the employer and employee are in dispute over the exact amount due and the dispute gets resolved in court years after the employee did the work. Or suppose backpay is awarded in connection with a discrimination suit or an unfair labor practice complaint. Should the employer treat the wages as paid when they were *originally due* or as paid in the year they were *actually paid*? (The question can make a big difference if the tax rate or FICA ceiling has changed.) The IRS has long taken the position that the wages should be treated as paid currently. The Supreme Court recently affirmed that position.

Other taxable benefits subject to withholding include bonuses, commissions, expense reimbursements (unless the reimbursement is pursuant to an arrangement that requires the employee to verify expenses), payments in kind, meals, and lodging (unless provided for the employer's convenience on the employer's premises).

TIPS

In addition to withholding for wages, the employer must withhold on account of *tips*. Employees are required to report tips to their employer no later than the 10th of the month after the tips are received, unless tips for the month are less than $20. The report should include not only cash tips the employee receives directly from customers, but also tips received in a sharing arrangement with other employees and tips paid by the employer on charge slips. Employees may use *Form 4070* (contained in IRS Publication 1244) or a similar statement to report tips to their employers.

The employer then must figure tax withholdings, payroll taxes, and garnishments just as if the tips were wages paid by the employer. However, the employer is not liable to taxing authorities or garnishers for more money than actually comes into the employer's hands. Employers who operate *large food* and beverage establishments (defined as employing more than ten people, who work more than 80 hours per week in the aggregate), must file *Form 8027* annually with the IRS showing total tips.

It should be no surprise that employees who receive cash tips do not always make full reports to their employers. The IRS has addressed the problem in a number of ways.

8 Percent Rule

The *8 percent rule* is applicable to food and beverage establishments that have more than ten employees on a typical business day. Under the rule, if total reported tips are less than 8% of gross receipts, then the employer must assume that tips have been under-reported to the extent of the difference and allocate that difference among those employees who customarily receive tip income. However, if the IRS can be convinced that average tips for the particular business are less than 8% of gross receipts, then the percentage will be reduced, but not below 2%.

Aggregate Estimation Method

For payroll tax purposes (FICA, FUTA, and Medicare), the IRS sometimes uses an *aggregate estimation* method to determine an employer's liability—a method recently approved by the Supreme Court. To illustrate, suppose a restaurant's employees report tips totaling $100,000 in a particular year, which in turn are reported to the IRS by the restaurant. Suppose further that during a compliance audit the IRS discovers that the $100,000 represents only tips shown on charge slips and does not include tips by cash-paying customers. The IRS may assume that cash customers tip at the same rate as charge customers, use that assumption to determine total tips, and allocate total tips among the restaurant's service employees. In other words, the IRS may use a *top down methodology*. It does not have to estimate on an employee-by-employee basis.

EMPLOYER TIP

Tips may be counted against the employer's federal minimum wage requirement, but only up to $2.77 per hour at this writing, regardless of the actual amount of tips received and reported. (see Chapter 5.)

Tip Rate Determination Agreement

The IRS has developed a form agreement (known as a *TRDA*) pursuant to which the IRS and the employer determine and agree in advance on the rate of tips to be reported by employees. TRDAs require that at least 75% of the affected employees to join in the agreement.

Tip Reporting Alternative Commitment

The IRS has developed another form agreement (known as a *TRAC*) for food and beverage industry employers under which the employer promises to establish an education program for its employees and to establish procedures designed to assure accurate tip reporting. In return, the IRS promises to assess payroll taxes based solely on reported tips.

Restaurants do not like to act as tax police over their employees. They argue that the IRS has used the *aggregate estimation method* to coerce restaurants into participating in tip reporting programs. Congress has been sympathetic to restaurants' complaints. For one thing, Congress included in the *Internal Revenue Service Restructuring and Reform Act of 1998* a prohibition against IRS threats to audit a restaurant in an attempt to coerce it into a tip-reporting program. Second, federal tax law allows restaurants a dollar-for-dollar credit against their own income tax for any FICA tax they pay on employee tips. Finally, penalties and interest do not begin to run for FICA tax on unreported tips until the IRS actually assesses the amount it claims is due.

OTHER TAXABLE PAYMENTS

Suppose an employee is laid off under circumstances that could give rise to a claim of abusive discharge. Fearing a claim, the employer obtains a written release of claims from the employee and, as consideration for the release, makes a lump sum payment to the employee. Or suppose the employee refuses to sign a release and instead files a lawsuit that results in a money judgment against the employer for which the parties settle for a cash payment prior to trial. Are those payments deductible by the employer and taxable to the employee? Are they subject to withholding requirements? Are they subject to *W-2* or *1099* reporting requirements?

It has long been the rule that the proceeds of a personal injury action (a suit claiming injury to the body or person of the plaintiff) are *excluded* from taxation and from any withholding or reporting requirements. In the past, the parties to an employment dispute often characterized payments in settlement of the dispute as damages for emotional distress, for injury to reputation, etc., to avoid tax obligations.

In 1996, the Internal Revenue Code was amended to narrow the exclusion. The Code now states that gross income does not include damages received on account of personal *physical* injuries or *physical* sickness. A private letter ruling by the IRS defines personal physical injuries as direct unwanted or uninvited physical contacts resulting in observable bodily harms such as bruises, cuts, swelling, and bleeding.

EMPLOYER TIP

The settlement of an employment dispute should be in writing and it should include a provision by which the employee, former employee, or applicant for employment clearly releases all employment-related claims against the employer. If the release is intended to cover an actual or potential age discrimination claim, the release must conform to special rules contained in the *Age Discrimination in Employment Act.* (see Chapter 16.)

EMPLOYER TIP

Workers' compensation benefits are
exempt from income tax.
(see Chapter 11.)

As a result of the 1996 amendment, most payments in employment dispute situations will be includible in the recipient's gross income for federal income tax purposes. At the same time, the payments will be deductible by the employer. In addition, since damages in an employment dispute usually are based on *lost wages*, the payments are generally viewed as the equivalent of employee compensation and therefore subject to withholding and reporting requirements.

When an employer agrees to settle an employment dispute or agrees to a severance payment in the face of a potential claim, the agreement should state that the payments are subject to withholding and reporting. If the agreement attempts to characterize any portion of the payment as nontaxable and not subject to withholding or reporting (a risky arrangement), the agreement should at least contain a provision requiring the recipient to indemnify the employer should the IRS later recharacterize the payment as taxable.

When an employer satisfies a garnishment by paying a portion of the employee's salary to the employee's creditor, the employer is discharging a debt the employee owes. Economically, it is as if the employer paid wages to the employee and the employee, in turn, paid down the debt. So for tax withholding and reporting purposes, a garnishment payment is treated just like a wage payment to the employee.

STATE WITHHOLDING REQUIREMENTS

Most states impose their own taxes on income and require employers to withhold against that tax. State withholding requirements can get confusing, particularly when there are employees who commute to work from out of state. For each employee, the first step is to determine the state or states in which the employee *may* have to file a state income tax return. If the employee both lives and works in the same state, then only that state's withholding requirements apply. If the employee lives in one state but commutes to work in another state, then *both* states' withholding requirements need to be considered, since the employee potentially has tax filing obligations in both states. (Those few states that do not have any income tax at all can be ignored.)

Even though an employee may have a tax filing obligation in a particular state, the employer might not be required to withhold under that state's law. This could occur if the employer itself is not *subject to the jurisdiction* of that particular state because the employer has no office in that state and does not do business in that state. Take, for example, a Maryland company whose employees all work in Maryland, but some of whom live in Virginia. Virginia might like the company to withhold for the company's Virginia employees, but if the company is not subject to Virginia's jurisdiction, Virginia has no power to compel the company to withhold. At the same time, Maryland, where the company *is* subject to jurisdiction, has no interest in enforcing Virginia's tax laws.

The company could withhold Maryland income tax from all its employees. But this would mean that its Virginia employees would face a big Virginia tax bill not covered by withholdings, plus they would need to deal with Maryland to get some or all of their Maryland withholdings back. To resolve this situation, Maryland and Virginia have entered into *reciprocal agreements* with each other. Under these agreements, the Maryland company in the example above withholds Maryland tax from its Maryland employees and Virginia tax from its Virginia employees.

Many other states that have common borders have entered into reciprocal agreements similar to those between Maryland and Virginia. Contact your state employment tax office for details.

EARNED INCOME CREDIT

The *Earned Income Credit* (EIC) is a tax credit available to low-income employees. The amount of the credit ranges from a few hundred dollars for an employee with no dependent children to more than $4,000 for an employee with two or more dependent children. The credit is *refundable*, meaning that if the credit reduces the employee's tax liability below zero, not only does the employee owe no tax, but the government pays the amount of the *negative tax* to the employee. The employee claims the credit when his or her federal tax return is filed.

The EIC is normally a matter just between the employee and the IRS. However, when an employee expects to be in a negative tax situation at the end of the year, he or she may notify the employer of that fact, using *Form W-5*. The employer then is obligated to advance the negative tax to the employee with his or her pay checks. Only employees with one or more dependent children are eligible for advances. The IRS's Circular E contains tables for determining the amount to be included in each pay check. The employer is reimbursed for the advances by claiming them as a credit on the withholding tax deposits.

DEPOSIT AND REPORTING REQUIREMENTS

The timing and method of depositing withheld taxes and the employer's portion of FICA and Medicare taxes depend on the amount of taxes involved. In general, if the annual amount is less than $50,000, the deposits are made monthly to an authorized financial institution such as a national bank. (An employer owing less than $2,500 in employment taxes per quarter may remit those taxes with its quarterly return rather than depositing the taxes separately.)

If the amount is $50,000 or more, the deposits are made semi-weekly and must be made electronically through the IRS's *Electronic Federal Tax Payment System* (EFTPS). However, if an employer accumulates a tax liability of $100,000 or more on any day during a deposit period, the deposit must be made by the next banking day. Nonelectronic deposits must be accompanied by a *Federal Tax Deposit coupon, Form 8109*. Employers are also required to file *Form 941, Employer's Quarterly Federal Tax Return*, each quarter. All this is spelled out in Circular E.

FUTA (federal unemployment tax) is generally deposited quarterly, although if the amount due in any one quarter is $100 or less, it may be carried forward and added to next quarter's liability. Again, see Circular E.

Trust Fund Penalty

Taxes withheld from employees are considered to be held by the employer in trust. Rather than just owing the money to the IRS, the employer is treated as having a *fiduciary duty* to assure that deposits get made as required by law. If the employer fails to do so, the IRS may impose a *trust fund penalty* equal to the amount of the undeposited tax *in addition* to collecting the tax itself. Further, the corporate shield offers no protection when it comes to withholding taxes. So even an employer who has incorporated will be *personally liable*.

The trust fund penalty may be imposed on any person responsible for collecting, accounting for, and depositing the tax, who willfully fails to do so. *Responsible persons* can include corporate officers, employees, directors, anyone who signs checks or has authority for spending business funds, and even volunteers of nonprofit organizations. (Volunteers of tax-exempt organizations are relieved of personal liability if they are serving in an honorary capacity; if they do not participate in the day-to-day or financial operations of the organization; and, if they had no actual knowledge of the failure to withhold or make the required deposit—so long as there are at least some remaining responsible persons left to pay the taxes.) Liability for withholding taxes and for trust fund penalties is *not* dischargeable in bankruptcy.

W-2s

No later than January 31 of each year, employers must issue a *W-2 Form* to each employee reporting the employee's compensation for the prior calendar year. Copies of those *W-2 Forms* are then transmitted to the Social Security Administration using *Form W-3*. If an employee quits or is terminated during the year, the employer must, if so requested by the employee, issue a *W-2* within thirty days. *W-2s* may also be filed electronically. For more information, go to **www.ssa.gov/bso/bsowelcome.htm**.

The employee's name and social security number (SSN) shown on the *W-2* must match the Social Security Administration's records. When they do not, the Administration issues a *no match* letter. Receipt of a no-match letter does not necessarily mean that the employee is an illegal alien or that he or she has falsified the *W-4* Form submitted when hired. The mismatch could be the result of an employer error in recording the employee's SSN on the *W-2*, an employee name change through marriage or divorce, or an error on the employee's *W-4*. On receipt of a no-match letter, the employer should:

> ## EMPLOYER TIP
>
> Firing the employee or taking other adverse action against him or her solely on the basis of a name/SSN mismatch could be discriminatory.

- ◆ check the employer's own records for errors;
- ◆ provide a copy of the no-match letter to the employee and ask the employee to check his or her records;
- ◆ promptly report corrected information to the Social Security Administration; and,
- ◆ if no obvious errors in the employer's or employee's records are apparent, suggest that the employee contact the Social Security Administration for help.

The Administration has a number of procedures available for verifying social security numbers beforehand. The procedures are explained at **www.ssa.gov/employer/ssnv.htm**.

1099s

Independent contractors who have been paid more than $600 during the prior calendar year are issued *Form 1099-MISC* by January 31.

K-1s

Partners in general partnerships, members of limited liability companies that have elected to be taxed as partnerships, and shareholders of corporations that have elected S status, are issued *K-1 Forms* at the time the partnership, LLC, or S corp files its own tax return. (see Chapter 1.)

Payroll Services

For very modest charges, a commercial payroll service will:
- calculate each employee's deductions and withholdings;
- issue net checks to employees using the employer's preprinted check stock (or make deposits directly to the employees' bank accounts);
- provide a check stub to each employee showing current and year-to-date earnings, deductions, and withholdings;
- make all required federal and state tax deposits;
- prepare all federal and state reports; and,
- prepare *W-2 Forms* and appropriate transmittal forms.

Particularly for smaller employers, this service is difficult to beat. Be cautioned, however, that the employer will be held responsible if the payroll service fails to make required tax deposits. For that reason, it is a good idea to check with the IRS periodically to be sure no deficiencies exist. The address on file with the IRS for mailing deficiency notices should be the employer's address, not that of the payroll service.

CREDITS FOR EMPLOYING THE DISADVANTAGED

The Internal Revenue Code has long provided incentives for employing the disadvantaged. Current programs include the *empowerment zone employment credit*, the *work opportunity credit*, and the *welfare-to-work credit*. In general, wages that are counted for one of the credits cannot be counted for either of the other credits or claimed as a deduction on the employer's federal income tax return. (see IRS Publication 3991.)

Empowerment Zone Employment (EZE) Credit

The first $15,000 of compensation paid to persons who both live and work within an empowerment zone constitutes *qualified zone wages*. The credit is equal to 20% of all qualified zone wages. So employers can claim a credit of up to $3,000 per qualified zone employee per year. Payments to certain employees do not qualify, such as relatives, persons who own 5% or more of the business, and employees at golf courses, country clubs, massage parlors, race tracks, and liquor stores. (See IRS Form 8844 and instructions.)

More information about the EZE credit, the specific zones that qualify, contact information, and applicable expiration dates is available at:
www.hud.gov/offices/cpd
/economicdevelopment/programs/rc/index.cfm

Work Opportunity Tax Credit

The *Work Opportunity Tax Credit* (WOTC) applies to *qualified first-year wages* paid to *targeted group employees* who typically suffer high unemployment. In general, the first $6,000 in wages paid for work during the first year of employment qualifies for a 40% ($2,400) credit. Summer youth employees are limited to a 25% ($1,500) credit. Targeted groups include recipients of assistance under *TANF* (Temporary Assistance for Needy Families), veterans, ex-felons, summer youths, food stamp recipients, and supplemental security income (SSI) recipients. (See IRS Publications 954 and 3991 and Form 5884 and instructions.) To be considered a member of a targeted group, the employee must first be certified by the employer's state employment security agency (SESA). Certification is obtained by submitting IRS *Form 8850* and U.S. Department of Labor *Form ETA 9061* to the applicable SESA.

Welfare-to-Work Credit

The *Welfare-to-Work Credit* is available to employers who hire long-term family assistance recipients. As with the WOTC, certification by the employer's SESA is required. Certification is obtained by submitting IRS *Form 8861* and U.S. Department of Labor *Form ETA 9061* to the applicable SESA. The first $10,000 in wages paid to a certified employee in the first year of employment qualifies for a 35% credit. For the second year of employment, the first $10,000 in wages qualifies for a 50% credit the second year. The maximum credit over two years is $8,500.

At this writing, both the WOTC and the WtW credit expire after 2003, although Congress may continue extending the deadline, as it has done in the past. The IRS publications, forms, and instructions are available at **www.irs.gov**. *Form ETA 9061* is available at **www.doleta.gov**.

States have a variety of tax credits as well. More information can be obtained from each state's employment security agency.

–8–

LEAVE POLICIES

With a few exceptions discussed later in this chapter, there is no obligation for an employer to offer any leave at all. Of course, most employers do so because it is customary, it is humane, and not doing so would place the employer at a competitive disadvantage in the marketplace.

VACATION AND SICK LEAVE

A typical vacation formula for regular, full-time employees might give ten days (two weeks) per year after the first two or three years of employment and fifteen days (three weeks) per year after the third or fourth year. Limitations are commonly placed on the amount of vacation that can be carried forward—a *use-it-or-lose-it policy*. This encourages employees to take regular vacations, which in turn improves morale. It also avoids the disruption of extra-long absences.

Sick leave is often ten days per year. Employers need to specify in their employee handbooks what is covered by sick leave and what is not. For example, must the actual employee be sick or does a sick child or spouse also qualify? How about routine,

> ## EMPLOYER TIP
>
> For employers covered by *Title VII* of the federal *Civil Rights Act* or equivalent state law, a temporary disability caused by pregnancy or childbirth must be treated the same under the employer's sick leave policy as a temporary disability caused by other medical conditions. (see Chapter 15.)

EMPLOYER TIP

An employer policy that requires a health care provider's certification to state a diagnosis of the condition that gave rise to the absence may violate the *Americans with Disabilities Act.* A federal appellate court recently ruled that since a diagnosis might reveal an underlying disability, the requirement runs afoul of the ADA's prohibition on inquiring about disabilities. (see Chapter 17.)

nonemergency medical and dental visits for the employee or for the employee's child? And believe it or not, the policy needs to address sick pets as well.

When time off for an injury or illness extends more than a few days, employers may want to require written verification from the employee's health care practitioner. After a serious illness or injury, *certification of fitness* for duty may be required on the employee's return. These policies, too, should be spelled out in the employee handbook and applied uniformly to avoid claims of favoritism or discrimination.

To eliminate any implication that employees are hired for a year period, it is good practice to express vacation and sick leave as the number of hours accrued per pay period rather than the number of days accrued per year. For example, for an employer that pays semi-monthly (twenty-four times a year), ten days of vacation per year translates to 3.33 hours per pay period. For the same reason, *vacation* rather than *annual leave* is the preferred term.

EMPLOYER TIP

Vacation and sick leave benefits that an employer provides out of its general assets are exempt from *Employee Retirement Income Security Act* requirements. However, if the employer establishes a dedicated fund to cover those benefits, ERISA may apply. (ERISA is covered in Chapter 9.)

In general, a terminated employee must be paid wages accrued up to the time of termination. If the employer's announced policy is to cash out accrued leave at termination, then the employee has earned the contract right to be cashed out, just as the right to wages has been earned. On the other hand, in most states, the employer is free to adopt a policy of not paying for unused leave at termination or limiting the amount of leave which will be paid.

Some employers have a policy that if an employee quits without giving the normal two-weeks' notice, or is fired for cause, any accrued but unused vacation leave is forfeited. Such a policy is enforceable in most states so long as it is explained to employees *beforehand*.

FMLA COVERAGE AND ELIGIBILITY

Some employers consider the *Family and Medical Leave Act* (FMLA), the *Americans with Disabilities Act* (ADA), and workers' compensation laws to be a three-legged stool upon which their employees rest while milking the employer. It is true that prior to those laws, an employer could fire an employee for taking extended leave, no matter how good the reason, and had no obligation to offer a returning employee his or her old job or any job at all. It is also true that under certain circumstances, an employee could now be entitled to the protections of all three laws *at the same time*. The real problem for employers, however, is not so much that these laws give employees too many rights, but that the laws are complex and compliance can be tricky.

When leave qualifies under FMLA, a covered employer must:
- grant an eligible employee up to twelve weeks of unpaid leave, including intermittent leave as needed, within a 12-month period;
- restore the employee to his or her former job upon return to work, or to an *equivalent job* (a job that is virtually identical to the former job in terms of pay, benefits, and other employment terms and conditions); and,
- maintain group health insurance coverage for the employee, including family coverage, on the same basis as if the employee had continued to work.

Employers are covered under the FMLA if they have fifty or more employees for at least twenty weeks during the current or preceding calendar year. (From time to time Congress considers lowering the threshold to twenty-five or more employees, but has not done so as of this writing.) An employee is potentially eligible for FMLA leave if each one of the following conditions is met:

- the employee works for a covered employer;
- the employee has been on the job for a year or more;
- the employee has worked at least 1250 hours during the previous year; and,
- there are at least fifty employees who work at the location where the employee works or within 75 miles of that location.

The only exception to the duty to grant FMLA leave is for *key employees* whose absence would cause substantial and grievous economic injury to the operations of the employer—a tough standard to say the least. If the employer intends to deny leave on this basis, the employer must first notify the affected employee and give the employee an opportunity to change his or her mind about taking FMLA leave.

An eligible employee is entitled to FMLA leave when the employee:

- has a serious health condition;
- needs to care for a spouse, child, or parent with a serious health condition;
- needs to care for a newborn child; and,
- adopts a son or daughter, or has a child placed with the employee for foster care.

Serious health condition is defined as an illness, injury, impairment, or physical or mental condition that involves:

- treatment as an in-patient in a hospital, hospice, or residential medical care facility;
- a period of incapacity requiring absence of more than three days from work, school, or other regular activity and that involves continuing treatment by a health-care provider;
- any period of incapacity due to pregnancy or for prenatal care;

◆ any period of incapacity due to a chronic, serious health condition;

◆ a period of incapacity that is permanent or long-term, even if there is no effective treatment; and,

◆ absences to receive multiple treatment where the underlying condition, if left untreated, would likely result in incapacity of more than three consecutive days.

U.S. Department of Labor (DOL) regulations expand on the statutory definition. DOL regulations say that a condition qualifies as *serious* if the employee is incapacitated for more than three consecutive calendar days and the condition requires treatment two or more times by a health care practitioner. Even the flu can satisfy this test, according to a recent decision of the Fourth Circuit Court of Appeals.

The *Family and Medical Leave Act* requires employers to respond promptly to employee requests for leave under FMLA. Employers may require a *medical certification* of the serious health condition from a *health care provider*. The employer must allow the employee fifteen days to obtain the certification. The employer may, at its own expense, obtain a second opinion from another health care provider of the employer's own choosing, so long as the health care provider is not under contract with, or regularly used by, the employer. If the two opinions differ, the employer and employee together choose a third health care provider, whose opinion is final and binding. Optional *Form WH-380*, developed by the Employment Standards Administration of the U.S. Department of Labor, may be used for these medical certifications. The form is available at **www.dol.gov/esa/whd**.

> # EMPLOYER TIP
>
> For employers covered by the *Family and Medical Leave Act*, unexplained or undocumented leave should never result in automatic discipline. The employer should first make efforts to determine whether the leave qualifies as FMLA leave and, if so, whether the employee wishes to take FMLA leave. (see Chapter 8.)

The list of health care providers whose medical certifications can trigger FMLA leave is long and somewhat surprising. As might be expected, it includes doctors of medicine and osteopathy, but they need to be licensed only in the state in which they practice, not necessarily in the state where the employer or employee is located. The list also includes: podiatrists; dentists; clinical psychologists; optometrists; chiropractors; nurse practitioners; nurse midwives; and clinical social workers (so long as they are practicing within the scope of their licenses); Christian Science practitioners; and any health care provider recognized by the employer's health care benefits manager. Foreign, as well as U.S.-licensed health care providers are also included.

> ## EMPLOYER TIP
>
> For disabilities covered by the ADA, the employer may be required to offer leave as a reasonable accommodation, so long as doing so does not cause an undue hardship. A requirement to offer ADA leave is separate from FMLA leave requirements and may even extend beyond the 12-week FMLA obligation.

FMLA BENEFITS

An employee on FMLA leave is entitled to no more that 12 weeks' leave within a 12-month period. The employer has some options in determining when the 12-month period begins and ends. For example, a calendar year may be used, the employer's fiscal year may be used, an *employment year* based on the employee's start date may be used, or a rolling 12-month period that looks back from when the employee requests FMLA leave may be used. Under a rolling 12-month period, the employer may deny a new FMLA leave request if, during the immediately preceding 12-month period, the employee has taken the full 12-week entitlement. Whatever option the employer chooses must be applied consistently to all employees.

An employer must continue group health insurance coverage during FMLA leave on the same basis as if the employer had continued to work. This means that if the plan was noncontributory (where the employer pays 100% of the premium), the employer must continue to do so for employees under FMLA leave. On the other hand, if the plan is *contributory* (that is, if the employees pay some portion of their premiums), the employer may require an employee on FMLA leave to continue contributing on the same basis. The employer has a right to recover the employer's portion of the premiums if the employee does not return to work when FMLA leave ends. If the employer has no group health plan, the employer does not have to provide health insurance during FMLA leave.

The employer may, but is not required to, continue other benefits for employees on FMLA leave. Seniority, for example, need not accrue. The employer may also insist that the employee use vacation, sick leave, or other leave before going on unpaid FMLA leave.

> ## EMPLOYER TIP
>
> When a husband and wife are employed by the same employer, they are entitled only to a combined total of 12 weeks' FMLA leave if the leave is based on the birth of a child or the placement with them of a child for adoption or foster care.

When FMLA leave ends, the employer is required to restore the returning employee to the same or an equivalent position. Department of Labor regulations define *equivalent position* as one that is virtually identical to the employee's former position in terms of pay, benefits, and working conditions, including privileges, prerequisites, and status. Assignment of an employee to a different shift on return from FMLA leave violates the equivalent position requirement.

Employers who are covered by FMLA should follow these guidelines:

- post the FMLA notice (WH Publication 1420) required by the U.S. Department of Labor;
- adopt a FMLA policy and publicize it to your employees (DOL's Fact Sheet No. ESA 95-24 will satisfy this requirement);

◆ if the employer has an employee handbook or a collective bargaining agreement, set out the policy in those documents;

◆ be alert to leave that may qualify under FMLA and make inquiry to determine whether FMLA might apply whenever an employee requests any type of leave;

◆ never discipline an employee for unauthorized absence without first determining whether FMLA might apply;

◆ when an employee requests FMLA leave, notify the employee promptly (within one or two business days) whether the leave will qualify under FMLA, whether you require a medical certification or other documentation in support of the leave, and what the employee's rights and responsibilities are while on FMLA leave (DOL *Form WH-381* satisfies the employer's notice requirements);

◆ maintain group health insurance for the employee during FMLA leave on the same basis as if the employee has continued to work (the cost of which may be recovered from the employee if the employee does not return to work after FMLA leave expires); and,

◆ upon termination of FMLA leave, restore the employee to the same or an equivalent position.

The Department of Labor documents mentioned above are available at **www.dol.gov/esa/regs/compliance/whd/1421.htm**.

FMLA leave may be terminated for employees who state, unequivocally, that they do not intend to return to work or who fail to comply with their employer's requirement to furnish periodic reports justifying continued leave.

A Department of Labor regulation requires employers to notify their employees when leave is being treated as FMLA leave. The regulation goes on to say that if an employer fails to do so, the leave taken does not count against an employee's FMLA entitlement. The validity of the regulation was recently tested before the Supreme Court. The Court upheld the regulation's *notice* requirement, but it struck down, as contrary to the FMLA, the *penalty* for failing to give notice. In other words, employers are required to notify employees when leave is being treated as FMLA leave, but failure to do so does not necessarily result in disqualification of the leave as FMLA leave.

The question of whether an employer may discipline an employee while on FMLA leave does not arise frequently. But it can arise where, for example, the employee's misconduct occurs before he or she takes FMLA leave. It is clear that an employer cannot discipline an employee *because* he or she is on FMLA leave, but nothing in the law prevents an employer from pursuing disciplinary action unrelated to FMLA *while* an employee is on leave.

Example: In one recent case decided by the Sixth Circuit Court of Appeals, the question of misconduct did arise while an employee was on FMLA leave. In that case, the employer had a policy prohibiting employees from performing outside work without the employer's permission. The employee in the case requested and was granted four weeks' FMLA leave in connection with his wife's childbirth, but while on leave he managed a restaurant that his wife had recently purchased. The employer fired the employee when he returned from leave and the court upheld the firing. The court pointed out that the right to reinstatement under FMLA is not absolute, since an employer need not reinstate an employee who would have lost his job even if he had not taken FMLA leave. That was exactly the case here—the employee was fired for violating the company's outside work rule, not because he took FMLA leave.

The Sixth Circuit decision relied on the Department of Labor's FMLA regulations that list a number of circumstances under which an employer may refuse to reinstate or delay reinstatement.

♦ If an employee fails to provide a requested fitness-for-duty certification to return to work, an employer may delay restoration until the employee submits the certificate.

◆ An employee has no greater right to reinstatement or to other benefits and conditions of employment than if the employee had been continuously employed during the FMLA leave period.

◆ An employer may require an employee on FMLA leave to report periodically on the employee's status and intention to return to work.

◆ An employee who fraudulently obtains FMLA leave from an employer is not protected by FMLA's job restoration or maintenance of health benefits provisions.

◆ If the employer has a uniformly-applied policy governing outside or supplemental employment, such a policy may continue to apply to an employee while on FMLA leave.

DOL regulations prohibit employers from discriminating against employees and applicants who have taken FMLA leave. So an employer may not base a job decision on the fact that an existing employee, or a former employee who is reapplying, exercised rights under FMLA. Similarly, if a job applicant took FMLA leave while with a *different* employer, the new employer cannot use that fact in deciding whether to hire.

MILITARY LEAVE

The *Uniformed Services Employment and Reemployment Rights Act* (USERRA), adopted in 1994, requires employers to carry service members on leave status for benefit and seniority purposes while on active duty, and to reemploy them when they return. USERRA also prohibits employers from discriminating against veterans and persons in the uniformed services. USERRA applies to all service members except those who receive dishonorable or bad conduct discharges or who are discharged under less than honorable conditions. To be eligible for USERRA protection, the service member must notify the employer that he or she has been called to active duty, unless he or she is precluded from doing so by military necessity or unless it is otherwise impossible or unreasonable to do so.

Employees on active duty are considered to be on furlough or leave of absence. As such, they are entitled to whatever benefits other similarly situated employees receive. In addition, an employee on active duty:

- ◆ may (but cannot be required to) use any accrued vacation or other leave with pay;
- ◆ may elect to continue any employer-sponsored health insurance coverage for up to eighteen months. (For employees on active duty for less than thirty-one days, the employee can only be required to pay the portion of the premium normally charged to employees. For employees on active duty for more than thirty days, the employee can be charged up to 102% of the full premium.);
- ◆ may continue to contribute to any retirement plan to which he or she was contributing prior to active duty; and,
- ◆ must be treated as continuing to work for the employer for purposes of computing the employer's pension plan funding obligation and benefits under any pension plan in which he or she participated. (This would be significant for defined benefit plans that use a formula that includes a years-of-service component.)

A returning service member is entitled to be reemployed unless the employer can show that the employer's circumstances have so changed as to make reemployment impossible or unreasonable or that reemployment would impose an undue hardship. This right applies to service members who have been on active duty for as long a five years, and, in some cases, even longer.

The returning service member is entitled to be placed in the position that he or she would have been employed but for the call to active duty (or in a position with equivalent seniority, status, and pay). Under this *escalator* provision, the employer must take into consideration any promotions or advancements the member would have received if he or she had continued to work.

If a member who has been on active duty for more than ninety days is not qualified for an escalated position, the employer must make reasonable efforts to help the member become qualified. For returning service members who became disabled while on active duty, the employer must make reasonable efforts to accommodate the disability.

To be eligible for reemployment, the returning service member must, after release from active duty, notify the employer of his or her intent to return to work. Strict time limits apply to this notice requirement.

- ◆ If the period of active duty was less than thirty-one days, the returning member must report to work on the first regular workday after release from duty (after allowing for an 8-hour rest period and safe transportation home).
- ◆ If the period of active duty was between thirty-one and 181 days, the returning member must apply for reemployment within 14 days after release from duty.
- ◆ If the period of active duty was more than 180 days, the returning member must apply for reemployment within ninety days after release from duty.

These time limits can be extended for up to two years or more in cases of returning service members who are hospitalized or convalescing from an illness or injury suffered while on active duty.

Once the employer has reemployed a returning service member, the employer is restricted in its ability to discharge the member. Except for discharges for cause, members who have been on active duty for 180 days or less cannot be fired for a period of 180 days after reemployment. Members who have been on active duty for more than 180 days cannot be fired for one year.

EMPLOYER TIP

Docking the salary of exempt employees who are on temporary military leave will cause loss of the exemption for *Fair Labor Standards Act* purposes, although an employer may offset any compensation received by the employee for military service. (see Chapter 5.)

OTHER TYPES OF LEAVE

State laws frequently have their own provisions regarding required leave. Be alert to the following possibilities in your state.

Disability Leave

Little FMLA laws are becoming increasingly popular at the state level, although eligibility and leave periods do not necessarily coincide with federal law. California is even experimenting with *paid* extended leave.

Jury Duty

Most states protect the jobs of employees who are absent from work for jury service. Some even require salary continuation during periods of jury service. Even where salary continuation is not required, it is common for employers to pay full salary or at least make up the difference between juror fees and regular salary. Docking the salary of exempt employees who are on jury service will cause loss of the exemption for FLSA purposes, although an employer may offset any juror fees received by the employee.

> ## EMPLOYER TIP
>
> Asking an employee to lie about his or her availability for jury service is a criminal offense.

Testimony

Some states protect the jobs of employees who are subpoenaed to appear in court as witnesses or who are attending court under a *victim's right* law. Docking the salary of exempt employees in these circumstances will cause loss of the exemption for FLSA purposes, although an employer may offset any witness fees received by the employee.

NOTE: *Maternity and paternity leave is covered in Chapter 15.*

PAID TIME OFF

Some employers have abandoned the various forms of voluntary leave—vacation, sick leave, emergency leave, personal leave, etc.— and replaced them with a *Paid Time Off* or PTO plan.

Suppose, for example, that traditional company policy grants ten days paid vacation per year, ten days paid sick leave per year, three days leave without pay for a death in the immediate family, three days personal leave without pay, and up to three days hazard leave with pay for weather-related absences. Keeping track of all these categories is an administrative nightmare. Worse, determining in which category a particular day off should be placed imposes a substantial burden on supervisors and engenders endless bickering and hard feelings among employees.

After switching to a PTO plan, the company now grants twenty paid days off per year (6.67 hours each semi-monthly pay period) that employees can use for any purpose. In addition to reducing administrative burdens and morale problems, the PTO plan discourages employees from taking sick leave, because doing so uses up vacation time. Instead, employees now schedule most of their leave in advance, giving the employer an opportunity to arrange for coverage or an opportunity to require that the leave be taken at a time more convenient for the employer.

PTO plans can be fine-tuned, depending on a particular employer's experience and needs. For example, a day of *scheduled* leave might cost the employee only six hours out of his or her PTO bank, but *unscheduled* leave might cost the full eight hours. The employer might also impose a cap on the amount of PTO that can be accumulated in the PTO bank. Allowing employees to draw prescribed amounts of PTO in cash in lieu of leave time tends to limit overall absences. PTO time can also be cashed out with *pre-tax* dollars in the form of employer contributions to a 401(k) retirement plan or cafeteria plan.

Other details need to be considered in implementing a PTO plan. For example, what happens to accumulated PTO at termination of employment—is it forfeited or cashed out? How is PTO time coordinated with FMLA—is the employee required to exhaust PTO before taking FMLA leave or may he or she take FMLA leave first? Of course, these same questions arise with any leave policy the employer may have.

PTO plans seem to have all the advantages over traditional leave arrangements. They are simpler to administer; they are more flexible; they can be fine-tuned to meet the employer's specific needs; and, they discourage unscheduled sick leave. PTO plans deserve serious consideration.

–9–

DEFERRED COMPENSATION AND ERISA

For a typical employer, the cost of employee benefits, together with other payroll costs like FICA and workers' compensation insurance, may be 20% or more of payroll. So, for every salary dollar promised an employee, the employer actually incurs at least $1.20—a significant factor when considering hiring an additional employee or raising an existing salary.

On the other hand, benefit plans help an employer attract and keep quality employees. Their costs are also generally tax deductible by the employer, just like wage and salary payments. Some benefit plans enjoy especially favorable tax treatment. For example, even though the employer gets a current tax deduction for the cost of providing a cash benefit, the employee need not include the value of the benefit in current gross income for tax purposes. In other words, the benefit has a tax postponement feature. Where taxation of earnings on benefit contributions is postponed—called *inside build-up*—the benefit fund can grow much more rapidly than the employee's other investments. Many deferred compensation arrangements qualify for this favorable tax treatment.

If properly designed and administered, some plans give the employer a current tax deduction for the cost of providing the benefit, but the benefit is *never* taxed to the employee. Group health insurance and life insurance plans, for example, can fall in this category.

These tax morsels come at a price. Employee benefit plans are highly regulated under tax and labor laws administered by the IRS and the U.S. Department of Labor. For example, a qualified plan cannot discriminate in favor of highly compensated individuals—it cannot give all the benefits to the boss and leave little or nothing for the rank-and-file. Qualified retirement plans must also meet strict funding and vesting requirements, so that the promised benefit is not illusory.

EMPLOYER TIP

One of the risks of classifying workers as independent contractors is that if the IRS disagrees and re-classifies them as employees, these new employees may demand pension plan contributions for prior years. Worse, if a plan fails to include workers who should have been covered, the plan may lose its tax-qualified status. (see Chapter 7.)

The design and operation of benefit plans are among some of the most complex tasks you are likely to face as an employer. It is best to hire an experienced *benefits consultant* who is familiar with the range of available options, can project your future costs in managing and funding various plans, can guide you through tax and labor law requirements, and will be available to help with plan administration.

DEFERRED COMPENSATION

Various arrangements fall under the general rubric of *deferred compensation*. In most cases, the employer will want the arrangement to qualify for the favorable tax treatment discussed above. These arrangements include:
- pension plans;
- profit-sharing plans;
- employee stock ownership plans (ESOPs);
- 401(k) plans;
- SIMPLE plans;
- tax-sheltered annuities (403(b) plans); and,
- cash balance plans.

Some common characteristics of each of these plans are: contributions to the plan within specified limits are deductible for tax purposes by the employer but are not includible in the employee's gross income until later, upon actual receipt of benefits by the employee; the accumulated benefits must vest (become nonforfeitable) within a specified time period; and, plan income is exempt from taxation. In the case of qualified retirement plans, the right to withdraw funds from the plan is restricted prior to retirement, which can be as early as age 59½. Withdrawals become mandatory when the plan participant reaches age 70½ or later retires. (Retirement plan participants who hold a 5% or greater ownership interest in the sponsoring employer must begin mandatory withdrawals at age 70½ even if they keep working.)

Pension plans generally fall into two broad categories.

Defined Contribution (Money Purchase) Plan

In a *defined contribution plan*, a *separate account* is established for each employee, to which the employer (and sometimes the employee) make regular contributions according to an established formula, such as a percentage of salary. When it comes time for an employee to retire, the employee's retirement benefit is whatever has been contributed to his or her account, plus any income the account has earned through investments (but less any investment losses the account has suffered). 401(k) plans and profit-sharing plans are defined contribution plans.

Defined Benefit Plan

In a *defined benefit plan*, there are no separate accounts for employees. Instead, there is simply a *common fund* out of which each retiring employee is entitled to a specified monthly benefit. The amount of the monthly benefit is usually based on a formula, such as years of service, times highest annual income, times some factor such as 1.5%, divided by 12. So for an employee earning $50,000 who retires after 30 years, the monthly benefit might be 30 x 50,000 x .015 / 12 = $1875. The employer is obligated to keep sufficient assets in the fund, based on actuarial computations, to enable payments of the benefits when they come due.

Differences Between the Two Types of Plans

In addition to the existence or absence of a separate account, other major differences between defined contribution and defined benefit plans include:

- *investment risk.* In a defined contribution plan, the employee wins if the market goes up and loses if the market goes down. In a defined benefit plan, the employer bears the investment risk.

- *mortality risk.* If the employee lives for many years after retirement, he or she may use up all the funds in the defined contribution account. But if he or she had a defined benefit plan, the monthly annuity continues for life. In short, the employer bears the mortality risk in a defined benefit plan. The employee usually bears that risk in a defined contribution plan.

- *insurance.* Defined benefit plans are insured by the federal Pension Benefit Guaranty Corporation, for which the employer pays an insurance premium. Defined contribution plans are not insured because there is no guaranteed benefit at retirement.

- *settlement options.* Defined benefit plans simply pay the prescribed monthly benefit. In a defined contribution plan, the retiring employee can usually use the amount in his or her account to purchase an annuity or, optionally (and subject to spousal consent, as discussed later) take the account in a lump sum or roll it over to an individual retirement account (IRA) from which he or she may make periodic withdrawals.

- *funding.* Defined contribution plans are always fully funded (assuming the employer actually makes the contribution promised), because the benefit is based on whatever is in the account. Defined benefit plans may become underfunded if, for example, investments do not turn out as expected or if retirees live longer than their life expectancies. For that reason, the employer must do an annual actuarial study of the plan and cover any shortfalls. Of course, if investments have performed better than expected, the employer's funding obligation will be reduced.

◆ *loading.* Defined benefit plans that use a years-of-service/highest-pay formula to determine benefits are said to be *back-loaded* because the size of the benefit produced by the formula tends to increase significantly in the last few years of employment. Defined contribution plans tend to be more *front-loaded* because the benefit amount grows at a more even rate.

Cash Balance Plans

Another item in the plan menagerie that has recently been in the news is the *cash balance plan.* Technically classified as a defined benefit plan, a cash balance plan has characteristics of both defined benefit and defined contribution plans. For that reason, cash balance plans are sometimes called *hybrid plans.*

In a cash balance plan, the employee establishes a hypothetical account for each employee. The account is hypothetical because there are no actual specific assets that belong to the employee. The account is really just a *bookkeeping entry*.

The employer credits the hypothetical account with a specific dollar amount each year, usually based on a percentage of the employee's salary. In addition, the employer credits the account with interest earned on the account balance—either a fixed interest rate or a rate tied to treasury bills or some other index.

EMPLOYER TIP

When an employer converts from a defined benefit plan to a cash balance plan, employees lose the back-loaded boost they had anticipated from their defined benefit plan. Since this loss is borne most heavily by older workers who are near retirement, some have argued that such conversions amount to age discrimination.

Example: An employer establishes a cash balance plan under which he credits 8% of salary and which is deemed to earn interest at 7% per year. For an employee who earns $35,000 per year, the balance in the hypothetical account will be $2,800 at the end of the first year (8% of $35,000). At the end of the second year, the balance in the account will be $5,796: the original $2,800, plus 7% interest on that amount ($196), plus another $2,800 credited at the end of the second year. When the employee retires, his benefit is based on whatever is then in the hypothetical account.

Because each employee does have an account—albeit hypothetical—and because the amount of the ultimate benefit depends on what is in the account at retirement, cash balance plans look like defined contribution plans. Other characteristics, however, make them look like defined benefit plans. For example, the employer bears the investment risk since if the fund earns more than the interest rate promised to employees (7% in the above example), the employer's funding obligation is reduced.

Profit-Sharing Plans

Profit-sharing plans allow an employer to share company profits with employees. At the same time, they give the employer some flexibility in determining how much to contribute to the plan. Although the employer's contribution must be substantial and recurring in order to maintain the plan, the employer can change the contribution from year to year to track business cycles. Profit-sharing plans are defined contribution plans, since each employee has an individual account and the ultimate benefit is a function of what is in the account. They are often used as retirement plans or at least as a component of a retirement plan, but they can also provide benefit payments at other times, such as after a fixed period of years, without regard to retirement.

401(k) Plans

401(k) Plans (so-called because they are authorized by Section 401(k) of the Internal Revenue Code) are a special type of defined contribution plan. Typically, the employee makes an election each year to contribute a certain percentage of salar., The employer then matches that election in some ratio, such as 100% of the employee's contribution up to 3% of the employee's salary and 50% of the employee's contribution that is between 3% and 5% of salary. (The elective component of the plan is sometimes called a *cash or deferral arrangement* or CODA.) Neither the employee's contribution nor the employer's match is subject to tax. In addition, 401(k) plans include a *profit-sharing* component, by which the employer agrees to pay some additional percentage of employee salaries that the employee can elect to take in cash (which is taxable to the employee), or in the form of an additional contribution to the plan (which is nontaxable).

SIMPLE Plans

SIMPLE plans (SIMPLE stands for Savings Incentive Match Plan for Employees) are available to employers with 100 or fewer employees. All employees who receive compensation of $5,000 or more per year must be eligible to participate. SIMPLE plans may take the form of either 401(k) plans (discussed above) or Individual Retirement Accounts. In their IRA form, a SIMPLE plan must permit each eligible employee to elect to have the employer contribution (expressed as a percentage of compensation and subject to statutory limits) either paid to the employee in cash or paid into an IRA account. If taken in cash, the payment is immediately taxable to the employee. If taken as an IRA contribution, tax is deferred and the account is subject to usual IRA rules. The employer may also make a matching, tax deductible contribution to the IRA account.

Tax-Sheltered Annuities

Tax-sheltered annuities (sometimes called 403(b) annuities) are only available to organizations that are exempt from income tax under Section 501(c)(3) of the Internal Revenue Code, such as educational organizations, churches, public and private schools, etc. (These plans are discussed in Chapter 20.)

ERISA

The Employee Retirement Income Security Act (ERISA) was passed in 1974 in response to abuses in the handling of pension funds. Before ERISA, it was not unusual for employers to make grossly unwise investments with pension funds, to underfund pension plans, to adopt a drawn-out vesting schedule, or to borrow from pension plans to cover operating expenses and then be unable to pay promised benefits when the time came. Employers also sometimes fired their senior workers just before those workers were to retire and become eligible for benefits. Top-heavy plans that favored owners or upper management were also common.

To cure these abuses, Congress enacted ERISA. ERISA has parallel labor law and tax law aspects. For example, ERISA has minimum participation and vesting requirements. It contains detailed reporting and disclosure requirements. It imposes fiduciary (trustee) standards on plan administrators. It requires defined benefit plans to be fully funded, meaning that the employer must contribute sufficient amounts on a current basis so that the promised benefits will be available at retirement time. It even requires defined benefit plans to carry insurance against any shortfall in promised benefits should the plan terminate.

But ERISA goes far beyond pension plan abuses. Although it applies to employee benefit *pension* plans, it also applies to employee *welfare* benefit plans. Emloyee welfare benefit plans are defined as any plan, fund, or program established or maintained by an employer for the purpose of providing benefits for:

◆ medical, surgical, or hospital care;
◆ sickness;
◆ accident;

- disability;
- death;
- unemployment;
- vacation;
- apprenticeship or other training programs;
- day care centers;
- scholarship funds; or,
- prepaid legal services.

In short, it applies to almost every on-going plan or program an employer has for providing group benefits to employees. The only exceptions are plans that are maintained solely to comply with workers' compensation or unemployment insurance laws, plans maintained by tax-exempt churches or associations of churches, and certain unfunded plans.

Example: A grocery store chain in the New Orleans area issued vouchers to its retired employees, which they could use instead of cash to purchase goods at the chain's stores. When the chain decided to sell its business, it canceled the voucher arrangement and retirees who had been receiving the vouchers sued. The Fifth Circuit Court of Appeals ruled that the plan was subject to ERISA, so that the retirees were entitled to money damages for loss of their vested *pension* benefit.

On the other hand, the Supreme Court concluded that an employer policy of cashing out accrued vacation when an employee terminates was *not* covered by ERISA. In that case, the State of Massachusetts brought criminal charges against the employer for violating that state's wage payment laws by refusing to pay certain employees for unused vacation. Since ERISA did not apply, the State was free to pursue criminal charges against the employer.

What makes ERISA particularly powerful is its *preemption provision*. By its own terms, ERISA shall supersede any and all State laws insofar as they may now or hereafter relate to any employee benefit plan. One of Congress' purposes in enacting this preemption provision was to create a uniform body of *federal* law governing the administration of employee benefit plans. To the extent *state* laws (which vary considerably from state to state) purport to regulate employee benefit plans, those laws are unenforceable.

Subject to the exceptions mentioned above, ERISA requires every employee benefit plan to:

◆ be in writing;

◆ place its assets in a trust (except where the assets of the plan consist of insurance contracts or policies);

◆ name one or more fiduciaries to administer the plan;

◆ describe how the plan is to be funded;

◆ describe the basis on which benefits are paid; and,

◆ describe claim procedures.

Employers must provide employees with a *Summary Plan Description* (SPD) for every benefit plan covered by ERISA. SPDs describe plan eligibility requirements and they describe procedures for claiming benefits and for appealing benefit denials. SPDs must be provided within ninety days after an employee becomes a participant in the plan and after any significant modification of the plan. SPDs must also be provided every five years if there have been any amendments to the plan and every ten years if there have not been any amendments. The actual plan documents must be made available to participants and beneficiaries on request.

Employers must also file *Form 5500* with the IRS each year for most types of benefit plans. The form is due on the last day of the 7th month after the end of each plan year. For plans that operate on a calendar year, the due date is July 31. The form calls for information as to the plan's financial condition, participation, and funding.

ERISA prohibits employers from interfering with employee rights under a plan or retaliating against employees for exercising plan rights. Employers are also prohibited from firing employees or taking other adverse action in order to avoid paying benefits. While an employer can, by amendment, reduce benefits under a plan (assuming the plan document permits such amendments) or even terminate a plan entirely, such actions cannot affect vested or accrued benefits.

The *fiduciary responsibilities* imposed on persons who manage ERISA plans deserve mention. ERISA places managers in a special trust relationship with plan participants and beneficiaries. For example, plans must be managed in the best interests of participants and beneficiaries. They must segregate plan assets from the employer's operating funds. The plans are prohibited from engaging in transactions with the employer. Employers and individual managers can be held *personally liable* for a breach of these fiduciary duties.

When an employer communicates with employees about an ERISA benefit plan, the employer may be acting in a fiduciary (trustee) capacity. If so, the employer will be held to a much higher standard of truthfulness, accuracy, and completeness than if communicating just in an employer capacity. The dangers are especially great for *Employee Stock Ownership Plans* (ESOPs), where company owners who also serve as fiduciaries routinely find themselves in conflict-of-interest situations.

Employers can also get into trouble in the area of pension plan investments. Suppose a plan allows the participating employee to direct investments within his or her account, or it provides the participant with choices among a number of mutual funds, each of which has a different objective or investment strategy. In general, employers should not give investment *advice* to their employees, because doing so may make them liable as fiduciaries and because the advice may lack objectivity or a sound research basis. On the other hand, plan sponsors have an obligation to provide *sufficient information* about investment choices so that the employees themselves can make informed decisions.

The Department of Labor has issued guidelines to help an employer walk the fine line between too much and too little information. Under DOL guidelines, an employer may provide the following in satisfaction of the affirmative obligation, without becoming a fiduciary:

- *plan information,* such as the benefits of plan participation, the benefits of increasing plan contributions, the impact of pre-retirement withdrawals, investment alternatives, and historical return information;

- *general financial and investment information*, including invest-ment concepts like diversification, risk and return, compounding, investment time horizons, etc.;
- *asset allocation models* that provide hypothetical results based on differing assumptions of age, age to retirement, life expectancy, inflation rates, time horizons, risk profiles, etc.; and,
- *interactive investment materials*, such as worksheets and soft-ware that enable the participant to estimate future retirement income needs and to assess the impact of different asset alloca-tions.

When an employee becomes eligible for a pension plan distrib-ution, plan administrators are also required to provide a written explanation of distribution options. An employee at a prominent chemical company, for example, successfully sued the company based on bad advice the company gave about the tax consequences of a roll-over distribution from one of its pension plans.

SPOUSAL RIGHTS TO PENSION BENEFITS

ERISA intentionally makes it difficult for pension plan participants to divert benefits from their spouses. The law requires that when a plan participant retires and he or she has a spouse, benefits must be payable in the form of a *joint and survivor annuity*—an annuity that will be paid to husband and wife jointly and that will continue to be paid (at a 50% rate) to the surviving spouse if the plan participant dies first. In order for benefits to be paid in some other fashion, such as to a different beneficiary or in a lump sum, the spouse must con-sent and the consent must satisfy the following statutory requirements:

- be in writing;
- designate some other specific beneficiary, which may not be changed without the spouse's further consent (unless the spouse expressly agrees to further changes without consent);
- acknowledge the effect of the change; and,
- be witnessed by a plan representative or notary public.

Courts require strict compliance with these spousal consent requirements and will not enforce a consent where requisite procedures have not been followed.

Issues arise when parties who are about to be married enter into a prenuptial agreement in which each party waives any legal claim he or she might otherwise have in the other's property, including claims to the other's pension benefits. Several courts have ruled that only a *spouse* can execute a valid consent, so that in a prenuptial agreement, where the parties are not yet married, a waiver of pension plan benefits is ineffective. Other courts have reached a contrary conclusion.

A similar issue arises in the case of a voluntary separation agreement where a divorcing couple resolves property and support issues, including claims to each other's pension plans. At least one federal court of appeals has indicated that ERISA's statutory requirements are *not* applicable in a divorce context, so that a voluntary separation agreement in which one spouse gives up any claim against the other's pension is effective so long as the agreement specifically refers to the plan involved.

Until the Supreme Court definitively resolves these issues, pension plan administrators are in a quandary. Suppose that a plan participant dies, the participant's child claims benefits based on a separation agreement or prenuptial agreement that waives all spousal rights, and the surviving spouse (who has since had a change of heart) also claims benefits, arguing that the waiver is invalid. If the plan administrator pays one of the claimants, the other might sue and force the administrator to pay again. So the safest course may be for the plan administrator to go to court and ask a federal judge to decide who is entitled—thereby incurring exactly the kind of expense and delay ERISA was designed to avoid.

Qualified Domestic Relations Order (QDROs)

ERISA requires plans to contain a provision insulating plan benefits from an employee's creditors. In other words, if an employee fails to pay some personal obligation, is sued, and a court judgment is entered against the employee, the party who holds the judgment cannot go after pension plan assets to satisfy the judgment. But again, spouses get special protection. In a divorce proceeding, even if the parties have not reached agreement on how pension benefits should be allocated, the divorce court can issue a *qualified domestic relations order* (QDRO), awarding one spouse a portion (or all) of the other spouse's pension plan as alimony, child support, or simply as a division of marital property.

EMPLOYER TIP

One way to avoid the uncertainty surrounding the effect of a voluntary separation agreement (but not a prenuptial agreement) is to ask the divorce court to bless the agreement by entering a QDRO incorporating the provisions of the agreement that address pension plan rights.

To be recognized as a QDRO, an order must be made pursuant to state domestic relations law that relates to alimony, child support, or marital property rights for the benefit of someone who qualifies as an alternate payee—a spouse, former spouse, child, or other dependent. A separation or property settlement agreement between divorcing spouses will not qualify as a QDRO unless the agreement's provisions otherwise satisfy ERISA requirements *and* the agreement is approved by an order of the domestic relations court. (The term *court* here includes administrative agencies if they have the power under state law to issue support orders.)

QDROs must:

◆ contain the names and mailing addresses of the plan participant (employee) and each alternate payee covered by the order;

◆ identify the plan to which the order applies;

◆ state the dollar amount or percentage interest of the alternate payee, or at least the method by which the amount or percentage can be calculated; and,

◆ state the number of payments or time period to which the order applies.

QDROs cannot:

- ◆ require a plan to provide the alternate payee with any type of benefit, option, or form not otherwise provided under the plan;
- ◆ require the plan to provide increased benefits;
- ◆ conflict with a previously issued QDRO; or,
- ◆ order payments in the form of a joint and survivor annuity for the lives an alternate payee and his or her subsequent spouse.

When presented with a QDRO that complies with the above requirements and prohibitions (there are some additional technical requirements that apply in special cases), a pension plan administrator must honor it. Every qualified pension plan is required to have written procedures for determining whether an order is a QDRO. Plans may, but are not required, to develop *model* QDRO forms to assist participants and potential alternate payees. Disputes as to whether an order is a valid QDRO are subject to resolution in federal court. Because ERISA preempts state law regarding pension plan administration, a state domestic relations court does *not* have the right (at least according to the U.S. Department of Labor) to determine whether its own order qualifies as a QDRO.

The Department of Labor takes the reasonable view that even before a QDRO is entered, the employer or plan administrator has an obligation to furnish a potential alternate payee (spouse, dependent child, etc.) with information about the pension plan and the participating employee's benefit status and interest in the plan. No such information should be furnished, however, without first obtaining satisfactory evidence that a domestic relations proceeding is in fact pending and that the potential alternate payee is attempting to obtain a QDRO in that proceeding. It also makes for good employee relations to notify the participating employee that plan information has been requested.

Another aspect of ERISA's preemption provision is illustrated by a recent Supreme Court case. The case involved a Washington State statute that said a divorce decree had the effect of automatically revoking a beneficiary designation in favor of a former spouse. Presumably, the Washington legislature felt that after a plan participant gets divorced, he or she probably does not want an ex-spouse to receive plan benefits, even if he or she forgets to submit a beneficiary change. The Supreme Court invalidated the statute, saying that under ERISA, the plan documents themselves govern the determination of who is the right beneficiary.

TOP HAT AND EXCESS BENEFIT PLANS

Suppose that a company wants to hire away the star employee of one of its competitors and make that person its new CEO. (Before making any final commitments the company will, of course, have the good sense to check whether the star employee is bound by a noncompete agreement. (see Chapters 19 and 23) The company is willing to pay whatever salary or bonus may be necessary to attract the star, but because of his or her tax status, the star does not really want or need more current taxable income. And making additional contributions to the company's qualified retirement plan for the star will not work because of the maximum contribution limits imposed by law. So the company promises to pay the new CEO deferred compensation *on some future date*. The amount promised may be a specified sum together with imputed earnings on that sum over the deferral period or it may be tied to company performance or determined by some other formula.

In terms of the tax consequence of this arrangement, all the new CEO is getting is a mere promise of compensation in the future. Since no actual compensation is received and there is no control over it, the star does not have to report the compensation as current income. At the same time, however, since all the employer has given is a mere promise, the employer gets no current deduction. Of course, when the CEO eventually receives the compensation, it will have to be reported as income and the company may then claim it as a deductible expense.

In terms of ERISA, since the arrangement is not a *plan*, it is unfunded, and it only benefits one employee, it is not subject to any ERISA requirements.

But suppose the company decides to establish more formal deferred compensation arrangements for the benefit of a number of high-level company executives. Will that trigger the tax and labor law provisions of ERISA? ERISA itself offers two techniques for avoiding or at least reducing, the compliance burdens and limitations imposed by the statute.

A *top hat plan* is an *unfunded* plan the employer maintains *primarily* for the purpose of providing deferred compensation to a select group of management or highly compensated employees. Top hat plans are exempt from ERISA's vesting, participation, funding and fiduciary rules, but they are subject to ERISA's enforcement provisions. This means that an employee who is a beneficiary of a top hat plan can sue the employer in federal court to collect promised benefits.

An *excess benefit plan* is an *unfunded* plan the employer maintains *solely* for the purpose of providing benefits for certain employees in excess of the limitations on contributions and benefits imposed by Section 415 of the Internal Revenue Code. Excess benefit plans are not subject to either the substantive or the enforcement provisions of ERISA.

The italicized terms—*unfunded, primarily,* and *solely*—are critical. As used here, *unfunded* refers to whether the employer has actually set money aside, typically in a trust, to make good the promise of deferred compensation. If benefits are paid out of the employer's general assets and if employees have no greater rights to the fund than the employer's general creditors, the plan will be considered *unfunded.*

The purpose or purposes of the plan are also determinative. A top hat plan may have a number of purposes, including avoidance of various limitations imposed by the tax code. But in order to be an excess benefit plan, the plan must be limited to the single purpose of providing benefits in excess of I.R.C. Sec. 415 limitations.

RABBI TRUSTS

Although top hat and excess benefit plans must be unfunded, the IRS has approved arrangements under which the employer can actually establish a trust as a repository for accumulating benefits, so long as trust assets remain subject to claims by the employer's creditors. The trust documents may establish broad investment policies, although specific investment authority must remain with the employer-designated trustee of the trust and cannot be given to the employee-beneficiaries. (This type of trust is known as a *rabbi trust* because the first IRS ruling on such an arrangement involved a retirement plan adopted by a congregation for its rabbi.)

To facilitate the adoption of rabbi trusts (and to reduce the IRS's burden of responding to ruling requests), the IRS in 1992 issued a Revenue Procedure that sets out a model trust form that employers may use.

While a rabbi trust may give participating employees some level of assurance that the employer will eventually make good on its promise of deferred compensation, employees need to realize that trust assets still remain subject to claims by the company's creditors and that the employees may end up with nothing if the company fails.

–10–
GROUP HEALTH AND OTHER VOLUNTARY PLANS

Group health insurance competes with retirement plans as the most common type of employee benefit plan. A variety of funding arrangements are available. For example, the employer may pay the entire premium, in which case the plan is called *noncontributory*. Or the employer may adopt a *contributory* plan requiring the employees to contribute some of the premium. For qualified health insurance plans, whatever portion of the premium the employer pays is deductible to the employer. Even better, the employee does not include either the premium, or the value of the medical services when received, in his or her gross income.

Various risk-sharing and administrative arrangements also are available. For smaller companies, probably the most common arrangement is for the health insurer both to administer the plan and to assume the full risk, subject only to deductible and co-pay requirements. As companies get larger, they may want to undertake some of the administrative burdens and they may also want to self-insure some or most of the risk. Some companies self-insure as to routine claims and buy a *stop loss policy* that kicks in when claims reach an unusually high level. Companies that self-insure may self-administer, they may hire their stop-loss carrier to administer the plan, or they may hire a third-party administrator (TPA) to handle claims and other administrative burdens.

When the plan participants—the employee and any covered family members—choose their own health care providers and the insurance company reimburses the employee or pays the provider directly according to some policy formula, the plan is known as an *indemnity plan.* In the last fifteen or twenty years or so, there has been explosive growth in a new type of plan known as *managed care*, driven largely by efforts to contain health care costs. In a managed care plan, the employer contracts with a *health maintenance organization* (HMO) or with an insurance company that has established a network of participating physicians, psychologists, hospitals, etc. This network is sometimes called a *preferred provider organization* (PPO). The plan participant is required to stay within the network and pays nothing or only a nominal amount when medical care is received. If the participant goes *out of plan*, he or she may not be covered at all or may have a substantial co-pay obligation.

Managed care plans attempt to contain health care costs in other ways as well. For example, some plans use general practice physicians as gatekeepers who must approve referrals to specialists. Precertifications for hospitalizations are also common, both in managed care plans and in indemnity plans.

Group health plans usually impose a participation requirement that allows for cancellation of the group contract unless at least a minimum number of employees (such as 75%) participate in the plan. This helps assure that the group is broadly representative of the work force. It avoids *anti-selection* where only less healthy employees elect to participate. Also, participation is usually limited to employees who work more than a specified number of hours per year, such as 1000.

EMPLOYER TIP

Provisions in group health plans that exclude or limit coverage for particular disabilities could violate the *Americans with Disabilities Act.* (see Chapter 17.)

Group health plans are subject to a variety of special requirements not applicable to other benefit plans. These special requirements—all highly technical—are discussed in the following sections. Employers should look to their health insurance company or an experienced broker or third party administrator for guidance through the group health plan labyrinth.

COBRA

Employers who have twenty or more employees and who provide group health coverage need to know about one of the strangest acronyms in the employment field—COBRA. It stands for *Consolidated Omnibus Budget Reconciliation Act* (of 1985). The Act was really a catch-all piece of legislation that just happened to include an amendment to ERISA. That amendment requires employers to continue health coverage for employees and their dependents who, for various reasons, would otherwise become ineligible.

Before COBRA, an employee who quit or was fired would automatically lose health coverage for him or herself and for any participating family members. Similarly, a spouse's coverage would terminate on divorce, as would a child's coverage upon completion of his or her education or reaching a specified age. Most group policies had *conversion privileges*, which entitled the departing employee to purchase an individual policy, but the individual policies were usually very expensive and provided only limited coverage. Conversion privileges were usually not available to the divorced spouse or graduated child.

> ## EMPLOYER TIP
>
> For employees subject to *Title VII* of the federal *Civil Rights Act* or equivalent state law, pregnancy and childbirth must be treated as medical conditions under any health insurance plan maintained by the employer. (see Chapter 15.)

COBRA changed all that. Now, when a *qualifying event* occurs, the employer must offer continuing coverage at the participants' cost to those who would otherwise lose benefits. Examples of qualifying events are:

- the employee voluntarily quits;
- the employee is fired (except in cases of gross misconduct);
- the employee becomes ineligible for coverage because of a reduction in hours of work;
- the employee dies leaving a covered spouse or dependent;

◆ a covered spouse is divorced or becomes separated; and,

◆ a covered dependent ceases to be a dependent.

COBRA contains various deadlines within which notice must be given after the occurrence of a qualifying event. Once on notice that a qualifying event has occurred, the employer must, within fourteen days, offer continuing coverage. The employee, spouse, or dependent who is otherwise losing coverage then has sixty days within which to elect COBRA benefits.

EMPLOYER TIP

Employers must continue health insurance coverage for an employee on *Family and Medical Leave Act* (FMLA) leave on the same basis as if the employee had continued to work. Health insurance continuation requirements also apply to employees on military leave.

(see Chapter 8.)

What if a participant's coverage ends *in anticipation* of a qualifying event? Say, for example, that an employee with family coverage is in the midst of a divorce but, before the divorce is final, instructs his employer to drop his wife from the plan. Assuming the employee's instructions are consistent with plan requirements, and the employer is not on notice of a court order prohibiting the employee from dropping his wife's coverage, the employer has no choice but to comply. But, under IRS regulations, once the divorce is final, the employer must then give the usual COBRA notice to the employee's ex-wife. It does not matter that the wife was not in fact participating at the time of the divorce, since she was dropped in anticipation of that event.

The cost of the continuing benefits must be paid 100% by the participant (the employee, spouse, or dependent), even if the employer was paying all or a portion of the premium before the qualifying event. The employer may also charge an additional 2% of the premium to cover administrative costs.

COBRA benefits do not continue indefinitely. For a terminated employee and his or her spouse and dependents, benefits last for only eighteen months. For a spouse or dependents who lose benefits due to divorce or separation from the employee or due to the employee's death, benefits last up to thirty-six months.

Many states have *little COBRA* laws that apply to employers who do not meet the 20-employee threshold under federal law.

HIPAA

The federal *Health Insurance Portability and Accountability Act* (HIPAA) imposes a variety of requirements on group health plans in order to make health coverage more *portable*, so that when an employee changes jobs he or she will more quickly qualify for full coverage from the new employer. For example, HIPAA limits to twelve months the time period for which preexisting conditions may be excluded. The 12-month limit is further reduced by the employee's *creditable coverage*, meaning coverage under a prior individual policy, under a prior group policy, under COBRA continuation benefits, or under Medicare or Medicaid.

To enable an employee to prove prior coverage, the previous employer or insurer must issue a *Certificate of Credible Coverage* containing information about the prior plan and the employee's participation.

EMPLOYER TIP

Department of Health and Human Services regulations under *HIPAA* impose strict confidentiality requirements on the handling of protected health information (PHI) relating to employees. (see Chapter 18.)

HIPAA also requires plans to have special enrollment periods during which employees or dependents who previously declined coverage can sign up. Unlike COBRA, which applies to employers with 20 or more employees, HIPAA applies to all employers who have group health plans.

Additional information about portability is available at:

www.dol.gov/ebsa/faqs/faq_consumer_hipaa.html#

A form of Certificate of Credible Coverage is set out in the Department of Labor's regulations, available at:

www.dol.gov/ebsa/regs/fedreg/final/97_8275.pdf

MANDATED BENEFITS

The federal *Newborns' and Mothers' Health Protection Act* prohibits group health plans from cutting off hospitalization benefits for a mother and her newborn child for the first 48 hours of hospitalization after a normal vaginal delivery and for the first 96 hours of hospitalization after a cesarean section.

The Act also prohibits health plans and insurers from offering financial incentives to mothers or health care providers to encourage hospital stays shorter than these minimum stays. Of course, in consultation with her physician a mother is free to leave sooner if it is medically appropriate. The Act does not require that births take place in a hospital.

The insurance laws of most states specify certain coverages that must be included in group health plans. Mental health coverage is a typical mandated benefit. Additional examples include chiropractic treatment and other treatments that have not always been considered in the health care mainstream.

For the most part, the courts have upheld these requirements, despite claims that they are preempted by ERISA.

QUALIFIED MEDICAL CHILD SUPPORT ORDERS

ERISA requires that group health plans contain provisions to recognize *Qualified Medical Child Support Orders* (QMCSOs). QMCSOs are somewhat similar to QDROs (Qualified Domestic Relations Orders), discussed in Chapter 8, in that they give alternate payees—persons other than participating employees—rights with respect to an employer-sponsored benefit plan.

Under a QMCSO, an employee who has child support obligations may, as part of the obligation, be ordered to provide any available health insurance coverage for the dependent children. Assuming the employer's plan includes family coverage, delivery to the employer of such an order has the effect of requiring the employer to enroll the employee's dependent children. The costs of such coverage are covered by deductions from the employee's pay. The employer may not disenroll the children unless the employee quits or obtains replacement coverage or unless the employer eliminates family coverage from the plan. However, the employer is *not* required to provide any type or form of benefit, or any option, not already provided under the plan. For example, if a plan limits participation just to employees and does not cover other family members, than a QMCSO cannot require the plan to begin providing family coverage.

Under ERISA's QMCSO requirements, a plan must have procedures in place for determining whether a court or administrative order, entered in a domestic relations proceeding, in fact qualifies as a QMCSO. To simplify the process, the U.S. Department of Labor has issued a standard set of forms to be used by state enforcement agencies (called IV-D agencies) in connection with QMCSOs.

CLAIMS ADMINISTRATION

The Department of Labor has developed an elaborate set of regulations governing health plan claims procedures. Under these regulations, an insurer must process an initial claim:

- within seventy-two hours for urgent claim care;
- within fifteen days for pre-service claims (with one 15-day extension allowed); and,
- within thirty days for post-service claims (with one 15-day extension allowed).

Claimants have 180 days to appeal a claim denial, and the appeal itself must be decided:

- within seventy-two hours for urgent claim care;
- within thirty days for pre-service claims; and,
- within sixty days for post-service claims.

Plans are prohibited from imposing fees or costs as a condition to filing or appealing a claim. Appeals must also be decided by a person different from the decision-maker on the initial claim denial. Where an appeal involves a medical judgment, such as the medical necessity of a particular procedure or drug, appropriate health care professionals must also be consulted. Finally, plans must:

- provide participants with a full description of claim procedures;

- provide specific reasons for claim denials, including identification of and access to guidelines or rules relied upon in denying the claim, along with all other documents and records relevant to the denial; and,
- disclose the names of any medical professionals consulted as part of the claim process.

GENDER-SPECIFIC COVERAGE

In 1978, Congress passed the *Pregnancy Discrimination Act* (PDA) amending *Title VII* of the federal *Civil Rights Act*. The PDA expands the definition of sex discrimination to include *pregnancy, childbirth,* or *related medical conditions*. Under the PDA, a group health plan must cover pregnancy, childbirth, and related medical conditions to the same extent the plan covers similar medical conditions. Abortions need not be covered, except where the mother's life is endangered.

The EEOC has ruled that an otherwise comprehensive health insurance plan that excludes coverage for prescription contraceptives violates *Title VII*'s sex discrimination provision. At least one federal trial court has agreed with the EEOC. The idea is that unless a health plan is equally comprehensive for men and women, it discriminates on the basis of gender. However, in a recent federal court of appeals case, a plan that denied benefits for surgical fertility treatments was held *not* discriminatory, even though the surgical procedures are used only on women. The court reasoned that while the surgery itself is performed only on women, the underlying condition that the surgery is attempting to abate could be male infertility, female infertility, or both, so that the exclusion is equally adverse to males and females.

EMPLOYER TIP

Providing less comprehensive coverage for one gender than for the other may also violate federal anti-discrimination laws. (see Chapter 15.)

STOCK OPTIONS

More and more companies find it attractive to include, as part of their compensation package for key employees, some equity participation in the company. In a tight labor market, the opportunity to become a stockholder in the company may even be a necessary part of the recruitment and retention process. The idea is to provide an incentive to key employees by enabling them to share in the company's growth. The amount of stock involved is usually small enough that there is no significant effect on control of the company.

The company could simply give company stock to an employee as additional compensation or sell stock to the employee at some price that is below actual market value. However, any difference between the actual value of the stock and the amount paid by the employee will be income to the employee, immediately taxable at ordinary income (not capital gain) rates. The employee may have to sell some of the stock in order to raise cash to pay the tax, defeating the purpose of the arrangement. Worse, if there is no market for the stock or the stock declines in value, the employee may be stuck with a big tax bill and have no way to pay it.

A more typical approach is to use *stock options*, in which the company grants the employee a right, exercisable during a specified time period, to acquire company stock (or stock in a parent or subsidiary company) at a stated price, called the *option price* or *strike price*. While the *grant* of the option is not immediately taxable, the *exercise* of the option may or may not have tax consequences, depending on whether the arrangement qualifies as a *statutory* stock option or a *non-statutory* stock option. But regardless of the tax consequences at the time the option is exercised, the grant of the option itself gives the employee a tax-free opportunity to participate in the growth of the company.

Statutory Stock Options

A *statutory stock option* is an option that qualifies as either an *incentive stock option* (ISO) under Section 422 of the Internal Revenue Code or as an employee stock purchase plan under I.R.C. Sec. 423.

Under an ISO, when the employee exercises an option, pays the option price, and acquires company stock, no taxable income is incurred (but the company gets no tax deduction, either). Should the employee later sell the stock (after satisfying applicable holding periods), he or she is taxed at capital gain rates on the difference between the option price and selling price. In order to qualify for this favorable tax treatment, the option must meet the following requirements.

- The option must be granted pursuant to a written plan and approved by the company's shareholders. The plan must specify the total number of shares that may be issued under the plan and must identify the employees or class of employees eligible to receive options. (The identity-of-the-employees requirement can be met if the plan simply says that the employees will be chosen by a specified person or committee.)
- The option must be in the form of a written agreement between the company and the employee.
- The option must be granted within ten years after adoption of the plan.
- The option must state that the option can only be exercised within ten years after being granted.
- The employee cannot be eligible to exercise more than $100,000 in options within any twelve-month period.
- The option holder must be an employee when the option is granted and must continue to be an employee until three months before the option is exercised. (Special rules apply to employees who die or become disabled.)
- The option holder can own no more than 10% of the voting stock of the company. (This requirement does not apply if the option price is at least 110% of the fair market value of the stock and if the option cannot be exercised for at least five years.)
- The option price must be at least equal to the fair market value of the stock at the time the option is granted.
- The option cannot be exercisable by anyone other than the employee personally, and the option must be nontransferrable

during the employee's lifetime. (Special rules apply to the exercise of options by a deceased employee's estate.)

♦ After the option is exercised, the shares themselves must be held for at least two years after the option was granted and for at least one year after the option is exercised.

Under an *Employee Stock Purchase Plan* (not to be confused with an *Employee Stock Ownership Plan*, or *ESOP*, discussed later), an employer grants options to its general workforce in proportion to their compensation. The plan *must* exclude employees who own 5% or more of the company. It *may* exclude part-time and seasonal employees, employees who have worked less than two years, and highly-compensated employees. The

EMPLOYER TIP

ISOs are not subject to ERISA because their purpose is to provide a current incentive, much like salary, and not to defer compensation or provide retirement benefits.

option price cannot be lower than 85% of the value of the stock at the time the option is granted (or, alternatively, at the time the option is exercised).

Other restrictions apply, including a $25,000 per year limitation on the amount of stock for which a single employee can hold options. As with ISOs, the exercise of the option does not result in taxable income. The sale of stock acquired through the option receives capital gain treatment, so long as applicable holding periods are satisfied.

Nonstatutory Stock Options

In a *nonstatutory stock option* (NSO), the tax advantages shift to the employer. Specifically, when the employee exercises the option and acquires company stock with a value higher than the option price, the employer can take a deduction for the difference, but the employee must report the difference as ordinary income. An option will be nonstatutory if the option does not meet the statutory requirements listed earlier, or the option specifically states that it is *not* an ISO.

Although NSOs are not required to satisfy the conditions applicable to ISOs, a company may choose to impose certain conditions, such as holding periods, restrictions on transfer, etc.

One disadvantage of ISOs is that the company must determine the fair market value of the stock subject to the option in order to set the option price. If the company's stock is publicly traded, the trading value is used. But if the company is privately held, hiring an outside valuation expert may be necessary. (The company need only make a *good faith effort* to value its stock. However, restrictions on transferability *cannot* be considered as reducing the value of the stock.) The ISO agreement can state that the company will issue a special class of stock, such as nonvoting stock, to satisfy the exercise of an option, but this further complicates the valuation process because of the need to value the special class of stock separately.

Once the employee exercises the option and acquires company stock, the employee can sell it immediately if the stock was acquired through an NSO. (This is subject to any restrictions in the option agreement and to any securities law restrictions.) If it was acquired through an ISO, the employee can sell it after satisfying the ISO holding period requirements, any additional restrictions in the option agreement, and any securities law restrictions. But if the company is privately held, there is not likely to be any market for the stock. So in practical terms, the option plan must allow the employee to sell the stock back to the company. Such a repurchase obligation may entail yet another expensive valuation. If the employee sells back less than all the stock, he or she may be deemed to have received a dividend taxable at ordinary income rates.

Companies contemplating a stock option plan should consider the effect on employee incentive if the stock goes *down* instead of

EMPLOYER TIP

Businesses that grant NSOs to their employees must separately identify on the employees' W-2 forms any compensation received by the employees from the exercise of NSOs.

up. Employees whose primary compensation has been stock options may get discouraged and leave sooner than if their compensation had not included options. Companies should also consider their increased litigation exposure should a fired employee sue for wrongful discharge and claim not only the wages he or she would have received, but also the value of unvested stock options.

Publicly-traded companies should also be mindful of new SEC rules designed to protect against *dilution in the dark*. Under these rules, companies are required to provide detailed information about their equity compensation plans in their annual reports to the SEC. The information is also required to be included in proxy statements whenever the company is submitting an equity compensation plan for approval by shareholders.

EMPLOYEE STOCK OWNERSHIP PLANS

An ESOP, or *Employee Stock Ownership Plan*, is a form of defined contribution plan in which the plan's primary investment is in stock of the employer company. (Under ERISA's self-dealing rules, most pension plans are prohibited from holding significant investments in the sponsoring company. ESOPs fall within an exception to these rules.) Since ESOPs, along with other qualified pension plans, must be managed for the exclusive benefit of participating employees and their beneficiaries, an ESOP is a way for employees to own the company, or at least own a significant part of the company.

Advantages

ESOPs have a number of advantages over other pension plans, particularly when the company is a closely-held corporation whose stock is not publicly traded. Among the advantages are the following.

+ Employees are more highly motivated, since

> **EMPLOYER TIP**
>
> Employee ownership of company stock, whether obtained through the exercise of stock options or otherwise, requires attention to insider trading restrictions. (see Chapter 23.)

they have an ownership interest in the company and their productivity increases the value of their stock.

♦ The added control and bargaining power employees have through stock ownership may dissuade them from unionizing.

♦ When an ESOP acquires its stock by purchase of newly issued company shares, the company can, in effect, use pension plan contributions as a source of capital for company operations or expansion.

♦ When an ESOP acquires its stock by purchase from existing shareholders, the ESOP provides a market for those shares and provides liquidity to existing shareholders. (If the ESOP is acquiring at least a 30% interest in the company from existing shareholders, the selling shareholders may defer recognition of capital gain on those shares.)

♦ An ESOP can *leverage* its stock ownership by borrowing money from a bank or other lender to purchase stock, thereby providing additional capital to the company or liquidity to its selling shareholders. Future pension plan contributions by the company to the ESOP to service the loan are fully tax deductible, in effect enabling the company to deduct otherwise nondeductible principal repayments.

♦ An ESOP provides continuity of ownership and management of the company. Without an ESOP, the death or retirement of a principal shareholder often means liquidation of the company or the involvement of new owners who are strangers to the company.

♦ Premiums for *key person* life insurance owned by an ESOP are fully tax deductible. (A key person is an employee whose death would cause substantial financial harm to the business.)

There are some disadvantages to an ESOP. When the company's stock is not publicly traded, the company must pay for expensive stock valuations to determine the fair market value of the stock being contributed or sold to the ESOP. These valuations are typically required on an annual basis.

Then there is the question of who will serve as trustees of the trust that holds the ESOP stock. Banks and other financial institutions are increasingly reluctant to assume the trustee role because of the fiduciary responsibilities and risks involved. But if company officers or directors are appointed as trustees, they may find it difficult to subordinate their own self-interest to the interests of participating employees (for whose benefit the ESOP is supposed to be managed).

The conflict of interest is heightened when the company is considering out-of-the-ordinary corporate actions, such as implementing a nonqualified deferred compensation plan for senior executives or responding to a merger proposal. In these instances, it may be necessary for the company to obtain outside advice as to the reasonableness of deferred compensation or the fairness of a proposed transaction.

NOTE: *ESOPs may not be for everyone, but their unique advantages deserve serious consideration.*

OTHER PLANS
Retirement and group health plans are probably the most significant employee benefits, both in terms of tax savings and in terms of popularity with employees. Other arrangements are available, however, and should not be overlooked. As with retirement and group health plans, these other arrangements generally must satisfy applicable tax and ERISA requirements.

Group Term Life Insurance
An employer may provide group term life insurance to employees, either as part of a group health plan or as a separate plan. The first $50,000 in coverage is tax free to the employee. The premium for coverage in excess of $50,000 is taxable income to the employee.

Disability Insurance
Premiums on employer-sponsored group disability insurance, if paid by the employer, are deductible by the employer, but are not includible in the employee's income. However, if an employee becomes disabled and collects benefits under the policy, the benefits

are taxable income to the employee. Alternatively, if the employee pays the premiums with after-tax dollars, then the benefits are not taxable to the employee.

Under one clever arrangement, the employer paid the disability insurance premiums but gave each employee an election between having the premium amounts included or excluded in the employee's gross income. The IRS concluded in a private letter ruling, that if the employee becomes disabled in a plan year in which he or she has elected to include the premiums in gross income, then the benefits are not taxable. However, if the employee becomes disabled in a plan year in which he or she has elected to exclude the premiums, the benefits are taxable.

Long-term Care Insurance

Premiums on employer-sponsored group long-term care insurance are deductible by the employer. If the coverage qualifies as medical care and the premiums are below certain limits specified in the Internal Revenue Code, the premiums are not includible in the employee's income. Benefits, when paid, are not taxable.

Cafeteria Plans

Sometimes referred to as Section 125 plans (because they are authorized under that section of the Internal Revenue Code), *cafeteria plans* give each employee a choice between taking cash or receiving qualified benefits such as health insurance, group term life insurance, long-term care insurance, etc. If the employee elects cash, he or she must report the benefit as taxable income. If he or she elects a qualified benefit, the benefit is excludible to the extent allowed by law.

Cafeteria plans are attractive in that they allow each employee to tailor benefits to his or her particular circumstances—as, for example, when an employee does not need health insurance due to coverage through his or her spouse's employer, but would like life insurance for which he or she cannot otherwise qualify because of a medical condition.

Flexible Spending Arrangements

Flexible Spending Accounts (FSAs) allow employees to put aside before-tax dollars to cover *dependent care expenses, uninsured medical expenses,* or both. Once an employer has approved inclusion of an FSA in its cafeteria plan, each employee individually designates a portion of income each year, in

> ## EMPLOYER TIP
>
> Although the IRS permits employers to enroll employees automatically in cafeteria plans (subject to the employee's opting out), state wage-and-hour laws may prohibit an employer from making payroll deductions without the employee's express consent.

the form of regular payroll deductions, for payment into a special trust fund. The amount designated is up to the employee, subject to any outside limits imposed by the plan. The amount so designated is not includible in the employee's gross income for income tax purposes.

During the year, if the employee incurs dependent care expenses or medical expenses not covered by the health plan, the employee submits receipted bills to the administrator of the fund and is reimbursed. The reimbursement is also not included in gross income, so the net effect is that the employee pays dependent care expenses and uninsured medical expenses with before-tax dollars rather than with after-tax dollars.

In the case of medical expenses, the tax result achieved with an FSA is similar to taking a deduction on the employee's tax return for uninsured medical expenses. However, medical expense deductions are limited to employees who itemize and are further limited to expenses that are greater than 7.5% of the employee's adjusted gross income. Therefore, from the employee's viewpoint, the practical benefit of an FSA is that it allows him or her to deduct *all* uninsured medical expenses, rather than just those that are above the 7.5% floor, *whether or not* he or she itemizes.

The downside of an FSA for employees is that any money left in their accounts at year-end is forfeited to the employer. For that reason, employees should be conservative in their estimates of uninsured medical and dependent care expenses.

The downside for employers is that if an employee has substantial reimbursable expenses early in the plan year, before enough funds are accumulated to cover the expenses, the employer must advance the reimbursement to the employee. If the employee then quits, there will be no more payroll deductions and the employer will be left holding an FSA with a negative balance. To guard against this possibility, employers usually limit the size of each employee's FSA to no more than several thousand dollars.

Health Reimbursement Arrangements

Health Reimbursement Arrangements (HRAs) are employee-directed health care plans. In a typical HRA, the employer sponsors a group health insurance policy with a high deductible amount. Policy premiums, which are low because of the high deductible, can be paid by the employer, the employee, or partly by both, as specified in plan documents. The employer then establishes an additional plan to reimburse employees for the employees' uninsured medical expenses. The reimbursement amount usually approximates the amount of the deductible under the group policy, so that employees end up paying little or no medical expenses out of their own pockets.

Employer reimbursements under an HRA are tax-deductible to the employer, but they are not taxable income to the employee. And unlike FSAs, which have a use-it-or-lose-it rule, unused HRA reimbursements can be carried over from plan year to plan year. The plan may permit former employees and retirees to have continuing access to unused reimbursement amounts (and it must do so when a former employee elects COBRA). Reimbursement amounts may even be used to purchase health insurance.

In order to enjoy favorable tax treatment, HRAs must satisfy certain IRS-specified requirements. They must:

- ◆ be paid for solely by the employer and cannot be funded pursuant to a salary reduction arrangement or under a cafeteria plan;

◆ limit reimbursements to *substantiated* (documented) medical expenses incurred by the employee or by the employee's spouse and dependents while the plan is in existence and while the employee is participating in the plan;

◆ limit reimbursements to medical expenses that would qualify for deduction as medical expenses on the employee's income tax return; and,

◆ comply generally with ERISA (including COBRA) and HIPAA.

Employee Assistance Plans

Employee Assistance Plans (EAPs) are designed to provide counseling and related services to employees who have emotional or substance abuse problems. Typically, the employer contracts with an outside agency to provide the services.

Child and Dependent Care Service Plans

These plans provide day care for an employee's child under 13 years of age and for a spouse or dependents who are unable to care for themselves. The first $5,000 in benefits is excludible from the employee's income for tax purposes. Amounts in excess of $5,000 are includible.

DOMESTIC PARTNERS

The term domestic partner as used here refers to someone with whom your employee lives and has a voluntary, committed relationship, other than a spouse or relative. In general, benefit laws and anti-discrimination laws do not recognize domestic partnerships. For example, the federal *Defense of Marriage Act* (DOMA) defines *spouse* as someone of the opposite sex, so that a domestic partner has none of the protec-

> **EMPLOYER TIP**
>
> EAP records relating to substance abuse services are subject to special confidentiality provisions of federal law. (see Chapter 18.)

tions or benefits provided to spouses under federal pension law. But there are a few exceptions.

Disability

The federal *Americans with Disabilities Act* prohibits discrimination against an applicant or employee who is known to be *in a relationship with or be associated with* someone who has a disability. That language is broad enough to cover a domestic partner.

Sexual Orientation

A number of states and local jurisdictions prohibit discrimination based on sexual orientation. When a domestic partner is a person of the same sex as the employee, adverse treatment of the employee could give rise to a claim of discrimination because of sexual orientation.

Marital Status

Regardless of the genders involved, adverse treatment of an employee who has a domestic partner could give rise to a claim of discrimination because of marital status, in violation of state or local law.

COBRA

COBRA benefits can include a domestic partner *if* the employer provides health insurance for domestic partners and *if* the employee has elected COBRA. However, a domestic partner has no independent right to elect COBRA benefits for him or herself.

Establishing Benefits

Local governments and private employers are beginning to recognize domestic partners. They do so because they see it as fair and equal treatment for their employees. Or they may agree to domestic partner coverage to stay competitive with other employers. Whatever the reason, domestic partner coverage poses a number of legal and practical issues that need to be addressed.

Who qualifies as a domestic partner? Employers need to develop a clear definition of *domestic partner*. The definition might, for example, include some or all of the following requirements:

- ◆ both persons in the relationship must be legally competent adults;
- ◆ the persons cannot be so closely related to each other that (aside from gender) they would be forbidden to marry under state law;
- ◆ the persons must have a committed, exclusive relationship and neither can be married or in a domestic partnership with someone else; and,
- ◆ the persons must live together and be financially interdependent.

The employer will also need to decide whether to cover only same-sex partners or include opposite-sex couples as well. In jurisdictions that prohibit sexual orientation discrimination, covering same-sex but not opposite-sex couples, or covering opposite-sex but not same-sex couples, could be discriminatory.

What proof will be required? Once the definition of domestic partner is settled, the employer will have to specify what documentation will be required to recognize a person as a domestic partner. Is an affidavit from the two partners sufficient? Or will the employer also want to see such items as deeds or leases showing that the partners jointly own or lease their residence?

What benefits will be offered? If domestic partners will be entitled to family coverage under the employer's group health policy, the employer will need to coordinate coverage with its insurer. Other benefits might include sick leave to care for an ill domestic partner, bereavement leave, the opportunity to participate in employer-sponsored recreational functions, health club memberships, conventions, and business trips, etc. (The *Family and Medical Leave Act* itself does not require employers to grant leave for the care of a domestic partner.)

Must an employer recognize same-sex marriages legally performed in another state? The answer to this question appears to be no, at least for the time being. At this writing, only Vermont has a law recognizing civil unions between same-sex partners. While each state is generally required by the U.S. Constitution to give *full faith and credit*—that is, to recognize—the laws of every other state, the *Defense of Marriage Act* gives states the choice not to recognize another state's same-sex marriage. So if you are an employer in a state that does not recognize same-sex marriages, you need not do so either. (It remains to be seen whether this provision of the DOMA is constitutional.)

What are the tax implications of providing domestic partner benefits? In general, an employer may claim an income tax deduction for the costs of a qualified benefit plan. And, in the case of health insurance provided to employees or to employees and their spouses or dependents, the employee need not treat the benefit as taxable income. However, the cost of providing health insurance to a domestic partner is taxable income to the employee, since the domestic partner is not a spouse and, in most cases, cannot qualify as a dependent. Therefore, the cost of such coverage must be included in the *W-2 Form* issued by the employer and it must be reported on the employee's income tax return.

-11-
WORKERS' COMPENSATION

Prior to the adoption of workers' compensation laws, an employer could, at least in theory, be held liable in court for work-related injuries suffered by employees. The employer might have to pay damages if, for example, he or she failed to provide a safe place to work or failed to provide a sufficient number of suitable fellow employees to accomplish the job at hand.

As a practical matter, however, the defenses available to the employer often prevented the employee from receiving any compensation for injuries. Those defenses included:

- *fellow servant doctrine*, which insulated employers from liability where the injury was caused by the negligence of a fellow employee;
- *contributory negligence*, which barred the employee from recovery if he or she contributed in any way to the cause of the injury; and,
- *assumption of the risk*, under which the employee was held to have assumed the risk of injury normally associated with the particular job.

In essence, workers' compensation acts are *no fault* laws under which the employer is automatically obligated to pay compensation and benefits for each employee who suffers a work-related illness or injury or who is killed in the course of employment. This obligation, which is usually funded by mandatory workers' compensation insurance, applies whether or not the employer was negligent and whether or not the employer could have raised one or more defenses to liability.

The trade-off for the employer is that workers' compensation benefits are the employer's *exclusive liability* for work-related injuries or illnesses. Unless the employer deliberately intended to injure or kill the employee—the employee cannot sue the employer in court; the employee cannot demand a jury trial; and, the employee cannot obtain open-ended damages for pain and suffering.

GENERAL COVERAGE

Workers' compensation acts broadly apply to all employers and, with few exceptions, all their employees. For purposes of these acts, the term *employee* means someone whose method of work the employer has a right to control. The acts apply to minors, even if they are employed unlawfully, and in some states to domestic workers in private homes.

The acts do not apply to independent contractors or to *casual employees*—employees who work irregularly, for a brief period only, doing work not normally performed by employees of the employer.

Workers' compensation acts require employers to *secure compensation* for their covered employees by maintaining insurance through authorized insurance companies or through self-insurance. Insurance premiums are calculated as a percentage of payroll. The actual percentage varies for each employer based on factors such as the employer's industry classification and claim history. Employers may *self-insure* if they can demonstrate their financial ability to pay compensation. Self-insurers usually must put up security or a *bond* to cover their compensation obligations.

> **EMPLOYER TIP**
>
> Workers' compensation programs are exempt from ERISA.
> (see Chapter 9.)

State laws generally require employers to post a notice in the workplace as to the existence of workers' compensation coverage and the procedure to be followed after an injury or death. It is ille-

gal for an employer to charge employees, such as by a wage deduction, for any part of the cost of providing workers' compensation. It
is also illegal for an employer to retaliate against an employee for filing a compensation claim or for testifying in a compensation
proceeding.

Personal Injury

Workers' compensation acts cover accidental *personal injury* that is
usually defined as:
- an accidental injury that arises out of and in the course of
  employment;
- an injury caused by the willful or negligent act of a third person in connection with a covered employee's employment;
- a disease or infection that naturally results from an accidental
  injury, such as frostbite or sunstroke; or,
- an occupational disease.

The acts *do not* cover injuries:
- that are intentionally self-inflicted;
- resulting from the covered employee's attempt to injure or kill
  another or other willful misconduct; or,
- resulting solely from intoxication while on duty and, in some
  states, from illegal drug use.

It is sometimes argued that the likelihood of injury in certain
occupations is so great that when an injury does occur, it cannot
fairly be called *accidental*. A professional football team, for example,
sought to deny compensation to one of its offensive linemen who
injured his ankle in a game. The team claimed that when injuries are
customary, foreseeable, and expected—in other words, are simply
part of the game—they are not accidental within the meaning of the
workers' compensation statute. The Virginia Supreme Court
rejected the team's argument, saying that just because an occupation is *high-risk* does not mean the compensation statute is
inapplicable.

COVERED EMPLOYEES

State law typically defines *covered employee* broadly as any individual (including a minor), while in the service of an employer under an express or implied contract of apprenticeship or hire. The statutes then go on to list a number of exceptions and special provisions. For example, sole proprietors, partners, and officers of closely-held corporations may not be covered at all or they may have a right to *opt in* or *opt out* of coverage.

COURSE AND SCOPE OF EMPLOYMENT

Workers' compensation laws cover employees who suffer accidental injuries *arising out of* and *in the course of employment*. Sometimes it is difficult to tell whether an injury did or did not arise out of and in the course of employment.

Take, for example, an employee who is injured while commuting to or from work. The general rule (sometimes called the *going-and-coming rule*) is that employees are not covered while commuting. But there are exceptions. Despite the going-and-coming rule, coverage will be provided when:

- ◆ an employee is going from one of the employer's places of business to another during the workday;
- ◆ an employee is exposed to a special hazard, which the public-at-large is normally not exposed to, while gaining access to the employer's place of business;
- ◆ the means of transportation are provided by the employer, or the employee is being paid while commuting; or,
- ◆ the employer requires the employee to commute in a specified way or follow a specified route.

When an employee is on travel for the employer, he or she generally *is* covered, even if not specifically engaged in work at the time of the injury. This includes hotel bathroom falls, choking on a meal, suffering a criminal assault, or being injured in a hotel fire. Only if the employee is injured while on a *distinct departure* from work and on a *personal errand* will there be no coverage.

CLAIM PROCEDURE

If an employee suffers a work-related injury or illness, he or she must both notify the employer and file a claim for compensation with the state agency that administers the compensation act. Once the employer learns of a compensable injury, the employer too must file a report with the state agency.

The time limits applicable to notification and reporting requirements vary from jurisdiction to jurisdiction. Failure to meet these deadlines may bar the employee's right of recovery, although the government agency that administers the law usually has authority to excuse a late filing.

After a claim is filed, the employer or its insurance carrier must either begin paying benefits or *controvert* (contest) the claim. If the claim is controverted, the government agency investigates, conducts a hearing if necessary, and then issues an award or denies coverage. Further appeal may be made to the courts. The parties are entitled to be represented by attorneys in a contested matter, but the amount of attorneys' fees charged the employee are often subject to approval by the administering agency.

BENEFITS

Workers' compensation acts provide for various categories of benefits including:

- disability benefits to the covered employee for lost wages or loss of earning capacity;
- medical benefits;
- death benefits to the employee's dependents;
- funeral benefits; and,
- vocational rehabilitation.

The actual amount of disability benefits is calculated from complicated statutory formulas based on the employee's average weekly wage. The following benefit formulas (subject to statutory maximums and minimums) are typical:

- for *temporary partial disability*—up to two-thirds of the employee's lost wage earning capacity;

- for *temporary total disability*—two-thirds of the employee's average weekly wage. If the disability lasts more than fourteen days, benefits are payable from the first day of disability. However, if the disability lasts fourteen days or less, the first three days of disability are not covered;
- for *permanent partial disability*—up to two-thirds of the employee's average weekly wage. If the injury falls in one of the categories listed in the act (such as loss of a specific appendage, loss of a sensory organ, or loss of various combinations of appendages and sensory organs), the benefit continues only for the number of weeks specified in the law; and/or,
- for *permanent total disability*, two-thirds of the employee's average weekly wage.

EMPLOYER TIP

Although the meaning of *disabled* for workers' compensation act purposes is not the same as under the *Americans with Disabilities Act,* employers should be alert to the possibility that an injured employee might qualify as disabled under the ADA. If so, taking adverse employment action or failing to reasonably accommodate the employee could constitute illegal discrimination. A workplace injury can also trigger *Family and Medical Leave Act* obligations. (see Chapters 8 and 17.)

Workers' compensation premiums are deductible by the employer for federal income tax purposes. Benefits paid to an employee are exempt from income tax.

Terminating an employee for excessive absenteeism where the employee is out on disability as a result of a work-related, compensable injury is allowable in most states. However, even where dismissal is permitted, firing an employee who is out on work-related disability is fraught with peril. Some of the potential problems are listed below.

- The employee may claim that the termination was abusive or in retaliation for having filed a workers' compensation claim.
- If the employer is subject to the *Family and Medical Leave Act*, the employee may be entitled to FMLA leave.

◆ If the disabling condition is not merely temporary and if it substantially interferes with one or more major life activities, the employer's duty of reasonable accommodation under the *Americans with Disabilities Act* may be triggered.

SECOND INJURY FUND

Suppose an employee has a serious, pre-existing condition, but the applicant is nevertheless able to work. Some employers may be reluctant to hire the person, fearing that a subsequent injury on top of the earlier condition, even if minor, could disable the employee and expose the employer to liability for permanent disability benefits.

Recognizing that the workers' compensation system may inadvertently discourage the hiring of employees who have suffered prior injuries, many states have created a *second injury fund* that pays a portion of the compensation benefits due a re-injured employee.

Since the purpose of second injury funds is to discourage employers from discriminating against employment applicants who have suffered prior injuries, the question arises whether an employer who was unaware of a prior injury can obtain reimbursement from the fund after paying full benefits to a re-injured employee.

Some courts have adopted the rule that the employee's prior injury must be *manifest* for the employer to recover from the fund. As a practical matter, this means that the employer must either have actual knowledge of the prior injury at hiring time or the prior injury must be obvious or documented in medical records available to the employer such that a reasonable person in the employer's shoes would have known about the prior injury.

> **EMPLOYER TIP**
>
> The ADA prohibits pre-employment physicals unless the employer has already made a conditional offer of employment to the employee.
> (see Chapter 17.)

The requirement that a prior injury be *manifest* for the employer to have access to the second injury fund in the event of a subsequent injury is one reason why an employer may require new employees to undergo medical exams.

RIGHTS AGAINST THIRD PARTIES

Although workers' compensation acts prohibit an employee from suing his or her own employer for a work-related injury, the acts do not prohibit an employee from suing a third party who may have caused the injury.

Example: Suppose an employee is a passenger in his employer's truck that is being driven by a fellow employee in the course of a delivery. If the truck is hit at an intersection because another vehicle ran a red light, the employee-passenger can sue the driver of the other vehicle. However, if the accident occurred because the employee-passenger's fellow employee ran the red light, the employee-passenger may or may not be able to sue his fellow employee, depending on state law.

In the above illustration, regardless of how the accident occurred, the employee-passenger can of course collect workers' compensation benefits. But the employee-passenger is not allowed to invoke the legal doctrine of *respondeat superior* and attempt to hold his own employer vicariously liable.

State laws differ as to whether the injured employee has to elect between accepting compensation or suing the negligent third party. In some states, by accepting compensation the employee in effect assigns to the employer the right to sue the third person, up to the amount of compensation paid by the employer. In other states, the employee may accept compensation *and* sue the third person, but if the employee's suit is successful, the employee has to reimburse the employer up to the amount of compensation paid by the employer.

If an injured employee enters into a settlement agreement with the third party and, in exchange for a cash payment, releases the third party from further liability, the employer may be able to raise the settlement as a defense to the employer's own workers' compensation obligation. The reason is that, by releasing the third party, the employee has also compromised the employer's subrogation right to recover against the third party. So the employee should obtain the employer's consent (and the consent of the employer's workers' compensation insurance carrier) before entering into any settlement agreement with a third party.

Independent Contractors

Suppose an employer engages an independent contractor to perform some function at the workplace and, as a result of the independent contractor's negligence, an employee suffers an injury on the job. Certainly the employee can recover workers' compensation benefits, but can the employee sue the independent contractor as well? In other words, is the independent contractor considered so connected with the employer as to enjoy immunity from suit? Or is the independent contractor a *third* party who is subject to suit?

The answer usually depends on whether the independent contractor is a stranger to the employer's business or whether the independent contractor was performing an essential part of the employer's business. The following examples illustrate this concept.

Example 1: A retail company hires an architect to design a warehouse for storing out-of-season merchandise. The architect negligently designs an overhead door at the warehouse that falls and injures one of the company's regular employees. The architect will in most instances be considered a *stranger* to the employer's business. The injured employee can sue him despite workers' compensation laws.

Example 2: But suppose that same retail company hires a cleaning company to assist with store maintenance and to perform cleaning and janitorial functions, both during and after normal store hours. Here the cleaning company is performing an essential part of the employer's business and will not be subject to suit for negligence that results in injury to the retailer's regular employees.

A related issue is the *dual capacity* doctrine. Take, for example, a hospital employee who is injured on the job and receives negligent medical treatment at the employer's hospital. Can the employee sue for the negligent medical treatment or is the suit barred by the exclusivity provision of the workers' compensation statute?

A few states take the view that when an employee is acting in a capacity other than as the employer, the employer becomes a third party and is no longer immune from employee suits for negligence. Other states have ruled that when an employer negligently renders first aid to an employee who was injured on the job, the employer enjoys protection under the workers' compensation act not only for the initial injury, but also for the emergency medical treatment.

> **EMPLOYER TIP**
>
> Health and safety laws require employers to provide medical first aid supplies and, in the absence of nearby medical facilities, assure the presence of a person trained in first aid. (see Chapter 13.)

–12–
UNEMPLOYMENT INSURANCE

Unemployment insurance benefits, together with workers' compensation, provide a safety net for employees. While workers' compensation protects employees who, through work-related injuries, suffer loss of earning capacity, unemployment benefits protect against involuntary job loss due to economic or other reasons not the fault of the employee.

The unemployment insurance system is a cooperative arrangement between the federal government and participating state governments. In essence, the federal government covers administrative costs of the system and state governments fund the payment of benefits. The system is financed through mandatory taxes (called *contributions*) imposed on covered employers by state unemployment insurance laws and, at the federal level, by the *Federal Unemployment Tax Act* (FUTA).

Each new business that has one or more employees must register under the unemployment insurance laws. Tax-exempt organizations described in Section 501(c)(3) of the Internal Revenue Code are exempt from FUTA, but not from state laws. Tax-exempt organizations may have the option under state law of making reimbursements for benefits charged against their account instead of making contributions in advance. (see Chapter 20.) A *successor employer*, an employer that takes over the business of another employer, also must register as a new business.

EMPLOYER CONTRIBUTIONS

At both the federal and state levels, an employer's unemployment insurance contribution is calculated as a percentage of wages paid in *covered employment* up to a cap. The amount of wages that are subject to tax is called the *wage base*. The federal wage base under FUTA is currently $7,000 per covered employee. Each state establishes its own wage base.

At the federal level, the tax rate applied to the wage base is normally 6.2%. However, the employer is entitled to credit its state unemployment tax against the federal tax (up to a maximum of 5.4% of taxable wages) *if* the state tax was paid on time. Federal unemployment tax is generally paid quarterly, with an annual return due on January 31.

At the state level, the tax rate depends on whether the employer is a *new employer* or whether the employer is entitled to an *earned rate*—a rate based partly on actual claims experience. A new employer is typically defined as an employer who has reported taxable wages for less than some specified period, such as three years. State unemployment contributions are usually due quarterly.

While earned rates are computed differently from state to state, in general they include these two factors: the employer's actual claims experience; and, an adjustment or pooling charge to cover shortfalls in the benefit fund. Because of the experience factor, hiring and firing practices can have a significant impact on the amount of future unemployment tax due.

In order to determine an employer's claims experience, the state agency that administers unemployment insurance maintains a separate account for each covered employer. Although specific accounting practices differ from state to state, in general, the account is charged with benefits that are paid out. The employer's earned rate is then determined based on benefits charged against its account over some prior period, such as three years.

Base Period

The process of determining which employer to charge for particular benefits gets complicated. One concept that needs to be understood is *base period.* The base period is the most recent four of the employee's last five completed calendar quarters prior to the filing of the claim for unemployment benefits. If a claimant had only one employer during the base period, then 100% of the benefits are charged against that employer's account. If a claimant had two or more employers during the base period, then, depending on the state:

- ◆ each base period employer is charged with a percentage of the benefits based on the ratio of the wages paid by that employer to the employee's total base period wages or
- ◆ the employer for whom the claimant last worked for thirty days is charged with 100% of the benefit.

If an employee works in more than one state, the employer should typically report the wages for unemployment insurance purposes:

- ◆ if all the employee's work is performed in one state, then the employee's wages are reported to that state;
- ◆ if substantial work (work that is not merely incidental, transitory, or occasional) is performed in several states, one of which is the employer's home office or a branch office, then that state is the state to which wages are reported; or,
- ◆ if no substantial work is performed in the state where the employer's home office or a branch office is located, then the employee's state of residence is the state to which wages are reported.

Unfortunately, these rules cannot always be clearly applied. In those instances, the employer should get competent advice or request a ruling from the state agencies involved.

NOTE: *Employers are prohibited from deducting any part of their required contributions from employee wages. Agreements between employers and employees to waive unemployment insurance benefits are illegal.*

COVERAGE AND ELIGIBILITY

By definition, independent contractors are not employees. Therefore, compensation paid to them is not subject to unemployment tax. (However, compensation paid to an employee who is *misclassified* as an independent contractor *is* subject to tax.) Under federal law, general partners in a partnership and students who perform services for their schools are also excluded from coverage. Household employees and agricultural workers are specially treated. Each state has its own list of additional jobs not covered by the unemployment insurance laws.

Employers do not have to pay state unemployment tax for employees who are not covered and such employees are not entitled to claim benefits if they become unemployed.

In order to receive benefits, a claimant must first have been employed in a type of job covered by the unemployment insurance law he or she must have been employed for at least two calendar quarters (not necessarily consecutive) within the base period, and he or she must have earned a specified minimum amount (which varies by state) during those two calendar quarters. In addition, the claimant must be *unemployed* (defined to mean not working at all for any wages) or be *underemployed* (working less than full-time and earning wages that are less than the benefit amount that would be payable to the claimant). The claimant must also be actively seeking work and must be available for and able to perform work. Failure to meet these qualifications or failure to accept suitable work, will temporarily disqualify the claimant from receiving benefits.

EMPLOYER TIP

An employee who is out of work due to an injury or illness is ineligible for unemployment benefits, since he or she is not able to work. However, he or she may be eligible for leave under the *Family and Medical Leave Act* and workers' compensation benefits. If the injury or illness is not work-related, benefits under a group disability insurance policy may also be available.

If an individual receives a severance package or dismissal payments covering some period of time after employment ends, he or she is also eligible for unemployment insurance depending on the form that the severance package takes. If an employer intends to offer a severance package, it makes sense to offer the package in the form of a specified number of weeks of continuing compensation and benefits. That should render the departing employee ineligible for unemployment insurance benefits during the severance period. Even better, if the departing employee finds new work during the severance period, he or she may not make any claim at all.

MISCONDUCT AND QUITTING *FOR CAUSE*

At the heart of unemployment insurance is the requirement that the person claiming benefits be out of work *involuntarily*, through no fault of his or her own. Therefore, state law often disqualifies an individual from receiving benefits if he or she is fired for misconduct or leaves work voluntarily without good cause.

> **EMPLOYER TIP**
>
> Quitting to escape discriminatory working conditions may be considered a *constructive discharge*.

Some states have gradations of misconduct, such as *aggravated misconduct*, *gross misconduct*, and *(simple) misconduct*. In states with gradations of misconduct, the most serious level may disqualify the employee from benefits entirely, whereas lesser degrees of misconduct may result in only temporary disqualification.

Normally, if an employee voluntarily quits, he or she is not entitled to benefits either. But unemployment insurance statutes usually specify that the disqualification only applies if the employee leaves work *without good cause*. Stated another way, if an employee voluntarily quits with good cause, he or she is not disqualified and may receive benefits.

In general, for there to be good cause, the cause must be connected in some way to the job the employee is leaving. A purely personal decision by the employee will not qualify. For example, leaving to take a better job, to become self-employed, to return to school, or to relocate with a spouse are not good causes. On the other hand, failing to pay the employee or maintaining discriminatory working conditions may amount to good cause depending on the circumstances. (see Chapter 4.)

Striking Employees

In general, benefits are denied to employees who are out of work because of a labor dispute at their worksite. However, a claimant is generally *not* disqualified despite the existence of a labor dispute at the worksite if the claimant is not personally involved in the labor dispute, and if the claimant does not belong to a grade or class or workers whose members are involved in the labor dispute.

An individual who is receiving benefits may turn down a job that has become vacant because of a strike and still continue to receive benefits. Unemployment laws do not force workers to become strikebreakers.

CLAIM PROCEDURE

An individual who loses his or her job or becomes underemployed must register for work and file a claim with the appropriate state agency. Since benefits are generally not paid retroactively, any delay in filing a claim results in loss of benefits.

When the state agency receives a claim, it notifies all the claimant's base period employers. All base period employers are required to submit separation information to the state agency, giving the reason why the employment terminated, the last day of employment, the claimant's wage rate, and other information that might affect eligibility for or the amount of benefits. Providing false information in order to disqualify a claimant is criminal.

Once the state agency makes an initial determination of entitlement to benefits, the employer may contest benefits by appealing the determination to a hearing examiner. When the basis for the contest is employee misconduct, the employer normally must prove:

   ◆ that the employer had a clear, well-established work rule;

◆ that the employee knew about the work rule; and,

◆ that the employee willfully violated the work rule.

The employee then has an opportunity to show that the employer frequently failed to enforce the work rule.

One obvious reason for an employer to contest benefits (assuming there are reasonable grounds to do so) is to protect the employer's *earned rate*. Recall that employers other than new employers are entitled to be rated based (in part) on the employer's actual claims experience. Each benefit payment pushes that rate higher and increases the employer's required contribution for future years.

A less obvious reason to contest a claim is to get a preview of any related claims the former employee may intend to bring against the employer. Suppose, for example, that the employee voluntarily quits but says in the claim for unemployment benefits that he or she had good cause to leave because he or she suf-

EMPLOYER TIP

The employer will have an easier time proving the existence of a work rule and the former employee's awareness of the rule if the rule is contained in an employee handbook. It will also be beneficial if the employee signed an acknowledgment that he received and would read the handbook.
(see Chapter 2.)

fered racial discrimination on the job. Or suppose the employee says he or she was fired for refusal to perform some illegal act such as lying to an OSHA inspector. In those circumstances, the employer can reasonably expect to be faced not only with an unemployment compensation claim, but also with a charge of discrimination or a suit for abusive discharge.

If benefits are contested, the state unemployment agency must conduct a hearing at which the employee may testify, call other witnesses, and present documents. The employer, usually with the assistance of an attorney, can cross-examine the employee and his or her witnesses and can examine documentary evidence.

BENEFITS

Assuming the claimant qualifies for benefits, the amount of the benefit is determined by complicated statutory formulas based on the claimant's base period wages.

Benefits last up to twenty-six weeks, which may be extended in certain circumstances. After using up the maximum benefit, the claimant is ineligible for additional benefits until he or she has worked in covered employment.

–13–
WORKPLACE SAFETY

Workers' compensation laws largely eliminated employer liability for failing to provide a safe workplace. Occupational safety and health laws, such as the federal *Occupational Safety and Health Act* (OSHA), restore that liability by imposing detailed safety and health standards on employers, by authorizing unannounced inspections, by authorizing issuance of compliance orders and injunctions, and by imposing civil fines and criminal penalties for violations. While safety and health laws impose obligations on employees as well as employers, generally, only the employer is subject to penalties.

SAFETY AND HEALTH STANDARDS
OSHA, passed in 1970, imposes on every employer the general duty to furnish to each employee, *employment and a place of employment which are free from recognized hazards that are causing or are likely to cause death or serious physical harm*—the so-called *General Duty Clause*. To assure that obligation is met, OSHA requires every employer to comply with specific occupational safety and health standards isued by the Secretary of Labor. OSHA also imposes posting, record-keeping, and reporting requirements on employers.

OSHA requires the Secretary of Labor to issue safety and health standards in three categories:
- *established federal standards*, meaning standards that were in effect when the Act was passed, either as part of some other act of Congress, or contained in regulations of a federal agency;

- *national consensus standards*, meaning broadly accepted standards adopted by nationally-recognized organizations; and,
- *additional standards*—additional occupational safety and health standards that the Secretary determines would serve the purposes of OSHA.

Employers are required to comply with all applicable standards issued by the Secretary. Many standards are industry-specific, such as those dealing with longshoring and the fishing industry. Many others are broadly applicable.

The standards adopted to date, fill thousands of pages in the Code of Federal Regulations. A comprehensive analysis is not possible here. What follows is a brief discussion of a few standards of more general applicability or interest. Employers may want to contact their trade associations or obtain copies of OSHA publications, for guidance as to specific standards or standards uniquely applicable to their industry or profession. Additional information is available at OSHA's website at **www.osha.gov**.

As examples of generally applicable standards, employers are required to:

- keep work areas clean, orderly and sanitary, and keep floors clean and dry;
- protect stairwells by guardrails and guard or cover other floor openings;
- provide free and unobstructed exit from all parts of a building or other structure when occupied; mark exits by lighted signs; and maintain and test fire alarm and sprinkler systems;
- provide readily accessible fire extinguishers; and,
- provide medical first aid supplies and, in the absence of nearby medical facilities, assure the presence of a person trained in first aid.

Handling of hazardous materials is the subject of extensive regulation. OSHA sets out detailed requirements for products such as flammable and combustible liquids, explosives, and liquefied petroleum gases. For highly hazardous chemicals (substances that are toxic, reactive, flammable, or explosive and are stored in sufficient quantities to cause a catastrophe if released), the employer must inform employees of the hazard involved and must consult with employees to develop safety management plans and training.

Hazardous Materials Standards

Closely associated with OSHA's hazardous materials standards are its hazard communication standards. Chemical manufacturers and importers are obligated to determine the hazards of each of their products. That information, along with protective measures for each product, is communicated downstream to distributors, who in turn distribute it to their customers. OSHA has developed a multi-page form for communicating this information, known as a *Material Safety Data Sheet* (MSDS). Use of the MSDS form itself is not mandatory, but the information it calls for must be provided. The MSDS form lists:

- manufacturer's name, address, and emergency phone number;
- specific chemical components that create the hazard;
- physical and chemical characteristics of the product, such as appearance and odor, melting point, boiling point, and solubility in water;
- fire and explosion hazards and any special fire-fighting procedures;
- reactivity data, such as how stable the product is and any hazardous products of decomposition;
- health hazards from exposure and recommended first aid procedures; and,
- precautions for safe handling and use, such as what protective clothing should be worn.

All employers along the way, from manufacturer to end-user, are required to communicate the MSDS information to their employees who come in contact with the product and to train their employees in handling the product. This communication and training program must be in writing. Sample programs are available from OSHA. The hazardous products themselves must be appropriately tagged or marked.

Employers must have on hand, and make available to their employees, copies of the MSDS (or equivalent) for each hazardous chemical at the workplace. The burden is on the employer to contact the manufacturer and obtain any missing MSDSs. However, once obtained, the employer may rely on the accuracy of the form as furnished by the manufacturer.

Lockout/Tagout Rule

Another widely applicable standard is OSHA's *Lockout/Tagout rule*. It is designed to prevent the accidental startup of machines and equipment while being serviced or the accidental release of hazardous energy. The standard requires that any machinery or equipment that is being serviced must be isolated from its energy source and the isolation device must be locked. If the device cannot be locked, it must be tagged with a warning such as DO NOT START. The lock or tag may be removed only by the person who put it in place. Before removal, he or she must conduct an inspection. After removal, but before startup, he or she must notify affected employees that the machine or equipment is about to be placed back in service. The standard also requires employers to train their employees in complying with lockout/tagout procedures.

Personal Protective Equipment

OSHA has adopted a number of standards dealing with use of *personal protective equipment* (PPE). PPE standards are designed to protect the eyes, face, head, extremities, respiratory system, and the body generally. For example, when exposure to noise in the workplace exceeds specified maximum levels or extends beyond specified maximum durations, protective devices must be worn to reduce effective exposure below permitted maximums. Respirators are required in dusty or smokey environments. Hard hats are common at construction jobs. Detailed information is available at **www.osha.gov/SLTC/personalprotectiveequipment/index.html**.

Current OSHA regulations require only that PPE must be *provided*. Some employers have read these regulations as allowing them to charge their employees for hard hats, wire-mesh gloves, ear plugs, etc. (Other employers cover the entire cost or charge the employee only if the employee loses an item.) OSHA has issued proposed regulations requiring the employers to pick up the cost of PPE except for items that have a use outside the workplace, like prescription safety glasses and steel-tipped boots. (At this writing, however, the proposed regulations have not been formally adopted.)

Blood-Borne Pathogen Standards

The health-care and medical research community may be particularly interested in OSHA's *blood-borne pathogen standards*. OSHA states the obvious when it says that HIV (human immunodeficiency virus) and HBV (Hepatitis B Virus) *merit serious concern* for workers occupationally exposed to blood, bodily fluids, human tissues and organs, and tissue and organ cultures.

> **EMPLOYER TIP**
>
> Safety considerations will justify placing limits on soliciting and distributing literature at the workplace. However, unless the rules are consistently enforced, the employer may be subject to unfair labor practice charges for prohibiting pro-union solicitations and literature. (see Chapter 21.)

To comply with the standards, employers must first determine who faces occupational exposure. Obvious candidates are medical personnel in an operating room or those who administer injections and are subject to needle-stick injuries. Less obvious are hospital laundry room workers, for example, who come in contact with contaminated bedding or clothing.

The next step is to inform those employees that they face occupational exposure to blood-borne pathogens. The employees must also receive training, to include:

- how to obtain copies of the OSHA regulation containing the standard;
- information on the epidemiology, transmission, and symptoms of blood-borne diseases;

◆ an explanation of the employer's exposure-control plan and the use and limitations of workplace practices, such as personal protective equipment;

◆ the safety and efficacy of HBV vaccinations (which the employer must make available free to all employees who face an exposure risk); and,

◆ emergency procedures and how to report an exposure incident.

The employer must also follow *universal precautions* that require *all* blood and bodily fluids be considered potentially infectious. Universal precautions include proper labeling, decontamination and disposal procedures and use of personal protective equipment such as gloves and eye protectors.

Telecommuters

Telecommuting (discussed in Chapter 22) raises questions as to what extent an employer has responsibility for a telecommuter's safety while working at home. OSHA issued a letter ruling that the Act applies to all worksites, including home worksites, but the ruling met with such a firestorm of objection from Congress and the public that OSHA withdrew the ruling. OSHA continues to take the position that the Act applies to hazardous or dangerous work assigned to telecommuters.

RECORD KEEPING

Employers who employ more than eleven employees must maintain an annual log and summary of all recordable occupational injuries and illnesses. A recordable injury or illness is one that results in:

◆ a fatality;

◆ a lost workday;

◆ a transfer or termination of employment or a restriction of work or motion;

◆ medical treatment beyond mere first aid; or,

◆ loss of consciousness.

The records are kept on an annual basis and each year's records must be retained for five years. OSHA provides a set of forms,

instructions, and worksheets for satisfying record keeping requirements, including:

◆ *Form 300*, Log of Work-Related Injuries and Illnesses;
◆ *Form 300A*, Summary of Work-Related Injuries and Illnesses;
and,
◆ *Form 301*, Injury and Illness Incident Report.

They are available on the Internet at:
www.osha-slc.gov/recordkeeping/OSHArecordkeepingforms.pdf

INSPECTIONS AND CITATIONS

OSHA inspectors (called Compliance Safety and Health Officers)
are authorized to enter and inspect any workplace at all reasonable
times to assure compliance with OSHA standards. The inspections
are unannounced (it is illegal for anyone to forewarn an employer
that an inspection will take place) and may include interviewing
employees in private, taking photographs and environmental sam-
ples, and reviewing records. A representative of the employer and an
employee representative may accompany the inspector during the
inspection.

An inspection may be initiated by OSHA itself or it may be conducted at the request of an employee who believes that a safety
violation exists. It is illegal for an employer to retaliate against an
employee for complaining about an OSHA violation or for giving
testimony or otherwise cooperating in an OSHA matter.

Inspections and other proceedings under OSHA present the risk
that an employer's trade secrets will be disclosed. The Act, as well
as Department of Labor regulations, contain special provisions to
protect the confidentiality of trade secrets. Inspectors also need
appropriate security clearances to inspect areas containing classified
information. They must also comply with the employer's health and
safety rules, such as wearing personal protective equipment.

Employers may refuse to admit an OSHA inspector and insist
that the inspector obtain a search warrant. Putting an inspector to
this added burden obviously does not create a cooperative atmosphere and it may, in fact, encourage the inspector to perform a more

detailed, intrusive procedure. Nevertheless, there are times when the employer should insist upon a warrant.

For example, if the employer suspects that a violation exists, a brief delay may provide just the opportunity needed to fix the problem. A delay might also be needed if a particular company official who should be present during the inspection is away. The company might also want advice from its attorney before permitting the inspection. (The attorney who will represent the company in connection with any citation that may result from the inspection should usually not participate in the inspection itself. This will make the attorney a witness to the process and if he or she has to testify about what was seen, he or she may be disqualified from further representation.) If an inspector anticipates that the company will insist on a warrant, the inspector may obtain one *beforehand*, thus defeating any advantage the employer had hoped to gain from delay.

At the conclusion of the inspection, the inspector must inform the employer of any apparent health and safety violations. The employer also has an opportunity to point out conditions or procedures related to the apparent violations. After the inspection, the inspector submits a report to OSHA's local Area Director. If the report indicates a violation, the Area Director issues either a citation or a notice of *de minimis violation* (a violation that has no direct or immediate relationship to health or safety). Citations and notices must be issued within six months of the inspection.

The Secretary of Labor may also go to federal court for an injunction to stop any practices or procedures that pose an imminent threat of death or serious physical harm. Citations must describe with particularity the nature of the alleged violation, including a reference to the safety or health standard allegedly violated. The citation must also fix a reasonable time within which to abate the violation. Employers are required to post a copy of the citation at or near the site of the violation for at least three days or until the violation is abated, even if the citation is being contested.

In addition to the citation, OSHA's Area Director also notifies the employer of a proposed penalty. (No penalty is proposed for *de minimis* violations.) Civil penalties can range up to $70,000 per violation, depending on the seriousness of the violation and whether it is willful. In assessing civil penalties, the Area Director is also required to consider the size of the business, the employer's good faith, and any history of previous violations. Failure to correct a violation can result in an additional civil penalty of up to $7,000 per day. The Act also provides for criminal penalties in cases of willful violations resulting in the death of an employee.

The employer has fifteen working days, after receipt of notice, to contest the citation, the proposed penalty, or the time allowed for abatement of the violation. Contests are initially handled through administrative proceedings, followed by a right of appeal to the courts.

FDA'S FOOD CODE

The federal *Food and Drug Administration's Food Code* is a set of model regulations offered by the FDA for adoption by state and local government agencies that have public health responsibilities. The regulations, in turn, govern food service industry procedures. Unless adopted by other government agencies, the Food Code itself is not a binding regulation. The Food Code (which the FDA updates every two years) is available at **www.cfsan.fda.gov/~dms/prime-con.html**. Jurisdictions that have adopted the Food Code are listed at **www.cfsan.fda.gov/~ear/fcadopt.html#adopt-03**.

RETALIATION AND REFUSAL TO WORK

OSHA prohibits retaliation against an employee because the employee filed an OSHA complaint, testified in a OSHA proceeding, or exercised any other rights afforded by the statute. However, the statute itself does protect an employee who walks off the job out of safety concerns. In that situation, the employee's remedy is to notify the employer of the danger and, if the employer fails to take appropriate action, to request an OSHA inspection. The statute does not authorize unilateral *self-help*.

There may be situations, however, where the employee faces an impossible choice of either immediately complying with a supervisor's instructions and risking serious injury or death, or not complying and being fired. In other words, the right to complain may simply not be a viable remedy. For those situations, the U.S. Department of Labor has adopted regulations that say if the employee, with no reasonable alternative, refuses in good faith to expose him or herself to the dangerous condition, he or she would be protected against subsequent discrimination.

The condition causing the employee's apprehension of death or injury must be of such a nature that a reasonable person, under the circumstances then confronting the employee, would conclude that there is a real danger of death or serious injury and that there is insufficient time, due to the urgency of the situation, to eliminate the danger through resort to regular statutory enforcement channels. In addition, in such circumstances, the employee, where possible, must also have sought, and been unable to obtain, a correction of the dangerous condition.

In a 1980 decision, the Supreme Court upheld this regulation in a case where an employee refused to work on a steel mesh that other workers had fallen through and suffered injury or death. Later court decisions have emphasized that the specific requirements of the regulation must be met—that the employee be acting reasonably and in good faith, that the danger be both real and serious, and that the employee has no opportunity to address the danger through regular channels.

The *National Labor Relations Act* (NLRA) protects workers who voice safety concerns or who engage in a job action to protest safety conditions. Under the NLRA, an employer may not take adverse action against employees who engage in *concerted activity* by complaining about safety issues or other job-related conditions. The NLRA also provides that employees who quit work in the *good faith belief* that their workplace is *abnormally dangerous* are not deemed to be on strike. That provision has been interpreted to mean that, like workers who are on strike to protest an unfair labor practice, or workers who are absent for safety reasons may not be permanently replaced. (In contrast, workers who are on strike for purely economic reasons *may* be permanently replaced. See Chapter 21.)

In a 1962 Supreme Court decision involving a factory in Baltimore, seven employees walked off the job on a bitter cold January day because their work area was unheated. The area was often uncomfortably cold anyway (a matter of repeated complaint) and, on the day in question, the furnace that usually supplied some heat had broken down. The Supreme Court ruled that the job action was protected under federal labor law, so that the employer had no right to fire the workers.

In more recent cases, fear of exposure to asbestos in an apartment complex and fear of exposure to radioactive depleted uranium dust have justified employee refusals to work.

STATE REQUIREMENTS

The *Occupational and Safety Health Act* provides that individual states may assume responsibility for occupational safety and health matters by developing a plan that is *at least as effective* as OSHA itself. State plans are subject to review and approval by the U.S. Secretary of Labor.

For a current listing of states that have approved state plans, go to **www.osha.gov/fso/osp/index.html.** Once a state plan has received final approval, enforcement of workplace safety and health matters shifts to the state.

SMOKING

Most of the issues relating to smoking involve the rights of non-smokers to be free from second-hand smoke. Many states and local jurisdictions have laws requiring employers to restrict smoking in the workplace. Some employers have responded by prohibiting smoking altogether. Others have designated a specific area for smoking that is sealed from the remainder of the workplace or that is under negative pressure so that smoke-filled air does not escape.

Aside from state and local law obligations, employers could conceivably face liability to nonsmokers:

◆ based on a violation of OSHA's General Duty Clause;

◆ under the *Americans with Disabilities Act*, on the theory that an employee who is allergic to cigarette smoke is disabled and is entitled to reasonable accommodation; and,

◆ for unemployment insurance benefits, if the nonsmoker claims he or she is entitled to quit for cause to avoid a smoke-filled, unsafe workplace.

A prudent employer will adopt and enforce a smoking policy designed to protect the health of nonsmokers.

Smoke Breaks

With few exceptions, most state laws do not entitle employees to any breaks at all, so that a break policy (including cigarette breaks) is a matter within the employer's discretion. An employer who does permit short breaks cannot (in the view of the U.S. Department of Labor) exclude that time for purposes of computing hourly workers' wages.

Even though employers do not have to permit smoke breaks, they are prohibited by laws in some jurisdictions from discriminating against smokers, provided the smokers limit their smoking to off-duty hours.

EMPLOYER TIP

For unionized shops, a smoking policy is a subject of mandatory bargaining. (see Chapter 21.)

ERGONOMICS

Ergonomics is the branch of science that studies the relationship between workers and their work environment. While some have dismissed the entire field as poorly grounded, in fact, there is increasing evidence that the traumatic effects of repetitive motion and poor positioning over prolonged periods are cumulative and can result in discomfort, pain, and even disabling injury. The National Academy of Sciences, for example, concluded in a 1998 report that there is a higher incidence of reported pain, injury, loss of work, and disability in *high-exposure occupational settings*.

Ergonomic issues affect employers in a number of ways. Discomfort and pain obviously decrease performance and may result in lost time. If a connection with the work environment can be shown, lost time may result in a workers' compensation award.

Serious, disabling injuries may also trigger obligations under the *Americans with Disabilities Act*. In a 1996 ADA suit, an employee claimed that interosseous nerve syndrome—a disabling condition of the hands and arms, possibly related to her 7-hour days of key-boarding—required her employer to provide a split keyboard or a voice-activated computer. The court ruled, however, that the employee failed to prove either of these steps was a reasonable accommodation.

The U.S. Department of Labor has pushed for OSHA ergonomic standards, but its efforts have so far been delayed or over-turned by Congress. Despite Congressional resistance, OSHA never abandoned the field and has been studying ergonomics ever since. As part of that process, it announced, in April 2002, a protocol for developing industry as well as task-specific guidelines. It then announced that nursing homes would be the first industry for which guidelines would be issued.

OSHA has now issued nursing home guidelines in final form. Grocery stores, poultry processing, and shipyards will be the focus of the next of industry-specific guidelines, according to OSHA. The guidelines, along with additional ergonomics information, are available at **www.osha.gov/SLTC/ergonomics.**

Although the guidelines are nonbinding in the sense that OSHA will not rely on them for enforcement purposes, employers still have a duty under the *General Duty Clause* of the *Occupational Safety and Health Act* to provide a safe workplace. Despite their nonbind-ing status, the guidelines could conceivably be used to show that an employer has violated the *General Duty Clause.*

Employers should anticipate that ergonomics litigation will increase and that federal or state safety standards in some form will eventually be adopted.

VIOLENCE IN THE WORKPLACE

According to the Occupational Safety and Health Administration, homicide is the second leading cause of fatal occupational injury in the United States. OSHA also reports that nonfatal violence is a widespread and growing phenomenon, particularly in jobs involving the exchange of money with the public (retail, home delivery, etc.), working alone, working late at night, guarding valuable property, and working in a community setting (taxicab drivers, health care workers, etc.).

OSHA does not have any specific standards for workplace violence. OSHA points out, however, that the *General Duty Clause*—that every employer furnish employment free from recognized hazards—may itself impose duties on employers whose workers are at risk. In consultation with the National Institute for Occupational Safety and Health, OSHA is developing guidelines for the health care and night retail industries, among others.

Whether or not employers owe a specific legal duty to prevent workplace violence, it makes good business sense to offer at least a minimum level of protection. Employers should:

- be alert to any history of violence in applicants;
- adopt, disseminate, and enforce a policy that any violence or threats of violence by employees will be met with dismissal;
- prohibit employees from bringing weapons of any kind to the employer's place of business or from carrying weapons during working hours (and make clear that this rule applies even though state law may allow the carrying of weapons);
- prohibit the use, possession, or being under the influence of alcohol and illegal drugs while on the job;
- for larger employers, require photo ID badges for all employees;
- secure non-public work areas and limit access to those with keys/passcards;
- secure *all* areas after normal working hours;
- provide adequate lighting for storage and garage areas;
- provide cell phones to employees who work off-premises;
- as necessary, contract with a security firm to provide security personnel, remote monitoring, alarms, etc.;

- restrict distribution of employee directories, particularly if they contain home addresses, home telephone numbers, names of spouse or children, or other personal information;
- establish an employee assistance program (EAP) and encourage its use;
- alert employees to any special risks the job may present;
- develop policies and train employees for responding to and recognizing emergencies; and,
- invite employees to express their concerns.

DISASTER PLANNING

Recent events have focused attention on responding to disasters of both the terrorist and the natural kind. While complete protection is impossible, advance planning can minimize injury and death.

An employer who owns the building in which the workplace is located must maintain the building in compliance with local and state *safety codes*. This includes, for example, fire alarm and sprinkler systems fire, extinguishers, and exit lights. Emergency exits must be accessible and unlocked.

Building owners can take additional steps that, though not required, may go a long way in protecting employees. The National Institute for Occupational Safety and Health (NIOSH), which is part of the federal Centers for Disease Control and Prevention, has issued its *Guidance for Protecting Building Environments from Airborne Chemical, Biological, or Radiological Attacks*, available for download at **www.cdc.gov/niosh/bldvent/2002-139D.html**.

> ## EMPLOYER TIP
>
> The EEOC has ruled that an employer may inquire about a worker's disability so that the employer can assist the worker in a disaster. However, it is up to the worker to decide whether assistance is necessary. Any information obtained about the worker's disability or need for assistance is subject to special confidentiality requirements.

NIOSH's recommendations regarding Chemical, Biological, or Radiological (CBR) attacks include:

- preventing access to outdoor air intakes, such as by relocating them on secure building roofs;
- securing roofs and other areas where mechanical equipment is located;
- isolating lobbies, mailrooms, loading docks, and storage areas;
- securing return air grilles;
- restricting access to information about building operations and systems;
- installing high-efficiency filters in the HVAC system; and,
- developing a response plan for a CBR emergency, such as shutting down the HVAC system entirely.

Employers who are not directly responsible for building maintenance and operation can also prepare for disasters, by means such as:

- maintaining duplicate employee information (names, addresses, payroll data, emergency contact, etc.) off-site;
- establishing a phone tree to alert employees about whether to report to work;
- determining in advance (in consultation with local disaster planning agencies) which emergencies require evacuation of the workplace and which require sheltering in place;
- conducting practice drills for various types of emergencies;
- if evacuation is appropriate, such as in response to a fire emergency, establishing a gathering point for all employees so an accurate count can be obtained and emergency personnel can be informed whether all persons are accounted for; and,
- identifying persons with disabilities or who may have special needs in an emergency and assigning appropriate personnel to assist them.

–14–
DISCRIMINATION IN GENERAL

The Civil War made clear that slavery would no longer be tolerated in the United States, but it did little to remedy rampant discrimination. It was not until 1964, through the efforts of Presidents Kennedy and Johnson and after bitter Congressional debate, that the first significant anti-discrimination laws were passed. Since then, numerous protections have been added, not only at the federal level, but also at state and local levels.

This chapter addresses employment discrimination in general. Subsequent chapters deal with discrimination on account of gender, age, and disability.

TITLE VII OF THE CIVIL RIGHTS ACT

The *Civil Rights Act of 1964* is the first modern piece of federal legislation to address discrimination generally. The Act deals not only with discrimination in employment, but also with discrimination in public accommodations. The Act was amended in 1991 to clarify and strengthen certain provisions and to expand the range of available remedies to include compensatory and punitive damages in cases of intentional discrimination.

Title VII of the Act addresses *employment discrimination*. It applies to all employers who have fifteen or more employees and to employment agencies and labor unions. The *Equal Employment Opportunity Commission* (EEOC) (created by *Title VII*), together with cooperating state and local agencies, enforce *Title VII* at the administrative level by investigating charges, recommending remedies, and conciliating disputes between employers and employees.

The EEOC can also bring suit against employers in federal court. EEOC guidelines interpreting *Title VII* are a useful resource.

At the heart of Title VII is the provision below.

It shall be an unlawful employment practice for an employer:

> *(1) to fail or refuse to hire or to discharge any individual or otherwise to discriminate against any individual with respect to his compensation, terms, conditions, or privileges of employment, because of such individual's race, color, religion, sex, or national origin; or*
>
> *(2) to limit, segregate, or classify his employees or applicants for employment in any way which would deprive or tend to deprive any individual of employment opportunities or otherwise adversely affect his status as an employee, because of such individual's race, color, religion, sex, or national origin.*

Those two paragraphs have generated whole libraries of commentary and thousands of court decisions. Many of the Supreme Court's landmark cases during the last forty years have involved *Title VII*. It would be impossible to digest that body of material here. What follows is a brief overview of *Title VII* principles and a discussion of some of the more important issues employers are likely to face.

Title VII is not limited to traditional minorities. Everyone—whites as well as blacks, males as well as females, Christians as well as Jews—is protected. In other words, *Title VII* does not protect *special groups* from adverse employment decisions. Rather, it prohibits an employer from using *irrelevant criteria* when making decisions. So, for example, a more qualified white male who is passed over for promotion in favor of a less qualified black female has a good *Title VII* claim if the employer was motivated by race or gender.

Reverse Discrimination

The discrimination that a nonminority member suffers when an employer discriminates *in favor of* a minority member is sometimes called *reverse discrimination*. Although the Supreme Court has made clear that such favoritism is plain and simple discrimination, the

Court's current views on this topic are not entirely clear. In a pair of widely-publicized decisions involving the University of Michigan, the Court ruled in June 2003 that the University's law school may consider race as a plus factor in evaluating individual applicants to the law school. According to the Court, the law school had a legitimate educational interest in assembling a diverse student body. Since employers, too, have a legitimate interest in a diverse workforce, the Court's reasoning would seem to be applicable to employment as well as higher education. It remains to be seen, however, whether the Michigan decisions are, in fact, applicable to the workplace.

Disparate Treatment and Disparate Impact

Discrimination under *Title VII* is sometimes classified as *disparate treatment* discrimination or *disparate impact* discrimination. The first category includes what immediately comes to mind—making a personnel decision, such as refusing to hire or promote a particular individual, because of race, color, gender, etc. That type of discrimination is prohibited by *Title VII*. So, too, is an employer practice of grouping employees by race, color, gender, etc., and treating the groups differently. Employment ads that indicate a preference for or against a particular race, color, or sex are also illegal, whether or not any actual discrimination is shown.

Disparate impact discrimination is a bit more subtle. Suppose an employer adopts a policy that on its face seems neutral, but that turns out to have an adverse impact on a particular ethnic group or gender. Take, for example, a private security company that has a minimum height and weight requirement for its patrol officers, the net effect of which is to exclude most females, but almost no males.

Other practices that could give rise to disparate impact claims include minimum education or experience requirements that do not serve a legitimate business purpose, use of tests scores in hiring or promoting where the test is culturally biased or is not related to job performance, or blanket exclusion of applicants who have criminal records or whose wages have been garnished.

Title VII prohibits discrimination in hiring, firing, compensation, and other *terms, conditions,* and *privilege* of employment. Ready examples of what is meant by terms, conditions, and privileges of employment include shift assignments, fringe benefits such as vacation, sick leave, insurance programs, and access to facilities such as the cafeteria and fitness center. But the courts have also ruled that the intangible *work environment* is covered by *Title VII* as well. Under those rulings, an employer who promotes or tolerates a workplace environment filled with demeaning racial or sexual slurs can be sued by the target of those slurs and by others who find the environment offensive, if a *reasonable person* would find the environment offensive. (Sexual harassment is discussed in Chapter 15.)

Trivial or inconsequential workplace actions by the employer will not support a *Title VII* action. The Supreme Court has said that a job action must amount to a *significant change in employment status.* The action must also be *objectively detrimental,* not just something a particular employee dislikes. As one court put it, not everything that makes an employee unhappy is an actionable adverse action, nor are changes that make a job less appealing but that do not affect a term, condition, or benefit of employment.

So, for example, a less-than-favorable evaluation, minor change in duties, or a change in title, with no effect on pay or status, even for allegedly discriminatory reasons, is not illegal. But if the evaluation leads to a loss of bonus or a demotion and the employee can show discriminatory motive, a good *Title VII* claim will result.

Bona Fide Occupational Qualification

An employer charged with discrimination on the grounds of sex, religion, or national origin (but *not* discrimination on the grounds of race) may, in theory, raise a defense of *bona fide occupational qualification* (BFOQ). However, the defense is very narrowly interpreted and as a practical matter is rarely available. In the airline industry, for example, an employer who fails to hire male applicants as flight attendants under the belief that passengers expect females in that role does not have a good BFOQ defense. On the other hand, an employer may rely on the BFOQ exception in hiring actors for male roles and actresses for female roles.

Testers

Private organizations and even the EEOC, sometimes use *testers* to obtain evidence of discrimination in the workplace.

Example: Suppose an employer who is suspected of having racially discriminatory hiring practices advertises a job opening. Two testers—one white, one black—apply for the job and give fake credentials that appear to be substantially similar. The employer interviews the black candidate first but says he needs to check references before making any offer. He then interviews the white candidate and makes an offer on the spot. If this pattern is repeated several times, the employer will have a difficult time explaining his actions in the discrimination suit that is sure to follow.

It should be noted that claims of discrimination by testers, and by the organizations that employ them, do not always fare well in court, since the testers were not really candidates and they cannot really claim to have been denied a job. According to recent press reports, the EEOC is also under pressure from Congress to stop using testers.

Retaliation

Title VII also prohibits *retaliation* against an employee who has complained about discrimination or who has assisted another complainant, such as by testifying on his or her behalf.

Whenever a discrimination charge is pending, even an informal one that is still at the internal investigation stage, employers should exercise extraordinary caution in making personnel decisions that affect the complaining employee or others involved in the matter. Any adverse action taken after the initial charge has been made is likely to generate a charge of retaliation. (see Chapter 4.)

PROTECTED EMPLOYERS

Title VII defines *employer* as a person or organization engaged in an industry affecting commerce who has fifteen or more employees for each working day in each of twenty or more calendar weeks in the current or preceding calendar year.

The term *industry affecting commerce* means any activity, business, or industry in commerce or in which a labor dispute would hinder or obstruct commerce or the free flow of commerce. In other words, just about any activity in which an employer might engage. (*Title VII* is tied to the Commerce Clause of the U.S. Constitution because all federal legislation must be based on one or another of the powers granted the federal government by the U.S. Constitution.)

EMPLOYER TIP

The employee-counting question is broadly applicable to a wide range of federal employment-related laws, even though they may have different numerical thresholds. (Appendix B lists many of the federal statutory thresholds.)

Counting employees to determine whether the 15-employee threshold is met is critical to a claim of discrimination. If the threshold is not satisfied, neither the EEOC nor the courts have jurisdiction to hear a *Title VII* claim. And, of course, the person making the claim must be an *employee* to invoke the benefit of federal anti-discrimination laws in the first place.

The discrimination laws themselves are not at all helpful in answering the counting question. They typically define *employee* as an individual employed by an employer. In the Supreme Court's words, that is a mere nominal definition that is completely circular and explains nothing.

One counting question involves how to deal with individuals who are carried on the employer's books as employees, but who are not physically at work for a full twenty weeks. In a 1997 Supreme

Court case, the employer had between fifteen and seventeen employees on its payroll for at least twenty weeks, but during eleven of those weeks, it was not actually compensating fifteen or more employees. The difference resulted from the fact that two of its employees were part-time who worked fewer than five days per week.

The Court ruled that the employer was subject to *Title VII*, adopting what has become known as the *payroll method* for counting employees. Under that method, if an employee appears on the employer's payroll records, he or she is counted whether or not he or she is actually being compensated on a particular day. In short, part-time as well as full-time employees, and presumably persons on leave, all count.

Employees vs. Independent Contractors

Another question involves the distinction between employees and independent contractors. In a case called *Darden* that arose under the *Employee Retirement Income Security Act* (ERISA), the Supreme Court concluded that the absence of a helpful statutory definition of *employee* meant that Congress intended to incorporate common-law principles in determining whether a worker was an employee or an independent contractor.

Professional Corporations

Yet another question involves shareholder-directors of professional corporations, such as doctors, lawyers, etc. While they may be classified as employees for federal tax and pension plan purposes, they also manage the professional corporation. (Professional corporations and other types of business entities are discussed in Chapter 1.)

In a recent Supreme Court case called *Clackamas*, an Oregon medical clinic was sued for discrimination by the clinic's bookkeeper. The bookkeeper argued that the clinic met the fifteen-employee threshold so long as four of its physician-shareholders were counted. The bookkeeper pointed out, for example, that the physician-shareholders had employment contracts, they were salaried, and they were treated as employees for tax purposes.

The clinic claimed otherwise—that the physician-shareholders were really more like partners in a partnership and should therefore not be counted. The Supreme Court, relying on its earlier *Darden* decision, ruled that common law principles should apply. Citing EEOC regulations, the Court in *Clackamas* listed six factors to be considered in determining whether a shareholder-director of a professional corporation is an employee for discrimination purposes. They are:

- whether the organization can hire or fire the individual or set the rules and regulations of the individual's work;
- whether and, if so, to what extent the organization supervises the individual's work;
- whether the individual reports to someone higher in the organization;
- whether and, if so, to what extent the individual is able to influence the organization;
- whether the parties intended that the individual be an employee, as expressed in written contracts; and,
- whether the individual shares in the profits, losses, and liabilities of the organization.

Whatever the merits of the *Clackamas* decision, the six factors the Supreme Court said must be considered are highly fact-specific. Having to deal with these additional factors adds further uncertainty to discrimination claims and increases associated costs and delays.

Extra-territorial Application

Activities by employers outside the U.S. could certainly affect commerce within the U.S. But the Supreme Court has held that *Title VII* does not have *extra-territorial application*, so that U.S. citizens employed abroad, even U.S. citizens employed by U.S. employers, have no *Title VII* protection. *Title VII* itself exempts aliens employed outside the U.S. and it permits employers operating in a foreign country to comply with that country's law, even if compliance amounts to a violation of *Title VII*.

Foreign Employees Doing Business in the U.S.

In general, foreign employers must comply with *Title VII* and other anti-discrimination laws as a privilege of doing business here, whether they employ U.S. citizens or their own foreign nationals. But there is an interesting exception based on treaties the U.S. has with many foreign countries. *Friendship, Commerce and Navigation* (FCN) *treaties* permit foreign companies doing business in the U.S. to engage, at their choice, high-level personnel essential to the functioning of the enterprise. These treaty provisions have been held to permit foreign companies to discriminate in favor of their own nationals, even though doing so would otherwise constitute race or national origin discrimination.

Foreign Sovereign Immunities Act

Another exception is based on the *Foreign Sovereign Immunities Act* (FSIA). Under the FSIA, *foreign states* are immune from the jurisdiction of courts in the U.S. so long as they are engaged in governmental-type activities (as opposed to commercial activities).

In a recent case under the FSIA, Saudi Arabia hired a Virginia security firm to work with the Saudi military in providing protection for the Saudi royal family at a family residence in California. A female employee of the security firm quit after the security firm refused to assign her to a command post position for which she was fully qualified. The security firm based its refusal on instructions of the Saudi military that such an assignment would be unacceptable under Islamic law, since the female officer would have to spend long periods working with her Saudi male counterparts.

The female officer filed suit against her former employer, claiming sex discrimination. The Fourth Circuit Court of Appeals ruled that providing security for members of the royal family is quintessentially an act *peculiar to sovereigns* and was therefore the type of government activity that fell within the FSIA's immunity protection. The Court went on to hold that the security firm, even though it was a U.S. company, was entitled to *derivative immunity* when following the instructions of the foreign sovereign not to assign the female officer to the command post.

RELIGIOUS DISCRIMINATION UNDER *TITLE VII*

Title VII makes it illegal for an employer to discriminate against an employee on the basis of his or her religion. *Religion* includes all aspects of religious observance, practice, and belief. This means, for example, that an employer cannot refuse to hire an applicant because the applicant is a member of a particular religious sect, any more than the employer can refuse to hire an applicant on the basis of the applicant's race or gender. Harassment based on religious beliefs or practices is also a violation of *Title VII*.

Special rules apply to religious discrimination. The First Amendment to the U.S. Constitution says that *Congress shall make no law respecting the establishment of religion, or prohibiting the free exercise thereof.* Based on the First Amendment, the courts have developed the so-called *ministerial exception* to *Title VII*, under which religious organizations *may* discriminate in connection with the selection and employment of their own clergy.

The term *clergy* has been broadly defined by the courts to include lay employees whose primary duties consist of teaching, spreading the faith, church governance, supervision of religious orders, or participating in religious ritual and worship. So, for example, a nun who was an assistant professor of canon law at Catholic University could not sue for sex discrimination when she was denied tenure. And a lay music teacher at a Catholic elementary school who directed a church choir also could not complain of sex discrimination because, as the court recognized, music is important in the spiritual and pastoral mission of the church and plays in integral role in religious tradition. (The ministerial exception is discussed more fully in Chapter 20.)

Even for nonclergy, *religious* organizations may discriminate against employees on *religious grounds*. Further, under *Title VII*, religious discrimination is similar to discrimination under the *Americans with Disabilities Act*. Employers have an affirmative duty to *reasonably accommodate* their employees' religious observances or practices just as they do their employees' disabilities. As with the ADA, the burden is on the employee to ask for a reasonable religious accommodation.

One difference between disability accommodation under the ADA and religious accommodation under *Title VII* is that under the ADA, the employer must, in effect, conduct a dialogue with a disabled employee to arrive at what is reasonable. Under *Title VII*, the employer gets to choose the accommodation and need not consider the employee's suggested accommodations.

The employer is excused from accommodating a religious practice if the accommodation would impose an undue hardship. While anything more than a minimal cost to the employer will qualify as an undue hardship, the hardship must be real and not merely speculative or hypothetical in order to excuse the employer from accommodating.

Following are examples of cases in which employees or applicants claimed that the employer failed to accommodate their religious observances or practices.

Sabbath Day

A number of cases have involved work on Sunday or other Sabbath day. The courts have ruled that an employer must attempt to accommodate a good faith belief prohibiting work on Sabbath, such as by allowing the employee to switch with another employee or by having a flexible leave policy that allows the employee to choose the Sabbath as a leave day. However, the employer does not have an absolute duty to accommodate such religious beliefs. If, due to the employer's workload, weekend work is necessary, and if excusing some employees completely from all weekend work would create disruption within the workplace, or would violate established seniority rules or a union contract, the employer may insist that employees participate in weekend work schedules despite their religious scruples to the contrary.

Religious Garb

If there is a good business reason, such as interference with job performance, or safety concerns, an employer may prohibit employees from wearing religious garb, such as crucifixes, yarmulkes, or chadors. Otherwise, the employer is likely obligated to accommodate the practice. One way to accommodate might be to transfer the employee from a position that deals with the public to a position that does not. (Dress codes are discussed in Chapters 2 and 15.)

Refusal to Comply with Tax Laws
When an applicant for employment refused, on religious grounds, to provide his social security number, the prospective employer was justified in rejecting his application. The court held that the prospective employer was not required to accommodate the applicant by violating IRS regulations or by seeking a waiver from the IRS.

OTHER ANTI-DISCRIMINATION LAWS
Although *Title VII* is by far the broadest and most significant federal anti-discrimination law, it is not the only one. Other federal laws apply in more limited, specialized circumstances.

Section 1981
A Reconstruction-era statute guarantees to all persons within the United States *the same right...to make and enforce contracts...as is enjoyed by white citizens.* (Lawsuits brought under this statute are known as *Section 1981 actions* because the statute is codified at Title 42, United States Code, Section 1981.) In 1989, the Supreme Court held that Section 1981 applies only to the formation and enforcement of contracts, not to racially discriminatory conduct by an employer *after* the employment relationship had come into existence. Two years later, Congress overruled the Supreme Court by amending the statute to cover the making, performance, modification, and termination of contracts, and the enjoyment of all benefits, privileges, terms, and conditions of the contractual relationship.

Section 1981 as amended now covers racial discrimination against employees who have employment contracts. The question of whether that covers at-will employees has not been fully answered. The Fourth Circuit Court of Appeals, in a case arising in Maryland, has ruled that an at-will employment relationship is a contractual relationship and Section 1981 therefore applies. In that case, an at-will employee who quit in the face of repeated and pervasive racial harassment was allowed to sue his employer under Section 1981. Other federal courts disagree with the Fourth Circuit's recent ruling. The dispute will likely be resolved by the Supreme Court.

Section 1981 is an important statute. Even though Title VII also prohibits racial discrimination, *Title VII* is limited to employers with fifteen or more employers. Section 1981 has no such limitation. In addition, claims under Section 1981 are not subject to the abbreviated time limits set by *Title VII* and they can be filed in court without first going through the administrative procedures applicable to *Title VII*.

Immigration

When Congress passed the *Immigration Reform and Control Act* in 1986, making it illegal for employers knowingly to hire persons who are not eligible to work in the U.S., Congress included a provision prohibiting discrimination on the basis of citizenship or national origin. (see Chapter 14.) The prohibition applies to employers with four or more employees. *Title VII*, in contrast, prohibits national origin discrimination by employers with fifteen or more employees, and it does not address citizenship status at all.

Military Service

Federal law prohibits any employer from discriminating against employees and applicants for employment on account of their military service. Persons who are members of the uniformed services, who have applied to become members, or who have obligations to one of the uniformed services are protected against discrimination in hiring, retention, reemployment, promotion, or the granting of any employment benefit.

EMPLOYER TIP

Nondiscrimination clauses are frequently contained in construction and other contracts, particularly in contracts with government agencies. (see Chapter 19.)

STATE AND LOCAL PROHIBITIONS

Most states and many local governments have their own laws prohibiting discrimination on grounds of race, color, etc. These laws are not just duplications of federal law, since they often prohibit additional forms of discrimination not covered by federal law (such as ancestry, marital status, sexual orientation, and genetics) and they reach small employers not covered by *Title VII*.

PROFESSIONAL CODES OF ETHICS

The *Codes of Ethics* of some professional groups contain nondiscrimination clauses. A professional who discriminates in employment may become subjected to disciplinary proceedings before his or her state licensing board and may suffer suspension or revocation of his or her license to practice.

DISCRIMINATION BASED ON GENETICS

By use of *genetic testing*, it is possible to calculate the probability that persons who are now symptom-free will develop a variety of disabling or fatal disorders. the *Human Genome Project* and related biomedical research will likely increase the number of conditions known to be genetically linked. While the existence of some genetic markers increase only slightly the statistical risk that an associated disease will become manifest, other genetic markers are virtual guarantees of eventual sickness or death.

> **EMPLOYER TIP**
>
> To the extent that a genetic marker is associated with a particular race or nationality, discrimination on the basis of genetics may violate other employment discrimination laws.

It is understandable that employers would want to know which of their existing employees or applicants for employment are at risk for genetically linked diseases. But are they entitled to know? There are some questions that employers may be asking themselves.

- ◆ May employers require genetic screening or obtain family health histories for genetic evaluation purposes?

◆ Do employers have access to health insurance records containing genetic test results?

◆ With genetic information in hand, may employers make employment decisions based on a genetic predisposition to illness?

ADA

The federal *Americans with Disabilities Act*, which applies to employers with fifteen or more employees, has long prohibited all *pre-employment* medical examinations (except drug testing). (see Chapter 17.) A test for genetic markers undoubtedly falls within this prohibition and is therefore illegal.

The ADA also prohibits *post-hiring* medical exams unless, among other things, the results are not used to discriminate against persons with disabilities. Determining whether a person who merely has a genetic marker, but who is not then afflicted with any disease, is a person with a disability is not totally certain.

The ADA defines *person with a disability* in three distinct ways. One definition involves a person who is substantially limited in one or more major life activities. A person with a genetic marker, but nothing more, probably does not meet this prong of the definition.

> **EMPLOYER TIP**
>
> A particular genetic marker that makes it difficult or impossible to have healthy children may, without more, amount to a disability, since reproduction is considered a major life activity.

The ADA's second definition of disability is having a history of an impairment. Again, since the genetic marker, without more, is usually not disabling, there is no history of an impairment.

According to the EEOC, the third definition—being regarded as disabled—does apply. In its *Compliance Manual*, the EEOC says:

> *This part of the definition of disability applies to individuals who are subjected to discrimination on the basis of genetic information relating to ill-*

*ness, disease, or other disorders. Covered entities
[employers, unions, etc.] that discriminate against
individuals on the basis of such genetic information are regarding the individuals as having
impairments that substantially limit a major life
activity. Those individuals, therefore, are covered
by the third part of the definition of disability.*

The EEOC's position is a bit of a stretch. The employer who
takes adverse action against an employee on the basis of genetic test
results does not regard the employee as impaired. Rather, the
employer regards the employee as statistically more likely to have
an impairment *in the future*. In short, notwithstanding the EEOC's
position, it remains at least arguable that the ADA does not, under
most circumstances, prohibit post-hiring genetic tests or prohibit
adverse employment actions based on test results.

HIPAA

The *Health Insurance Portability and Accountability Act* (discussed in
Chapter 10) prohibits a group health insurance plan from establishing eligibility rules based on *health status-related factors*, which
includes genetic information. Also under HIPAA, genetic information cannot be used to conclude that a person has a pre-existing
condition. The conclusion can only be based on a diagnosis of the
condition itself.

Recent Health and Human Services regulations under HIPAA
prohibit group health plans from disclosing protected health information to plan sponsors, except to enable plan sponsors to carry out
plan administration functions that the plan sponsor performs. This
would cover any genetic information obtained by the group plan.
The plan documents of employer-sponsored plans must contain a
provision prohibiting employers from using protected health information for any employment-related action or decision. Again, this
would cover genetic information, but only to the extent the information was obtained from the group plan.

Executive Order 13145

On February 8, 2000, President Clinton issued an Executive Order that prohibits all executive departments and agencies of the federal government from collecting *protected genetic information* about its employees or basing employment decisions on such information. Protected genetic information is defined as:

- information about an individual's genetic tests (that is, analyses of DNA, RNA, chromosomes, proteins, or certain metabolites in order to detect disease-related genotypes or mutations);
- information about the genetic tests of an individual's family members; and,
- information about the occurrence of a disease, or medical condition or disorder in an individual's family members.

The Executive Order is limited to federal employment. It does not apply to the general workforce.

State and Local Laws

A growing number of states prohibit an employer from using genetic information when making employment decisions or bar use of genetic information in connection with the rejection of applicants for health insurance or the pricing of health insurance policies.

CONTINGENT WORKERS

The term *contingent worker* is loosely defined as any worker who is outside the employer's core workforce of full-time, long-term employees. As used here, the term refers to independent contractors, part-time employees, job-sharing employees, temporary employees, leased employees, and joint employees.

In general, independent contractors are not covered by the employment provisions of the nondiscrimination laws because they are not employees. However, the *misclassification* of a true employee as an independent contractor is as disastrous for nondiscrimination law purposes as it is for tax and benefit entitlement purposes. (Independent contractors are discussed in more detail in Chapter 7.)

All other categories of contingent workers—part-timers, job-sharers, etc.—are fully protected by the nondiscrimination laws. For example, a company whose staff includes temporary workers furnished by an agency temps cannot direct the agency to furnish (or not to furnish) temps of a particular race or gender. Nor can the company accept temps from an agency when the company knows that the agency itself discriminates in selecting persons to be temps.

For certain categories of contingent workers, such as leased or joint employees, it is not always clear who the actual employer is—the staffing firm, the company that controls the actual worksite, or both. The EEOC has developed an elaborate set of definitions to determine who the employer is for purposes of applying the federal non-discrimination laws. The definitions turn on such factors as who does the hiring and firing, who handles payroll, who controls the employee's day-to-day work environment, etc. While it may be possible in any particular circumstance for either the staffing firm or the worksite owner to avoid being tagged as the employer, any company that tolerates or commits discrimination against a member of its workforce is exposed to substantial risk.

In one recent discrimination case, the Eighth Circuit Court of Appeals ruled that nurses who were hired by a staffing agency and assigned to the Missouri Department of Corrections were employees of *both* the staffing agency and the Department where they worked.

FORMER EMPLOYEES

The Supreme Court has held that the term employee as used in *Title VII* includes *former employees*. Under that holding, it was illegal for a company to give a bad reference to a former employee in retaliation for the former employee's filing a charge of race discrimination after he or she was fired.

RECORD KEEPING

Under EEOC regulations, employers with 100 or more employees are required to file an *Employer Information Report, Form EEO-1*, each year. *Form EEO-1* calls for a breakdown of the employer's workforce by race, sex, and national origin. The EEOC does not pre-scribe any particular records that must be kept to support the information contained in *Form EEO-1*. A sample form and instructions are available at **www.eeoc.gov/stats/jobpat/e1instruct.html.**

EEOC regulations permit employers to collect post-employ-ment records of race and national origin (unless doing so is prohibited by state law), but the EEOC recommends that any such records be kept separate from other personnel data, such as evalua-tions. Any records that are prepared to support submis-sion of *Form EEO-1* must be saved for at least one year.

Statutes of limitations, the time periods within which an employee or enforcement agency can bring a claim, should also be considered in establishing record retention policies. Those statutes differ from state to state and they may even vary for different types of claims. Although charges of *Title VII* discrimination must be initiated within a relatively brief time period (180 days or 300 days, depending on the particular federal, state, or local agency that has jurisdiction), other types of claims may be filed as late as three or even more years after the events take place. A five-year retention policy—that is, a policy of retaining all employment-related documents and information for five years after an employee terminates or an applicant is rejected—may seem a bit excessive, but can prove very helpful.

The retention policy should apply not only to documents and information that relate to individual applicants and employees, but should also include items such as employee handbooks and policy directives that have become out-of-date or superseded. That way, the employer can show what the rules were at a particular time, even if the rules have since changed.

> **EMPLOYER TIP**
>
> Additional record-keep requirements apply under wage and hour laws, income and withholding tax laws, laws regulating pension and other benefit plans, safety and health laws, and laws regarding the employment of non-U.S. citizens.

FOREIGN WORKERS

Foreign workers have long played a significant role in our workforce. Some claim that foreigners take positions from U.S. citizens. Others argue that they fill jobs U.S. workers either do not want or are not trained to do. Both perceptions are reflected in current law. On the one hand, employers face criminal penalties for knowingly hiring an undocumented alien. On the other hand, recent changes in visa policy make it easier for so-called high tech employees such as computer programmers to work in the U.S.

With terrorism now firmly planted in our collective consciousness, rules and restrictions affecting foreign workers are bound to play an increasing role.

Discrimination Protection

With passage of the law prohibiting employment of foreigners not eligible to work, Congress had concern that employers would discriminate against persons who are in fact eligible to work but who look or sound foreign. So at the same time, Congress made it illegal for employers having four or more employees to discriminate based on citizenship status or national origin. (Although *Title VII* addresses national origin, it only applies to employers having fifteen or more employees. *Title VII* does not address citizenship status at all.) Under that law, it is illegal for an employer to adopt a U.S. *citizens only* policy. However, it is not illegal for an employer to prefer a U.S. citizen over an eligible alien if the two are equally well qualified.

> ## EMPLOYER TIP
>
> Foreign employers doing business in the U.S. are generally subject to the same anti-discrimination laws as domestic employers.

Many employers require that their employees—particularly those who must deal with the public—be able to speak English. Even though such a policy might inadvertently exclude certain immigrant groups, it is usually a justifiable requirement. Employers cannot discriminate against those with accented English so long as the employee can communicate effectively.

Some employers go further and prohibit their bi-lingual employees from even *using* a language other than English while at work. It is difficult to see how that policy could be justified.

–15–
GENDER DISCRIMINATION

Sex discrimination in employment, along with discrimination based on race, color, religion, or national origin, is covered by *Title VII*. So it is just as illegal for an employer to reject an applicant on gender grounds as it is to reject the applicant on racial or religious grounds. Establishment of a glass ceiling, which limits promotion opportunities for women but not for men, is also illegal under *Title VII*. In other words, all the *Title VII* principles that apply to discrimination based on race, color, religion, and national origin generally also apply to gender-based discrimination.

But sex discrimination has some unique features. For one thing, sex discrimination is covered by two additional federal laws—the *Equal Pay Act* and the *Pregnancy Discrimination Act*—which do not apply to other forms of discrimination. For another thing, while the differences between persons of varying races, religions, or national origins are superficial at best, there are real biological differences between men and women. Finally, the term *sex* means *gender*. The special aspects of sex discrimination are discussed in the following sections of this chapter.

EQUAL PAY ACT

In addition to its minimum wage and overtime pay provisions, the federal *Fair Labor Standards Act* as amended by the *Equal Pay Act* prohibits employers from paying males and females at different rates for the same work. And while executives, administrators, and professionals are exempt from the minimum wage and overtime pay requirements of the FLSA, they are *not* exempt from its equal pay requirements.

So an employer who intentionally discriminates by paying males more than females for equal work not only violates *Title VII*, but also violates the *Equal Pay Act*.

PREGNANCY

In 1978, Congress enacted an amendment to the *Civil Rights Act* known as the *Pregnancy Discrimination Act* (PDA). As a result of the PDA, Title VII now defines *because of sex* as including:

> *because of or on account of pregnancy, childbirth, or related medical conditions; women affected by pregnancy, childbirth, or related medical conditions shall be treated the same for all employment-related purposes, including receipt of benefits under fringe benefit programs, as other persons not so affected but similar in their ability or inability to work.*

In other words, discrimination because of pregnancy, childbirth, or a related medical condition is sex discrimination, so that an employer cannot refuse to hire a pregnant woman or a woman of child-bearing age because of her pregnancy or because of the possibility she may become pregnant.

Nor may an employer have special rules for pregnant women. For example, sick leave must be available to pregnant women on the same basis as it is to others. Similarly, employers who have health or disability insurance plans must cover pregnancy-related expenses and disabilities the same as other medical expenses or disabilities.

EMPLOYER TIP

The federal *Newborns' and Mothers' Health Protection Act* prohibits group health plans from cutting off benefits for a mother or her newborn child after less than 48 hours of hospitalization following a normal vaginal delivery. This Act also prohibits cutting off benefits after less than 96 hours of hospitalization following a cesarean section. (see Chapter 10.)

Title VII does not require an employer to cover abortions in its group health insurance policies, except where the mother's life would be endangered if the fetus were carried to term and except where medical complications have arisen from an abortion. However, *Title VII permits* a plan to cover abortions.

Forced Leave

Generally an employer may not require pregnant women to take leave at a specified point in their pregnancies

> # EMPLOYER TIP
>
> For employers with fifty or more employees, extended leave without pay for complications of pregnancy and childbirth, and to care for new-born children, is required by the *Family and Medical Leave Act.* (see Chapter 8.)

unless the employer can demonstrate a *business necessity or bona fide occupational qualification* (BFOQ) for the rule. Compulsory leave policies for school teachers have routinely been held to violate *Title VII*. On the other hand, several cases involving the airline industry have held that mandatory maternity leave for flight attendants was justified by passenger safety considerations.

Job Reassignments

An important Supreme Court case involved the use of lead in battery manufacturing. Lead poses substantial health risks, including risks to fetuses carried by pregnant women who are exposed to the substance. When the manufacturing company discovered high lead levels in the blood of a number of its pregnant employees, the company adopted a policy barring all women of child-bearing age from jobs involving exposure to lead unless they could document that they were incapable of having children.

The Supreme Court held that the policy amounted to sex discrimination despite the company's benign motives. The Court said that the policy could not be justified as a BFOQ, since there was no evidence that pregnant women were less able than others to manufacture batteries. The Court concluded that the question of fetal safety should be for the mother, not the company, to decide, and it dismissed as only a remote possibility the company's fear of suit by children with birth defects attributed to fetal lead exposure.

EEOC Position

The EEOC takes the position that since pregnancy and childbirth are conditions unique to women, refusal to grant special leave to a pregnant employee may amount to sex discrimination.

In other words, according to the EEOC, the employer had better grant leave (assuming it is medically justified) unless the employer can show that the job cannot remain vacant and it cannot be filled by a temporary replacement. As of this writing, it remains to be seen whether the EEOC's position will be upheld in the courts.

Paternity Leave

If an employer grants maternity leave, at least one court has indicated it does not have to also grant *paternity* leave. However, for employers with fifty or more employees, fathers as well as mothers can qualify for leave under the FMLA.

HARASSMENT, IN GENERAL

When the authors of *Title VII* added the word *sex* to the list of characteristics that an employer could not consider in making personnel decisions, they probably intended the term to be synonymous with *gender*. In other words, employers cannot consider gender when establishing pay rates or deciding whether to hire, promote, or fire, just as they cannot consider other characteristics, such as race or color, deemed irrelevant to job performance.

But the courts and the EEOC have ruled that sexual harassment is also a form of discrimination prohibited by *Title VII*. According to the EEOC, unwelcome sexual advances, requests for sexual favors, and other verbal or physical conduct of a sexual nature constitute sexual harassment when:

- submission to such conduct is made either expressly or implicitly a term or condition of employment;

♦ submission to or rejection of such conduct by an individual is used as the basis for employment decisions affecting such individual; or,

♦ such conduct has the purpose or effect of unreasonably interfering with an individual's work performance or creating an intimidating, hostile, or offensive working environment.

The illegality of some forms of sexual harassment can probably be explained by traditional *Title VII* analysis. Take, for example, a male company supervisor who requests a female subordinate to sleep with him, promising her a promotion if she does and threatening to fire her if she does not. This type of sexual blackmail is discriminatory because the supervisor does not make the same request of any male subordinate. In other words, the supervisor has imposed on a female employee, because of her sex, a term or condition of employment that he has not imposed on a similarly situated male. Sex discrimination of this type has sometimes been called *quid pro quo* harassment.

Hostile Environment

The courts and the EEOC have gone beyond *quid pro quo harassment*, ruling that *Title VII* is violated by a *hostile environment* as well. To illustrate, suppose the branch manager of a bank requests sex from a teller who works for him, he touches her sexually, and he makes sexual jokes and comments directed to her or in her presence; *but, he never expressly promises any tangible job benefit, nor threatens to take any away.* The courts have held that the mere creation of an intimidating, hostile, or offensive work environment is a form of sex discrimination because, in effect, the employee must tolerate the hostile environment in order to keep her job. And if the employee finds the environment so hostile that she actually quits, she may have been constructively discharged and have a claim of *quid pro quo harassment* as well. (Constructive discharge is discussed in Chapter 4.)

The above example involves a male seeking sex from a female. But make no mistake—a male who is promised promotion or threatened with dismissal by a sex-seeking female supervisor has just as good an harassment claim. The EEOC even takes the position (not well supported in the case law) that when an employee is promoted because she sleeps with the boss, *other employees* who do not get the promotion suffer sex discrimination.

Same-sex harassment is also illegal under *Title VII*. In a case involving a male roustabout on an oil rig who was repeatedly subjected to sex-related, humiliating actions against him by other male members of the crew, including physical assaults and threats of rape, the Supreme Court ruled that sexual harassment *of any kind* is prohibited.

> # EMPLOYER TIP
>
> Although harassment is most often associated with sex discrimination, harassment based on any discriminatory factor—race, color, religion, national origin, age, or disability—is also illegal if it is sufficiently severe to create a hostile work environment.

Offensive Environment. An offensive environment must be *severe* and *pervasive*, but it need not be so intolerable as to force the employee to quit or to cause the employee to suffer psychological injury. It is an environment that the complaining employee finds offensive and that a reasonable person would find objectionable as well. (In other words, the environment must be both subjectively and objectively offensive to support a *Title VII* claim.)

A super-sensitive employee, for example, who takes offense at the retelling of an off-color TV episode, does not have a good claim. But note that the offended employee need not be the specific target of the harassment in order for the environment to be considered hostile. The routine exchange of pornographic email among a willing group of employees may create a hostile work environment for another employee who is not involved in the exchange, but who is simply exposed to the material.

Equal Opportunity Harassers

The above examples deal with male-female harassment, female-male harassment, and same-sex harassment. However, the work environment can be equally offensive to both male and female employees. This occurred in a strange case involving a supervisor who sought sexual favors from two of his subordinates (who happened to be husband and wife). The court ruling in this situation found no violation of *Title VII* because *Title VII* is premised on eliminating *discrimination*. Inappropriate conduct that is inflicted on both sexes, or is inflicted regardless of sex, is outside the statute's ambit.

Surrounding Circumstances

Title VII is a powerful tool against discrimination, but it does have limits. One such limit is that it is not intended as a code of workplace civility. That notion is reflected in a 1998 Supreme Court decision. Harassment is not *automatically discriminatory merely because the words used have sexual content or connotations*. Instead, the surrounding circumstances, expectations, and relationships must be examined. A simple recitation of the words used or the physical acts performed is not enough to find discrimination.

Example: A security guard supervisor working under contract at the Environmental Protection Agency disciplined two other guards at the site. The two guards, apparently infuriated by the discipline, launched a retaliatory campaign against the supervisor, that began by repeated slashing of his tires. Later they taunted him in a sexual manner, that included a variety of lewd gestures and comments.

In response to the supervisor's *Title VII* claim, the court ruled that the harassment he complained about, although *tinged with offensive sexual connotations*, was not based on his sex. The supervisor did not claim, for example, that the two guards were homosexual or that they were seriously proposing to have sex with him.

Nor did the supervisor show that the guards were motivated by general hostility to males in the workplace. Instead, according to the court, the guards were motivated by a workplace grudge having nothing to do with sex.

How can an employer possibly distinguish between sexual harassment that *is* discriminatory, and sexual harassment that *is not*? The short answer is that there is no way to distinguish. And despite pronouncements that *Title VII* was not intended as a workplace *civility code*, that is exactly what it has become. At the risk of incurring substantial liability, employers have little choice but to prohibit all teasing, horseplay, banter, and other conduct with sexual overtones, for fear that some court may view the conduct as discriminatory harassment.

EMPLOYER LIABILITY FOR HARASSMENT

Employer liability for sexual harassment has been a controversial issue in the courts. The controversy was heightened by the 1991 amendment to *Title VII* that added *compensatory* and *punitive damages* as available remedies in cases of intentional discrimination.

The Supreme Court has ruled that an employer is *always* liable for a hostile work environment created by a *supervisor* when the discrimination takes the form of a *tangible employment action*—defined as a significant change in employment status. Usually, but not always, a tangible employment action results in economic injury because it relates to matters such as hiring, firing, failing to promote, reassignment with significantly different responsibilities, or a significant change in benefits. The theory is that when a supervisor takes a tangible employment action with respect to a subordinate, he or she is exercising authority delegated by the employer company and the company is automatically responsible for how that occurs.

In a hostile environment case where no tangible job action is involved, the employer is only *presumed* liable for a supervisor's harassment. The employer may defend against the case and avoid liability if:

- the employer can show that it had and enforced a policy against sexual harassment *and*

- the complaining employee unreasonably failed to take advantage of preventive or corrective opportunities provided by the employer.

The courts are in disagreement whether a *constructive discharge*—being forced to quit because of intolerable working conditions—is a tangible employment action for purposes of employer harassment liability. (Constructive discharge is discussed in Chapter 4.) Some courts have ruled that a constructive discharge is *not* a tangible employment action, reasoning that in a constructive discharge situation the supervisor has not, in fact, made an employment decision and is not actually exercising any authority delegated by the employer. However, other courts held that a constructive discharge *is* a tangible employment action. The disagreement will likely be resolved by the Supreme Court.

Nonsupervisor Conduct

Workplace sexual misconduct is not limited to a supervisor's mistreatment of subordinates. The employer can also be liable for tolerating a hostile work environment created by an employee's fellow employees and even nonemployees, such as customers, if the employer knows (or should know) about the offensive work environment but fails to take appropriate remedial action. In effect, the law requires employers to make reasonable efforts to provide a working environment free from hostile or offensive harassment. The law does not necessarily care who is doing the harassing.

A number of court cases over the years have upheld the concept of employer liability for harassment by nonemployees. Some examples are below.

- A female blackjack dealer at a Las Vegas casino was repeatedly harassed by male customers who stared at her and made comments about her breasts and legs. The dealer complained, but her employer failed to take action and eventually fired her for being rude to customers. The court refused to dismiss her complaint, citing the EEOC's guidelines.

◆ An automotive manufacturer's representative was assigned to a Virginia dealership to promote sales. She was repeatedly harassed by several dealership employees. When she complained to the manufacturer and asked to be relocated, she was told to *put up with it* for the sake of the company. Eventually, she was fired after being told that she was *too cute* and would likely be harassed wherever she was assigned. The court said that the manufacturer was potentially liable, even though the harassment took place at an *independent dealership*.

◆ When a waitress at a pizza franchise complained about the behavior of two of her customers, the waitress' manager instructed her to continue waiting on the customers and took no other action. On her return trip to the customers' table, one of the customers grabbed the waitress sexually. The waitress then quit and successfully sued the franchise.

Protective Policies

Employers have tried different techniques to protect themselves from claims. Some employers require that employees who are involved in an office romance, particularly if the romance is between a higher-level supervisor and a lower-level employee, sign a *love contract* setting out the ground rules for the relationship. The contract might have the parties acknowledge, for example, that the relationship is consensual and that it can be terminated by either party at any time.

However, those measures seem extreme and may expose the employer to liability for invasion of privacy. The bottom line is that an employer must have an *effective* sexual harassment policy. While no list of *dos* and *don'ts* can completely protect employers from sexual harassment claims, the following suggestions should go a long way.

◆ Establish a *written* nondiscrimination policy, including a specific policy against sexual (and all other forms of) harassment. The policy should define sexual harassment. It should be published in the employee handbook and posted conspicuously at the workplace. *In the absence of a written policy, an employer has no chance at all of defending against a claim of hostile environment sexual harassment by a supervisor against a subordinate.*

◆ Include in the policy various means by which an employee can complain *in confidence* about sexual harassment. The complaint route should not be limited to the employee's immediate supervisor, since he or she may be the harasser.

◆ Consider installing an *anonymous* hotline or an interactive website for employees to report harassment and other types of workplace problems.

◆ Conduct regular *training seminars* on sexual harassment, attendance at which should be mandatory. (It usually makes sense to have separate sessions for supervisors and non-supervisory personnel.)

◆ Keep careful *records* of who attended each training session and what material was presented.

◆ Plan in advance *who* will be in charge of investigating complaints of sexual harassment and *how* the investigation will be conducted. (Making those determinations after a complaint is received will cause delay and could result in your harassment policy being ruled unreasonable or ineffective.)

◆ On receipt of a complaint of sexual harassment, review your *Employment Practices Liability Insurance Policy* and give notice of the complaint to your insurance carrier.

◆ If the complaint involves sexual assaults or other criminal conduct, suggest that the complaining party make a police report.

◆ Investigate *all* complaints of sexual harassment *promptly, thoroughly, and objectively.* Consider hiring experienced employment counsel to supervise the investigation.

◆ Include an interview with the complaining party in the investigation. Get as much detail from him or her as possible about what happened, when and where it happened, and who else saw or knows about the harassment. Also, ask the complainant how he or she would like the matter to be resolved (without making any promises about what action will be taken).

◆ Treat as confidential all information developed during the investigation. However, do not *promise* confidentiality, since complete confidentiality is probably not possible. Be careful about prohibiting your workforce from discussing the matter, since that may constitute an unfair labor practice.

◆ Make a contemporaneous, detailed written record of the investigation.

◆ If the investigation shows that the complaint is justified, take *immediate and appropriate* corrective action against the harasser. Inform the complaining party about the action taken and ask whether there is anything further he or she wishes to bring to the employer's attention.

◆ For serious, ongoing incidents, consider temporarily reassigning the alleged harasser or complaining party, or placing one or both of them on temporary leave with pay, to prevent additional incidents pending your investigation. (This could be a perilous step, if the reassignment or leave is construed as retaliation against the complainant or defamation of the alleged harasser.)

◆ If the investigation shows the complaint to be unfounded, inform the complaining party and the accused harasser and close the investigation.

◆ Do not take disciplinary action against the complainant unless it is clear that he or she intentionally lied about the matter. (Retaliation against an employee for exercising rights protected by law, such as the right to complain about harassment, constitutes illegal discrimination.)

EMPLOYER TIP

The complainant's own conduct is relevant to your investigation, such as whether the complainant willingly participated in the activity that he or she now claims was offensive. However, an investigation that focuses primarily on the complainant's own conduct may be viewed as retaliatory and may subject you to additional claims of discrimination.

SEXUAL ORIENTATION

Title VII coverage does not extend to discrimination based on being gay or a lesbian. A recent case involved a homosexual male nurse who worked for a hospital in Indianapolis. The nurse complained that one of his physician supervisors made fun of his homosexuality, yelled at him during telephone conversations, and otherwise treated him poorly, all based on his sexual orientation. The nurse was eventually fired, allegedly because of his complaint, although the hospital said it was for making an unauthorized entry in a patient's chart.

The court ruled that Congress used the term *sex* in *Title VII* to mean a biological male or biological female and not one's sexuality or sexual orientation. Therefore, said the court, harassment based solely on a person's sexual preference or orientation (and not on one's sex) is not an unlawful employment practice under *Title VII*. And even if the nurse's firing was in retaliation for his complaint of harassment, the nurse still did not have a valid *Title VII* claim, since the underlying conduct—harassment based on sexual orientation—was not itself covered.

> **EMPLOYER TIP**
>
> The *Federal Trade Commission* takes the position that, in the context of an harassment investigation, if an employer turns to an outside organization, such as outside counsel, for assistance in the investigation, the outside organization is a consumer reporting agency and the employer's obligations under the *Fair Credit Reporting Act* are triggered.
> (see Chapter 18.)

NOTE: *While Title VII may not prohibit discrimination based on sexual orientation, many state and local laws do.*

OTHER ISSUES

Title VII's prohibition of sex discrimination gives rise to additional workplace issues from time to time.

Dress Codes

A few federal court cases have ruled that employers have a certain amount of latitude in adopting dress and grooming standards that are not entirely gender neutral, and that minor differences in personal appearance regulations do not constitute sex discrimination under *Title VII*. As a caveat, however, the dress codes must be enforced even-handedly between men and women.

Many of the dress code cases have involved hair length. A few have involved earrings. The issue typically arises when a male employee is disciplined for violating policies that prohibit long hair for men but not for women, or that prohibit earrings on males but not females. The courts have said that while long hair and earrings on men may be fashionable in some circles, an employer may legitimately wish to present a more conservative image and need not tolerate the outer bounds of current fashion. But if the business justification for a gender-specific dress code is to present a more conservative image, application of the dress code to employees who have no contact with the public makes no sense.

> **EMPLOYER TIP**
>
> A dress code policy that prohibits clothing or accessories associated with particular religious beliefs or practices may constitute religious discrimination under Title VII. (see Chapter 14.)

Contraceptive Coverage

The EEOC has ruled that an employer-sponsored health insurance plan that provides comprehensive benefits, including drug coverage, but excludes contraceptive drugs, violates *Title VII* of the federal *Civil Rights Act*. A federal court in Washington state has reached the same conclusion. That court ruled that while:

*Title VII does not require employers to offer any partic-
ular type or category of benefit, any resulting plan must
not discriminate based on sex-based characteristics and
the plan must provide equally comprehensive coverage
for both sexes.*

Infertility Treatments

A group health plan that denied benefits for surgical procedures to
implant embryos was held nondiscriminatory, even though the particular treatment is only performed on women. A court reasoned
that even though the surgical procedure was limited to women, it
was not discriminatory because the underlying condition that the
surgery was attempting to abate could be male infertility, female
infertility, or both. In other words, the exclusion was equally adverse
to males and females.

Transgender Issues

Employees who identify with and adopt a gender opposite to his or
her traditional biological gender present unique problems.

For example, the Eighth Circuit Court of Appeals has ruled that
a Minneapolis teacher, who was a biological male but who considered himself a female, could use the women's faculty restroom
despite objection by a woman faculty member. The case was based
in part on Minnesota law, however, and does not necessarily indicate
how other courts might rule.

In another case, from the Second Circuit Court of Appeals, an
employee who suffered from *gender dysphoria* (discomfort with gender of birth) and underwent a sex-change surgery, was not entitled
to reimbursement from her group health plan. Since the surgery was
not medically necessary, the plan's denial of benefits was not a violation of *Title VII*.

Retirement Plans

An employer cannot provide smaller monthly retirement payments
to women just because women on average live longer than men and
collect benefits for a longer time.

Physique

A number of cases have involved size and strength differences between men and women. If an employer sets minimum height and weight standards that tend to exclude most women applicants but few men applicants, the standards will be deemed discriminatory unless the employer can show a business necessity for the standards.

–16–
AGE DISCRIMINATION

The federal *Age Discrimination in Employment Act* (ADEA) covers most employers with twenty or more employees. Specifically, it covers employers engaged in an industry affecting commerce who have twenty or more employees for each working day in each of twenty or more calendar weeks in the current or preceding calendar year. The coverage provisions track *Title VII* (except that the employee threshold for *Title VII* is fifteen employees instead of the 20-employee threshold of the ADEA). (See Chapter 14 for a discussion of the meaning of *industry affecting commerce* and the methodology for counting employees.)

The ADEA's expressed purpose is to *promote employment of older persons based on their ability rather than age* by prohibiting age-based discrimination against employees and job applicants. Consistent with that purpose, the ADEA only applies to persons 40 years of age or older, so that an age-based decision affecting a person under 40 does not violate the ADEA. (Many states and local jurisdictions have their own age discrimination laws that apply to all employees, not just those 40 years of age or older.)

Hiring or promoting a 35-year-old employee instead of a 45-year-old *for reasons other than age* is perfectly legal. However, the employer should identify the objective, job-related, nondiscriminatory criteria used in making the decision. In making personnel decisions, employers should avoid using terms such as *dead wood*, *fresh faces*, *new blood*, or *more energy*. These terms are often viewed as evidence of *discriminatory intent* and will hurt the employer in defending an age discrimination claim.

Harassment with respect to age can constitute age discrimination, just as harassment with respect to race or sex can violate *Title VII*. Employers should not tolerate workplace jokes or teasing aimed at older employees, their medical conditions, or other factors common to age.

A few courts have held that *reverse* age discrimination—favoring an older worker over a younger one, both of whom are at least 40 years of age—is also prohibited by the ADEA, although other courts disagree.

EXCEPTIONS

As with *Title VII*, there is an exception in the ADEA for a *bona fide occupational qualification* (BFOQ). However, the exception has been very narrowly applied by the courts. For example, an airline had a rule that its flight engineers must retire at age 60, on the theory that many persons over that age have limitations that preclude safe operation of aircraft. The airline argued that it would be impractical, if not impossible, to examine all flight engineers and identify those with limitations. A jury found the rule illegal under the ADEA and awarded damages. The Supreme Court let the jury verdict stand, saying that it was not enough for the airline to have a *rational basis* for its policy. Instead, the airline had to prove that its policy was *reasonably necessary* to the normal operation or essence of the particular business.

The ADEA also permits an employer to have a *bona fide seniority system* provided it is not intended to evade the purposes of the ADEA. A seniority system cannot be used to justify involuntary retirements.

The ADEA has other exceptions that make the Act unique among federal anti-discrimination laws. For one, the ADEA does not apply to persons under age 40, so age discrimination against persons younger than 40 is not illegal under the ADEA. (As pointed out above, it may be illegal under state or local laws.)

Although the Act generally prohibits compulsory retirements based on age, *bona fide executives* or *high policy makers* may be forced to retire. A bona fide executive is a person who exercises substantial managerial authority over a significant number of employees and a large volume of business. A high policymaker is an employee other than a bona fide executive who plays a significant role in developing and implementing corporate policy. The Act allows forced retirement of the bona fide executive or high policy maker if the person held the position for two years preceding retirement, is at least 65 years old, and is entitled to annual retirement benefits of at least $44,000 based solely on employer contributions.

> ## EMPLOYER TIP
>
> The definition of bona fide executive for ADEA purposes is different from the *Fair Labor Standards Act's* definition in connection with exemption from overtime requirements.
> (see Chapter 5.)

State and local governments are also permitted to establish mandatory retirement ages for firefighters and law enforcement officers.

BENEFIT PLANS

Almost all retirement plans make age-based distinctions. Plans stating that employees who have attained a specified age (such as 65) may retire and begin receiving benefits are lawful.

However, employers must take caution when changing the terms of plans to ensure that benefits are not being taken from a class of persons protected by the ADEA.

For example, when an employer *converts* from a defined benefit plan to a cash balance plan, employees lose the back-loaded boost they had anticipated from their defined benefit plan. Since this loss is borne most heavily by older workers who are near retirement, some have argued that such conversions amount to age discrimination.

PROVING AGE DISCRIMINATION

Although an older worker may be the victim of age discrimination, the worker still has to *prove* that the adverse employment decision was age-based. It is often difficult to find such direct evidence of discriminatory motive. In the more usual case, the boss's motive is unclear (or at least unexpressed) and circumstantial evidence is all that is available.

One type of circumstantial evidence is a significant age differential between the person fired and the replacement hired. Courts have come up with a variety of answers as to what is significant, ranging from three years to ten years. Five years seems to be emerging as a standard, so that an age differential of less than five years should not provide circumstantial evidence of age discrimination. But even when the age difference is less than five years, an employee could still prevail in court if he or she has *other evidence of age discrimination.*

EMPLOYER TIP

An employee can sue for age discrimination even if the job lost was to another person in the 40-plus protected class.

RELEASES OF ADEA CLAIMS

A *release* is a type of contract by which one party gives up a legal right or claim in exchange for valuable consideration—usually money. In general, no special form of contract is required to release most types of claims, including discrimination claims.

ADEA cases are different. Unlike other employment-related disputes, the release of an ADEA claim will be ineffective unless the employer follows very specific procedures spelled out in the law. For example, the employee must be advised in writing to consult with an attorney before signing the release, and the employee must be given at least twenty-one days to consider the release before signing it and an additional seven-day rescission period after signing it to change his or her mind.

The law does not require the employee to actually wait twenty-one days before signing the release. The employee can sign earlier, so long as his or her right to take a full twenty-one days is not restricted. However, the seven-day period after signing cannot be shortened.

The Supreme Court has ruled that where a release did not comply with ADEA requirements, an employee who received severance pay in exchange for a release of his or her ADEA claim was entitled to keep the severance pay and still sue his or her employer for age discrimination. Therefore, an employer who has required a release of all claims in exchange for a severance package should not begin making severance payments to the 40-plus employee until the 7-day rescission period has expired.

If a release of ADEA claims is requested in connection with an exit incentive or other employment termination program offered to a group or class of employees, the twenty-one-day period increases to forty-five days. In addition, the employer must provide all persons in the class or group with a description of the class or group. The employer must also inform them of the job titles and ages of all employees eligible or selected for the program. The ages of all employees in the same job classification or organizational unit who are not eligible or selected for the program must also be disclosed.

–17–
PERSONS WITH DISABILITIES

The latest entrant in the field of federal anti-discrimination law is the *Americans with Disabilities Act* (ADA). The statute is intended to be *a clear and comprehensive mandate for the elimination of discrimination against individuals with disabilities.*

In the employment context, the ADA applies to employers who have fifteen or more employees. It prohibits discrimination against a qualified individual with a disability with respect to application procedures, hiring, promotion, discharge, compensation, training, and other terms, conditions, and privileges of employment. A *qualified individual* is a person who, with or without reasonable accommodation, can perform the essential functions of the job he or she holds or for which he or she is applying.

ADA IN EMPLOYMENT

As used in the ADA, *disability* means a physical or mental impairment that substantially limits one or more major life activities. The *Equal Employment Opportunity Commission* that is charged with enforcing the employment provisions of the ADA, defines *major life activity* to include hearing, seeing, speaking, breathing, performing manual tasks, walking, caring for oneself, learning, and working.

The physical and mental impairments that can give rise to a disability would fill a medical encyclopedia. Generally speaking, any condition that can be diagnosed by a physician or psychotherapist (other than a mere temporary condition) is an impairment within the meaning of the ADA. If the impairment does not substantially limit one or more major life activities, however, it is not a *disability for* ADA purposes.

By contrast, the list of exclusions from ADA coverage is short. They include:

- ◆ homosexuality and bisexuality (because they are not considered impairments);
- ◆ transvestism, transsexualism, pedophilia, exhibitionism, voyeurism, gender identity disorders not resulting from physical impairment, or other sexual behavior disorders;
- ◆ compulsive gambling;
- ◆ kleptomania;
- ◆ pyromania; and,
- ◆ psychoactive substance abuse disorders resulting from current illegal use of drugs.

Diagnoses that are not generally accepted in the medical community will not trigger ADA obligations. For example, at this writing, multiple chemical sensitivity syndrome falls in this category, so that an employee complaining of that condition need not be accommodated under the ADA.

EMPLOYER TIP

Employees who suffer temporary illnesses and injuries from their employment may be entitled to workers' compensation benefits.
(see Chapters 8 and 11.)

It is important to note that the existence of even a significant impairment does not necessarily render a person *disabled*. An individualized, case-by-case inquiry is required to determine whether a particular employee is in fact substantially limited in one or more major life activities.

There is no such thing as a *per se disability* under the ADA, since each impairment, no matter how serious, must still be shown as substantially limiting a major life activity.

Conditions that manifest themselves intermittently may or may not be covered by the ADA, depending on the extent to which they limit major life activities. Short-term, temporary impairments generally do not trigger ADA coverage. An employee who is recovering from surgery, for example, or who breaks a leg, cannot claim ADA protection just because he or she cannot currently perform the usual job duties without help.

Special rules apply to substance abuse. Addiction to drugs or alcohol is an impairment that may trigger ADA coverage, depending on the particular individual's circumstances. However, employers *may* discriminate against current, illegal drug users and persons who traffic in drugs at the workplace, whether or not they are addicted. Employers may also prohibit intoxication or use of alcohol at the workplace and may impose discipline for poor performance or absenteeism related to alcohol use, even if the employee is an alcoholic.

MEDICAL EXAMINATIONS

The ADA has special rules for medical examinations. Prior to actually offering employment, an employer may *never* require an applicant to undergo a medical exam. While testing for illegal drugs is not considered a medical exam and is permitted prior to making a job offer, just about every other form of pre-offer medical test, including AIDS testing and genetic testing, is illegal.

When the employer actually *offers* employment, the offer may be conditioned on the results of a medical exam if:
- ◆ all entering employees in the job category are subject to examination;
- ◆ the exam requirement can be shown to be job-related and consistent with business necessity;
- ◆ the resulting medical information is separately maintained and treated as confidential; and,
- ◆ the results are not used to discriminate against persons with disabilities.

Closely related to medical examinations are disability-related inquiries. In general, an employer may not ask an applicant or employee about a disability and may not ask questions designed to elicit information about a disability. An employer may, however, ask whether an applicant or employee can perform job functions, ask whether an employee has been drinking, and ask about current illegal drug use.

The prohibition against disability-related inquiries invalidated one employer's sick leave policy. The policy required employees who were absent on sick leave to furnish a medical certification that included a general diagnosis of the condition that gave rise to the absence. The court ruled that since some diagnoses are bound to reveal underlying disabilities, the policy violated the ADA.

> ## EMPLOYER TIP
>
> The EEOC has ruled that an employer may inquire about a worker's disability in connection with disaster planning, so that the employee's need for special assistance can be identified in advance. However, it is up to the worker to decide whether assistance is necessary. (Disaster planning is covered in Chapter 13.)

Of course, once an applicant or employee discloses information about a disability and requests an accommodation, the employer not only *may* make disability-related inquiries, the employer is *required* to.

DUTY OF REASONABLE ACCOMMODATION

Included within the ADA's definition of *employment discrimination* is failing to make reasonable accommodations to the known physical or mental limitations of an otherwise-qualified applicant or employee. *Otherwise qualified* means a person with a disability who, with or without reasonable accommodation, can perform the essential functions of the particular position he or she holds or is applying for.

The key concept is *essential*. The employee has to be able to perform at least the essential functions of the job for ADA protections to apply. In determining what is essential and what is merely marginal, the employer's judgment is given substantial weight.

In understanding when the duty of reasonable accommodation applies, it is helpful to list the various degrees of impairment.

- ◆ An impairment that does not substantially limit any major life activity: *not covered by the ADA.*

◆ An impairment that would substantially limit one or more major life activities, but does not, in fact, because the effects of the impairment are controlled through treatment: *not covered by the ADA.*

◆ An impairment that substantially limits one or more major life activities, but the individual involved is able to perform all the essential functions of his or her job without any accommodation or with reasonable accommodation: *covered by the ADA.*

> ## EMPLOYER TIP
>
> An employer should determine the essential functions of a particular position and write them down, before advertising or interviewing for the position. A determination of essential functions after a disabled applicant has been rejected carries less weight.

◆ An impairment that substantially limits one or more major life activities, and the individual is not able to perform one or more essential functions of his or her job, despite reasonable accommodation: *not covered by the ADA.*

To *discriminate means*, among other things, to fail to make reasonable accommodations for the *known* physical or mental limitations of an otherwise-qualified applicant or employee. Under this definition, the *employee* has the burden of identifying his or her disability and requesting the accommodation, unless the need is obvious. The employer does not have an obligation to inquire about a nonobvious disability and in fact is prohibited from doing so. The employer may, however, make general inquiries as to the ability of an applicant or employee to perform job-related functions.

The duty to accommodate can sometimes give rise to difficult conceptual issues. In a case, where another employee was killed, an employee suffered from post-traumatic stress disorder, symptomized by insomnia and by anxiety when she attempted to return to work. So she asked to be accommodated by being assigned to another job location.

The court agreed that sleeping is a major life activity and that the employee was therefore disabled within the meaning of the ADA. However, her insomnia is separate from her inability to work. In other words, the accommodation she requested (reassignment to a different location) was unrelated to the major life activity in which she was limited (sleeping). The court therefore ruled that in the absence of a causal connection between the specific condition that limits a major life activity, and the accommodation requested, the employer has no duty to provide the accommodation.

> **EMPLOYER TIP**
>
> Psychological impairments can be tricky. An employer should address unacceptable behavior (moodiness, rudeness, short temper, etc.) and leave it to the employee to raise the matter of a psychological based disability and request reasonable accommodation.

REASONABLENESS OF REQUESTED ACCOMMODATION

If an employee informs the employer of a disability and requests the employer to accommodate, the employer must do so unless the accommodation would impose an *undue hardship*—that is, the accommodation would be significantly difficult or expensive.

It is often difficult to know whether a requested accommodation is reasonable or is an undue hardship. The ADA gives some examples of what is reasonable. For one, the employer's facilities must be readily accessible and usable. Wheelchair ramps may have to be installed and doorways and restroom facilities may need to be enlarged. Other examples might include:

- restructuring jobs;
- modifying work schedules;
- relaxing workplace rules;
- making reassignments to vacant positions; and,
- modifying or replacing existing equipment.

The list of what is reasonable goes on, but it is not limitless. The courts have ruled, for example, that an employer has no duty to grant indefinite leave, since the ADA covers people who can perform the essential functions of their job presently or in the immediate future. While reassignment to a vacant position may be reasonable, an employer is not required to create a new position tailored to an employee's abilities.

The courts have ruled that, generally speaking, an employer is not required to accommodate a disability by allowing the disabled worker to telecommute. The reason is that most jobs require the kind of teamwork, personal interaction, and supervision that simply cannot be performed at home without compromising the quality of the employee's performance. Only in a very extraordinary situation might a work-at-home accommodation be reasonable. (Telecommuting is discussed in Chapter 22.)

What employers need to remember is that when a disabled employee or applicant for employment requests an accommodation, the employer must engage in a good faith interactive process with the employee to identify accommodations that might enable him or her to perform the essential functions of the job. It could be that no accommodation will actually work, or that while a particular accommodation might work, it is unreasonable. Should that be the case, the employer is free to terminate the employee or reject the applicant. However, if the employer fails to engage in an interactive process, or delays in doing so, the employer will almost certainly lose any ADA suit that follows.

EFFECT OF REMEDIAL MEASURES

A person who suffers from a potentially incapacitating condition, but through the use of remedial measures is not in fact substantially limited in any major life activity does not qualify for protection under the ADA. The courts have ruled that the condition is not disabling because the person uses medication, or a prosthetic, or other device to mitigate the condition. Examples include a commercial truck driver whose high blood pressure is relieved with medication, and an applicant for a pilot's position whose severe myopia is corrected with glasses.

In those cases, the employer did not violate the ADA when it rejected the truck driver and pilot candidates, because those persons were not *disabled* within the meaning of the ADA.

> ## EMPLOYER TIP
>
> At least one court has indicated that failure to follow the advice of his or her doctor, when following the advice could have relieved an otherwise disabling condition, may bar an employee's ADA claim.

ACCOMMODATION AND SENIORITY

One form of reasonable accommodation involves assignment of a disabled employee from a job he or she cannot perform to a vacant position he or she can. However, seniority systems, will normally prevail over a disabled employee's interest in being assigned to a particular position. It is unreasonable, said the Supreme Court, to require an employer to violate a seniority system to accommodate a disability.

Seniority systems, whether imposed under a collective bargaining agreement or unilaterally imposed by management, provide important employee benefits by creating and fulfilling employee expectations of fair and uniform treatment, job security, and predictable advancement based on objective standards.

However, in *special circumstances* the disabled person's ADA rights will trump a seniority system. If an employee could show, for example, that the employer

> ## EMPLOYER TIP
>
> The seniority problem is further complicated when a union asks for copies of the disabled employee's medical records to determine whether a company's decision to override normal seniority rules is justified. Both the EEOC and the *National Labor Relations Board* take the position that disclosure of the records is a matter for good faith collective bargaining.

made frequent exceptions to its seniority system, then one more departure to accommodate a disabled employee might well be reasonable.

OTHER PROHIBITED CONDUCT

The ADA includes in its definition of impairment having a record of impairment and being regarded as having an impairment. In other words, an employer cannot reject an applicant because he or she has a history of being impaired, or because he or she is considered impaired, even if not actually so. (Most courts that have considered the question conclude that the ADA's duty of reasonable accommodation does not apply to a person who is not impaired but is mistakenly regarded as impaired, since the person does not, in fact, need any accommodation.)

Another form of discrimination prohibited by the ADA arises where an applicant or employee is known to be in a relationship or be associated with *someone else* who has a disability. Suppose an employer knows that a job applicant's spouse or domestic partner has a chronic condition that, the employer fears, may distract the applicant or require extra time off. A refusal to hire for that reason violates the ADA. As noted above, however, excessive absenteeism need not be tolerated, whatever the reason.

Many states and local governments have their own disability discrimination laws, which are similar, but not always identical, to the ADA. California, for example, defines *disability* as an impairment that *limits* one or more major life activities, as contrasted with the ADA's *substantially limits*. State and local laws often have a threshold lower than the ADA's fifteen-employee requirement.

DIRECT-THREAT DEFENSE

The ADA allows employers to exclude persons who pose a direct threat to the health or safety of the disabled person or to others in the workplace, when the threat cannot be eliminated by reasonable accommodation.

The food industry, for example, may exclude persons from food handling who have infectious or communicable diseases that are transmitted to others through the handling of food, if those persons cannot otherwise be reasonably accommodated. The ADA also permits enforcement of state and local laws dealing with food handling by persons with infectious or communicable diseases. The Secretary of Health and Human Services is required to publishes a list of such diseases and the manner in which they are transmitted at **www.cfsan.fda.gov/~dms/fc01-a3.html#a3-2**.

Other situations in which the *direct threat defense* applies include a worker with diabetes and hypertension, who is at risk for coma and stroke and who seeks employment as a bus driver; or a restaurant employee with epilepsy who is at risk for seizures and seeks a promotion to cook where she would be working with dangerous appliances and equipment. In both these situations, the employer may rely on the ADA's direct threat defense and refuse to place the worker in the position sought.

The conclusion that a direct threat exists, cannot be based on ignorance or irrational fear. When AIDS first came to public attention, but before the means of transmission were well understood, some employers simply fired or refused to hire infected individuals. The courts have held that practice to be illegal under the ADA.

EMPLOYER TIP

The direct threat defense is unique to the ADA and does not spill over to other areas of discrimination law.

–18–
EMPLOYEE PRIVACY

Privacy is the right to be left alone. When someone's privacy has been wrongfully invaded, he or she may have a claim for damages. The types of invasions that can give rise to a claim for damages are:

  ◆ unreasonable intrusion upon the seclusion of another;
  ◆ appropriation of another's name or likeness;
  ◆ unreasonable publicity given to another's private life; and,
  ◆ publicity which places another in a false light before the public.

Invasions of privacy do not usually arise in the employment context. After all, the workplace and the equipment in it belong to the employer. Those assets are there to promote the employer's business, not the employee's. When an employee is at the workplace, using the employer's equipment, he or she is supposed to be acting for the employer's exclusive benefit. His or her performance is constantly being evaluated, and, normally, there is no expectation that his or her activities are personal and private.

There are, however, exceptions.

PRIVATE PLACES

Most employees would expect their bodies, pockets, purses, wallets, and briefcases to be private and not open to inspection by their employer. If an employer intends to inspect those private places, a compelling business reason must exist and a clear written statement of this intention should be established and disseminated to all employers. In the diamond mining industry, for example, body cavity searches might be justified. Technicians working with lethal viruses might reasonably be put through decontamination at day's end. Perhaps retail workers should expect to have their packages inspected as they leave the store premises.

Less clear are places such as an employee's desk. An employer's right to go through an employee's desk without the employee's permission depends on the circumstances. If the employer has an announced policy of doing so, or if the employee shares the desk with others and could have no reasonable expectation of privacy, then the employer probably has the right. But if there is no announced policy, if the employer does not make it a practice of inspecting desk drawers, and if employees routinely lock their desks without objection from the employer, then the employer probably does *not* have the right.

SENSITIVE RECORDS

Employers frequently acquire highly sensitive, personal information about their employees. Examples include:

- drug test reports;
- results of medical exams;
- information about physical or mental disabilities that need to be accommodated under the *Americans with Disabilities Act*;
- medical information about the employee or employee's family in support of leave requests under the *Family and Medical Leave Act*;
- workers' compensation records;
- health insurance utilization records;
- substance abuse treatment records in connection with employee assistance programs;
- tax and financial information; and,
- information about family problems, divorces, separations, etc.

The confidentiality of some of these records is guaranteed by law. Even if no specific law applies, employees expect such information to be kept confidential and to be used strictly for its intended purpose. Employers should live up to those expectations. Sensitive records should be kept in a secure area and access should be limited to those with a legitimate need to know. Where sensitive information is stored electronically, appropriate computer security systems should be installed to prevent unauthorized access. Of course, an employer should guard against his or her own loose tongue at the water cooler or coffee machine.

ADA

The *Americans with Disabilities Act* prohibits pre-employment medical examinations (except drug tests) and it prohibits inquiries as to disabilities. The ADA permits an employer to conduct post-hiring medical exams so long as certain requirements are met, including the requirement that information obtained regarding medical condition or history be collected, maintained on separate forms and in separate medical files, and be treated as a confidential medical record. (See Chapter 17 for a more detailed discussion of medical examinations under the ADA.)

Drug and Alcohol Abuse Treatment

Substance abuse records may only be disclosed with the patient's consent, in cases of medical emergency, or when authorized by court order based on a showing of good cause for disclosure. This means that, in the absence of consent by the patient, even a subpoena issued to an employer is insufficient to justify disclosure. Instead, the party desiring the records must obtain a specific court order for disclosure.

HIPAA

There are extensive regulations implementing the privacy requirements of the *Health Insurance Portability and Accountability Act*. The regulations are expressly applicable only to health plans (except for plans with fewer than fifty participants that are self-administered solely by the sponsoring employer), health care clearing houses, and health care providers that electronically transmit health information. However, employers are affected by the regulations in important ways.

Health insurers and HMOs are prohibited from disclosing *protected health information* (PHI) to employers who sponsor health plans, except to enable plan sponsors to carry out plan administration functions that the plan sponsor performs, and then only upon certification that the plan documents have been amended as required by the regulations.

Employers in turn must:

♦ amend their plan documents to set out the permitted and required use of protected health information;

♦ require others who gain access, such as agents and subcontractors, to comply with use and disclosure restrictions;

♦ provide for return or destruction of information that is no longer needed;

♦ provide for separation between the group plan itself and the plan sponsor; and,

♦ describe those employees or classes of employees who have access to the information.

Employers are specifically prohibited from using protected health-care information for any employment-related action or decision.

SURVEILLANCE

An employer probably may install surveillance cameras around the workplace, so long as the cameras are located in places where there is no reasonable expectation of privacy. Having a stated legitimate business reason for installing cameras—safety in garage areas or to stop employee theft—is a good idea. Cameras installed in private areas, such as restrooms, would be difficult to justify.

Surveillance outside the workplace is slightly different. Take, for example, an injured employee who is on leave and collecting workers' compensation benefits. If the employer has a reasonable suspicion that the employee is malingering and hires an investigator to videotape the employee surreptitiously outside the workplace, there is no invasion. The employer had a legitimate business purpose in conducting the surveillance and did so in an unobtrusive manner. However, if the employer instructs the investigator to interview all the employee's neighbors, golfing buddies, bowling team, as well as take the video, the employer may have invaded the employee's privacy.

Some companies take surveillance to a whole new level by inquiring into or investigating an applicant's or employee's after-hours, leisure activities, and lifestyle in making employment decisions. Claiming a desire to hold down health insurance costs, or absenteeism, or negligent employment suits, companies have been known to inquire about tobacco and alcohol use, participation in dangerous sports like motorcycle racing or sky diving, and even sexual activities. Balancing the invasive nature of these inquiries against the questionable value of the information obtained suggests that such practices are ill-conceived. Some states prohibit an employer's using information about lawful after-hours activities to make employment decisions.

> **EMPLOYER TIP**
>
> In a unionized shop, the installation of surveillance cameras is a matter for mandatory bargaining. Surveillance to determine who is supporting a union organizing effort is an unfair labor practice.

ELECTRONIC MONITORING

Under the federal *Electronic Communications Privacy Act* (ECPA), it is illegal to intentionally intercept a wire, oral, or electronic communication. Intercept means the aural or other acquisition of the contents of any wire, electronic, or oral communication through the use of any electronic, mechanical, or other device. Telephone conversations, voice mail messages, face-to-face conversations, and email (probably) are all protected by the ECPA. Employers are subject to the ECPA just like any other interceptor.

The ECPA prohibition does not apply when one of the parties to the conversation has consented to an intercept. So at least under federal law, if two persons are engaged in a telephone or face-to-face conversation, one of them may record the conversation without the consent, or even the knowledge, of the other.

Many states have enacted laws similar to the ECPA. Be warned, however, that unlike the ECPA, which is a *one-party consent* statute, some states have *two-party consent* statutes. In a two-party consent state, both parties to the conversation (or all parties if there are more than two) must consent to the intercept. Two-party consent statutes are not preempted by the ECPA and are fully enforceable.

For example, a company that deals with the public must get the consent of both the *employee* and the *customer* if it is doing business in a two-party consent state. The employee's consent will be presumed if the employer notifies the employee of its intentions to record the communication beforehand. (It is a good idea to give the notice in writing and have the employee sign a receipt. A monitoring policy should also be stated in the employee handbook.) As for the customer, the employer should have a recorded announcement at the beginning of each telephone conversation that the conversation may be monitored. If the customer proceeds with the conversation, his or her consent is also presumed. Even in one-party states, it is a good idea to let both the employee and the customer know in advance that conversations may be monitored.

Stored Communication

The ECPA also prohibits unauthorized access to stored communications (as distinguished from real-time, on-going communications), but it has an exception for the provider of the communications service. This exception probably allows an employer to access employee emails that are backed up on the employer's own email server, as well as log data showing an employee's Internet surfing habits.

Word-processing and other data files stored on the employer's network server or on the employee's workstation hard drive are not covered by the ECPA, since they are not *communications*. However, even as to materials

> **EMPLOYER TIP**
>
> Posting employee photographs or other personal information about employees on a company website, if done without their permission, may not only be a privacy violation, it may increase the risk that employees will become crime victims—identity theft, violence, etc.

that are exempt from, or not covered by, the ECPA or comparable state statutes, employers need to be concerned about common-law privacy rights. As with searches of private places, the test is whether the employee had a reasonable expectation of privacy. To dispel any possible expectations of privacy, the employer should make clear in the employee handbook that the entire computer network, including individual workstations, belongs to the employer and that the employer may, at any time and without notice, inspect any files stored, processed, or transmitted on company computers.

Personal Use of Equipment

Some companies go so far as to prohibit any personal use of communications equipment. While such a policy is perfectly legal, it is difficult to enforce. Failure to enforce a policy consistently can give rise to employee expectations that the policy is one in name only. It probably makes more sense to recognize that some personal use will inevitably take place and to adopt a policy limiting personal use to no more than a few minutes a day. The policy should also prohibit any improper or illegal use.

If an employer discovers a computer file that appears to be personal, in violation of company policy, the employer should normally not study its contents except to determine that the file is in fact personal. Studying the file's con-

> **EMPLOYER TIP**
>
> Prohibiting employees from using the company email system for concerted activity relating to union organizing or conditions of employment could constitute an unfair labor practice. (see Chapter 21.)

tents beyond that point serves no legitimate business purpose, since the employer's interests are normally sufficiently served by instructing the employee to remove the file and imposing appropriate discipline. If the employer reasonably suspects that the employee is using office computers to engage in some illegal activity such as gambling, theft of trade secrets, or distribution of pornography, further inspection of the file's contents may be justified.

Telephone Equipment Exception. Provision of the ECPA exempts telephone equipment so long as the equipment is being used in the ordinary course of business. Extension telephones and speaker phones, for example, normally qualify under this exemption, even though they can be used to intercept electronic communication.

LIE DETECTOR TESTS

With very limited exceptions, a federal law known as the *Employee Polygraph Protection Act* (EPPA) prohibits use of lie detectors in employment situations. The term *lie detector* as used in the federal statute includes not only polygraph equipment (which measures pulse, respiration, and perspiration) but also any other device, such as a voice stress analyzer. The EPPA goes so far as to prohibit an employer's even requesting or suggesting that an employee submit to a lie detector test. Discharging an employee for refusing to submit to a test is abusive and subjects the employer to civil damages.

Exceptions

Exceptions to the EPPA include tests administered by federal, state and local government employers and tests administered by the federal government to employees of government contractors in connection with security, counterintelligence, and law enforcement functions. Exceptions for private employers include:

+ *Ongoing investigation.* An employer may request its employee to submit to a polygraph test in connection with an ongoing investigation involving economic loss or injury to the employer's business, such as theft, embezzlement, misappropriation, or an act of unlawful industrial espionage or sabotage. The employee had to have access to the property that is the subject of the investigation and the employer must have a reasonable suspicion that the employee was involved in the incident or activity under investigation.

+ *Security personnel.* Prospective employees may be required to undergo polygraph tests in connection with employment as armored car personnel, personnel engaged in the design, installation, and maintenance of security alarm systems, and security personnel whose functions include protection of facilities that have a significant impact on public health or safety (nuclear power plants, public water supply, etc).

◆ **Controlled substances**. Prospective employees who will be involved in the manufacture or distribution of controlled substances may be required to undergo polygraph tests. In addition, an existing employee may be required to undergo a polygraph test in connection with an ongoing investigation involving loss of a controlled substance, if the employee had access to the substance.

The EPPA goes on to specify a variety of requirements and procedures that must be met in order for the exemptions to apply. As a practical matter, most private employers will simply rule out lie detectors as a workplace tool.

DRUG TESTING AND DRUG-FREE WORKPLACES

More and more employers are requiring job applicants and even existing employees to take and pass a test—usually a urine test or a hair sample—for illegal drugs. In some industries, such as the transportation industry, the need for a drug-free workplace is obvious. In other industries, employers may justify drug testing on grounds of lower accident rates or less absenteeism.

Employers who decide to have a drug testing program should engage an outside consultant to set up the program and perhaps even administer it on an on-going basis. This will help assure that the program is run professionally and in accordance with any applicable law, that drug screens are accurate and reliable, and that medical information obtained in the process is handled appropriately. Using an outside consultant may also help insulate the employer from liability should a breach of confidentiality occur or should an employee be falsely reported as an illegal drug user.

Employers and employees have sharply competing interests over drug and alcohol testing. On the one hand, an employer has a strong, sometimes compelling interest in maintaining a drug-and alcohol-free workplace. The employer is concerned with the safety of employees, customers, and the public generally, and with the effect of drug and alcohol abuse on job performance and absenteeism.

> **EMPLOYER TIP**
>
> The *Americans with Disabilities Act* excludes current, illegal drug use from the disabilities that must be reasonably accommodated. Although the ADA prohibits medical exams prior to an offer of employment, a test for illegal drugs is not considered a medical exam and it may take place before an offer of employment is made. (see Chapter 17.)

In contrast, employees have privacy rights. They object to employer scrutiny of their off-hours conduct. They question the accuracy of testing procedures. They worry about the confidentiality of unrelated medical information obtained in the testing process. Public sector employees and employees in regulated industries additionally have a constitutional right against unreasonable searches and seizures by the government.

Drug-Free Workplace Act

Lawmakers have attempted to balance these competing interests. At the federal level, the *Drug-Free Workplace Act* (DFWA) requires federal grant recipients and most federal contractors to:

- ◆ adopt and publish a policy prohibiting the unlawful manufacture, distribution, dispensation, possession, or use of a controlled substance in the workplace, and specifying the disciplinary action that will be taken for violations;
- ◆ establish a drug-free awareness program to inform employees about the dangers of drug abuse and the availability of any drug counseling, rehabilitation, and employee assistance programs;
- ◆ require employees to notify the employer within five days of any criminal convictions relating to drug violations in the workplace;
- ◆ notify the federal granting or contracting agency within ten days after receiving notice of the conviction; and,

◆ either discharge the convicted employee or require him or her to participate satisfactorily in a drug abuse assistance or rehabilitation program.

> **EMPLOYER TIP**
>
> Employer records relating to substance abuse treatment are subject to special confidentiality provisions under federal law.

Department of Transportation

Employers in the various transportation industries regulated by the U.S. Department of Transportation (DOT) (aviation, mass transit, interstate pipelines, railroads, shipping, and trucking) are required to establish drug and alcohol policies for employees performing safety-sensitive jobs. Under these requirements, covered employees are prohibited from using, possessing, being under the influence of, or being impaired by drugs or alcohol while performing their jobs. Covered employees are subject to drug and alcohol tests:

◆ as part of their employment application process (drug testing required; alcohol testing permitted);

◆ when there is a reasonable basis to suspect drug or alcohol abuse;

◆ on a random basis; and,

◆ following an accident.

DOT regulations set out in detail the components of a comprehensive drug-testing program, with particular emphasis on fairness to the employees, collection and testing procedures, and record-keeping. Employers outside the transportation industry who are contemplating such a program should be guided by these regulations, found at **www.dot.gov/ost/dapc**.

Other federal agencies, including the Department of Defense, the Department of Energy, and the Nuclear Regulatory Commission, have drug and alcohol regulations governing their contractors.

DOT regulations have come under constitutional attack as a violation of the employees' Fourth Amendment right to be free from unreasonable searches and seizures. The Supreme Court has ruled, however, that while the Fourth Amendment applies to drug and alcohol testing conducted pursuant to government regulation, such testing is not unreasonable, even in the absence of a search warrant and even absent any basis to suspect the individual being tested.

Employers need to keep in mind certain federal-level restrictions applicable to their drug and alcohol programs. The *Americans with Disabilities Act* generally prohibits any pre-employment medical examinations. Although pre-employment tests for illegal drugs are expressly permitted under the ADA, pre-employment tests for alcohol are not.

The ADA also generally prohibits discrimination against, and requires reasonable accommodation of, persons with disabilities, including addictions. While persons with drug and alcohol addictions fall within these general ADA provisions, an employer:

- *may* discriminate against current users of illegal drugs;
- *may* discipline employees for use or possession of drugs or alcohol at the workplace in violation of company policy, even if the use or possession is the result of addiction; and,
- *need not* tolerate poor work performance, even if the deficiencies are the result of addiction.

EMPLOYEE MAIL

Federal law prohibits obstruction of mail correspondence. If a letter arrives addressed to a former employee to the company that is obviously personal—the envelope is the size and shape of a greeting card, the address is hand-written, it is addressed to the former employee *in care of* the company, it has a hand-written, non-business return address, and it was stamped rather than metered—then the employer's clear duty is to forward it unopened to the former employee.

However, if the envelope has all the earmarks of a business correspondence, including a pre-printed return address of one of the company's customers, most employers would not hesitate to open the letter, but their right to do so is not so clear.

An appropriate provision in the employee handbook should help resolve the matter. The provision should say:

> *mail arriving at the company's place of business that reasonably appears to be business mail intended for the company, may be opened by any authorized company employee, even if it is addressed to some other specific employee or former employee. By accepting employment, an employee grants permission to the company to open mail in accordance with the foregoing, and that the permission continues throughout the employment and after it ends.*

The provision should also prohibit employees from receiving personal mail at the company's place of business.

CONSUMER REPORTS

Federal law regulates the use by employers of credit and investigative reports prepared by consumer reporting agencies. The federal *Fair Credit Reporting Act* (FCRA) defines a consumer reporting agency (CRA) as a person or entity which, for a fee, assembles or evaluates credit information or other information on consumers for the purpose of regularly furnishing consumer reports to third parties (such as employers).

In general, employers may obtain consumer reports from CRAs, including investigative reports, to assess the character and general reputation for purposes of: evaluating an applicant, promotion, reassignment, or retention. The law places limits on how far back the credit reporting agency may go for various types of information, but those limits do not apply when highly compensated positions are being filled.

When requesting a consumer report, the employer must inform the applicant or employee in writing that such a report is being requested and must obtain the applicant's or employee's written authorization to obtain the report. The authorization should be a separate, stand-alone document and not be imbedded in the employment application or some other form. The applicant or employee may in turn make a written request to be informed of the full nature and scope of the report being requested, and the employer must then furnish that information.

EMPLOYER TIP

The FTC recently took the position that if an employer, in responding to a complaint of sexual harassment, turns to an outside organization for assistance in the investigation, the outside organization is a consumer reporting agency and the employer's obligations under the FCRA are triggered.

If the employer intends to make an adverse employment decision based wholly or partly on the consumer report, the employer must first inform the applicant or employee of this intention and must supply the applicant or employee with the name and address of the CRA that made the report, a copy of the report, and a statement explaining the applicant's or employee's rights under federal law to challenge the accuracy of the report. The Federal Trade Commission, which enforces the FCRA, has developed a form statement of employee rights under federal law which satisfies the employer's FCRA obligations. A copy is available from the FTC at **www.ftc.gov/os/statutes/2summary.htm**.

Additional information about the FCRA is available at **www.ftc.gov/bcp/conline/pubs/buspubs/credempl.htm**.

CRIMINAL RECORDS

In general, employers are free to ask applicants about criminal *convictions*, assuming there is a reasonable business purpose for doing so. However, the EEOC and some courts take the position that asking about *arrests*, when no conviction resulted, is discriminatory under *Title VII*.

Court records (except juvenile records) are open to the public and may be inspected at federal and state courthouses. Private companies can be hired to do state-wide or county-by-county searches.

DRIVING RECORDS

The federal *Driver's Privacy Protection Act of 1994* prohibits state motor vehicle departments from disclosing *personal information* without the consent of the person involved. Personal information is defined as information that identifies an individual, including an individual's photograph, social security number, driver identification number, name, address, telephone number, and medical or disability information. Excluded from the definition is information on vehicular accidents, driving violations, and driver's status.

When an employer decides to check driving records, the simplest procedure is to require the employee or prospective employee to personally obtain the record. As always, the decision should be supported by a reasonable business purpose and it should be invoked on a nondiscriminatory basis.

IDENTITY THEFT

Identity theft is a serious and growing national problem. According to some reports, the top cause of identity fraud is theft of records from employers or other businesses that maintain personal information on individuals. The information that employers necessarily obtain as part of the employment relationship—name, birthdate, address, and social security number—is the very information that enables an identity thief to do mischief. Employers need to safeguard that information. Failure to do so could result in legal liability.

Taking the following steps will help protect personal employee information.

- ◆ Keep records containing employee information in a secure room or file area and separate from other company records.
- ◆ If employee information is maintained electronically, be sure the files are passworded. Change passwords frequently and whenever an employee with password access leaves the company.
- ◆ Consider encrypting any employee information that is electronically stored; consider isolating the information from the office computer network and from the Internet.

- Perform thorough background checks on all employees who have access to personal employee information.
- Do not allow access by unauthorized employees, particularly temps who sometimes take jobs for the sole purpose of obtaining identity theft data.
- Do not use social security numbers for identification purposes or on employee badges, and do not print social security numbers on paychecks or other documents that could be available to the general public. (In some states, it is illegal for an employer to use social security numbers for employee identification purposes.)
- Limit distribution of company directories and allow employees to exclude personal information—home addresses, phone numbers, spouse's and children's names, etc.
- Develop a records retention policy that requires destruction of all obsolete records; shred obsolete records, rather than merely discarding them.
- Ask vendors who have access to personal information about your employees, such as your payroll service, third-party benefit plan administrators, etc., what steps they have taken to safeguard the information.
- Consider requiring contractual provisions with vendors, obligating them to maintain appropriate safeguards, to notify you immediately about unauthorized access or other problems, and to indemnify you if one of their employees compromises your information.

–19–
EMPLOYEE LOYALTY

Every employee owes a common-law duty of loyalty to his or her employer. The duty is an implicit part of the employment relationship unless the employer and employee agree otherwise. Under this duty, an employee is bound to serve his or her employer diligently and faithfully, to refrain from knowingly or willfully injuring the employer's business, and to avoid any conflict between the employer's interest and the employee's own self-interest.

Corporate officers and directors have heightened duties of loyalty to their employers. Officers and directors are generally considered fiduciaries, meaning that they must act for the benefit of their employer. They may not use corporate facilities or assets for personal gain. An even higher standard of loyalty and fiduciary duty is sometimes applied to trustees of charitable, nonprofit organizations.

COMPETING WITH AN EMPLOYER

In the absence of a contract that restricts an employee's right to compete with his or her former employer, the duty of loyalty ends when the employment relationship ends. So an employee is perfectly free to quit and go with a competitor or start a competing business.

As a general rule, an employee may *make plans* to compete while still employed. This includes gathering information, consulting with advisors, developing a business plan, creating a business entity, arranging for financing, purchasing a rival business, even let-ting existing customers and fellow employees know about his or her intentions.

But when the employee goes beyond the planning stages, or engages in some unfair, fraudulent, or wrongful conduct, he or she has crossed the legal line. Examples of improper conduct include:

◆ actually beginning business in competition with a current employer;

◆ misappropriating employer's trade secrets;

◆ pirating confidential customer lists;

◆ soliciting current customers or fellow employees for the new business;

◆ conspiring to bring about a mass resignation of key employees;

◆ usurping business opportunities, such as by diverting new business or asking a customer to delay a purchase until the employee's new company is operating; or,

◆ destroying current employer's records or computer files.

TRADE SECRETS

As a supplement to common-law duties of loyalty, most states have adopted the *Uniform Trade Secrets Act*, which prohibits the *misappropriation of trade secrets* by *improper means*. A *trade secret* is defined as information that has economic value because it is not generally known to others and that the employer makes reasonable efforts to keep secret. Examples include a closely-guarded process like the formula for *Coca Cola*, or *Windows* source code. *Improper means* includes theft, bribery, misrepresentation, breach of duty to maintain secrecy, and espionage. So if an employee steals information or documents while still employed, say in anticipation of leaving that job and going with a competitor, the company will have a claim under the Uniform Trade Secrets Act. (Theft of a trade secret is also criminal under the federal *Economic Espionage Act*.)

The Uniform Trade Secrets Act authorizes the courts to issue an injunction prohibiting an employee from misappropriating trade secrets. However, under the statute, there must be an *actual or threatened* misappropriation. Normally, to base an injunction on threatened disclosure, the courts at a minimum require evidence of intent to disclose. However, courts in a few states—most notably, Illinois and North Carolina—have adopted a legal doctrine known as *inevitable disclosure*. Under that doctrine, even when there is no actual or threatened disclosure, the court may issue an injunction against a former employee who had access to highly confidential, specifically identified trade secrets, if the employee's old and new companies are in direct competition, and if the employee's old and new jobs are so similar as to make disclosure of the secrets inevitable. Other courts have rejected the inevitable disclosure doctrine.

COMPUTER FRAUD

The *Computer Fraud and Abuse Act* (CRAA) is a potentially powerful weapon in an employer's hands. The CRAA covers virtually any computer that is connected to the Internet.

Under the CRAA, it is criminal for anyone to access a protected computer without authority or to exceed authorized access. Trafficking in passwords or similar information is also a crime if done with intent to defraud. Persons or companies injured by violations of the CRAA can sue in civil court for monetary damages.

What makes the CRAA so powerful is that when, for example, the data entry clerk takes a peek at his or her boss's personnel file using someone else's password, the CRAA is violated. High-level employees, who have access to the entire computer system can also be charged with a CRAA violation. If a high level employee accesses company information on behalf of a competitor, and the employee transmits the confidential information, he or she violates the CRAA.

Intentionally causing damage to a company's computer system by transmitting a program, information, code, or command, is a violation of federal criminal law. *Denial-of-service attacks* or deletion of valuable data are good examples. So is theft of confidential electronic information.

LOYALTY BY CONTRACT

An employer can gain protection beyond that provided by the common-law duty of loyalty, the *Uniform Trade Secrets Act*, and the *Computer Fraud and Abuse Act*. So long as the employer acts reasonably and for legitimate business reasons, an employer may require employees to sign binding contracts that go well beyond the limited protections provided by law. A typical contract might contain some or all of the following clauses:

- a *noncompetition clause* (sometimes called a *noncompete clause*, a *restrictive covenant*, or a *covenant not to compete*);
- a *nonsolicitation clause*;
- a *confidentiality clause*; or,
- a *work-for-hire clause*.

These clauses are discussed in the sections that follow.

Noncompetition

Contracts of involuntary servitude, that attempt to force an employee to work for a particular employer, are not enforceable. The law no longer recognizes the status of indentured servant. However, a contract that imposes restrictions on an employee's ability to compete with a former employer is enforceable if the restrictions are reasonable.

The general rule is that an employee's agreement not to compete with an employer upon leaving the employment will be upheld if:

- it is supported by adequate consideration;
- the restraint is confined within limits that are no wider as to area and duration than are reasonably necessary for the protection of the employer's business; and,
- the restraint does not impose undue hardship on the employees or disregard the interest of the public.

Noncompete agreements may be used to prevent unfair competition. They cannot be used to gain an unfair advantage.

The general public also has an interest in free competition. If your employee really can provide a service that is better, cheaper, and more reliable than yours, the public would certainly want him or her free to do so.

Examples of when an employer might want the protection of a noncompete agreement include:

- sales positions, when the business is heavily dependent on the relationship between the salesperson and the customers and where the customers would likely follow the salesperson to a new employer;
- professional practices, when the clients or patients tend to identify with particular professionals in the firm and not with the firm as a whole;
- jobs for which the employer must make a substantial initial investment in the employee's education or training or when the employee is unproductive while awaiting a security clearance or a special license or certification;
- jobs requiring unique skill sets;
- jobs involving access to highly confidential trade secrets; and,
- high-tech positions, in which the employee is likely to generate or have access to intellectual property such as computer programs or patentable devices.

The restrictions imposed by a noncompete agreement must be *reasonable*. Traditionally, the courts have looked to three factors in determining reasonableness:

1. the particular work that the employee is prohibited from doing;
2. the geographic area in which the employee is barred from competing; and,
3. the duration of the restriction.

A noncompete agreement that restricts an employee for six months from working for companies that compete directly with the employer, within a radius of ten miles of the employer's place of business, is likely to be held reasonable. A restriction of as much as two or even three years may be upheld as reasonable depending on the circumstances. But an agreement that prohibits an employee from working in any similar line of business, anywhere in the United States, for five years, is likely to be held an unreasonable restraint of trade. Drawing the line between reasonable and unreasonable is a case-by-case process.

The geographic restriction factor may be disappearing. As information technology assumes a greater role in the economy, and as the speed and ease of communications increase, it makes little difference whether a computer programmer works in the employer's office, in the employee's own mountain retreat, or in Bangalore, India. So merely prohibiting the programmer from competing within a ten-mile radius of the office will not be very effective.

Nonsolicitation

When an employee leaves with the intention of going into competition with a former employer, he or she will likely plan to contact former customers and invite them to become customers of the new business. Similarly, he or she will likely try to induce fellow employees to come work for the new business. A standard provision in noncompete and confidentiality agreements is a prohibition on soliciting customers and fellow employees.

A nonsolicitation provision may prohibit the departing employee from servicing *all* clients of the employer, not just the clients of the employer with whom the employee had contact or with whom he or she worked while employed.

A nonsolicitation provision may even be applied to customers that the employee brought to the employer, since relationships with those customers become part of the employer's goodwill. Thus, in defending a claim for breach of a nonsolicitation clause, it is no excuse that the customers for whom the employee did work after leaving the employer were also customers for whom work had been done before starting with the employer.

> **EMPLOYER TIP**
>
> Unlike noncompete clauses, in most states, a nonsolicitation provision need not be limited in duration or by geography.

One other aspect of nonsolicitation clauses deserves mention. Companies that provide contract services to other businesses know only too well the risk of having their business customers hire away their best employees to bring the contract work in-house. While nonsolicitation and noncompete clauses should help prevent that practice, the company is in an even stronger position if its *business-to-business contracts* prohibit nonsolicitation as well.

Confidentiality

In a typical confidentiality clause, an employee acknowledges that all company information, trade secrets, customer lists, business plans, procedures, cost structures, profit margins, etc., belong to the company. The employee promises to maintain the confidentiality of that information throughout his or her employment and after the employment ends.

Confidentiality agreements supplement the *Uniform Trade Secrets Act* in important ways. Such agreements demonstrate that the employer is making reasonable efforts to keep information confidential, thus bringing the information within the definition of *trade secret*. These agreements also impose a duty to maintain secrecy, so that breach of a confidentiality agreement may in certain circumstances be a violation of the statute as well. Finally, these agreements fill a significant gap in the statute.

As with nonsolicitation agreements, confidentiality agreements may last for an indefinite period, or at least until the confidential information becomes known to the public generally.

WORK-FOR-HIRE

In general, the right to patent an invention belongs to the inventor personally, and ownership of the copyright of a work belongs to the author personally. Federal patent law grants no rights to an employer whose employee is the inventor, even though the employee was being paid to create the invention.

While federal copyright law does provide that an employer is considered the author of a *work made for hire*—defined as a work prepared by an employee *within the scope of his or her employment*—a question can arise whether a particular work was prepared within or outside the scope of the employee's employment.

Example: Suppose a salesperson's job is to sell complex, expensive, medical equipment to hospitals and to train hospital personnel on the equipment. If the salesperson writes a 500-page manual on the maintenance and use of the equipment, who owns the rights to the manual—the salesperson or the employer? If the salesperson was instructed to write the manual and did so on the company's time and money, using a company word processor, then the manual is probably a work-for-hire, owned by the employer. But if the employee wrote the manual on his or her own time, at home, using his or her home computer, then probably the employee owns the manual, even though the employee acquired most of the information in the manual during the course of his or her work.

Employers should care about ownership of the manual because it likely contains valuable information not generally available to the public. The employer wants to profit from the manual, either by selling it to customers or by giving it to them as part of a service package. Alternatively, the employer may want to keep the manual secret and out of the hands of competitors. The employer gains no benefit and actually stands to be harmed if the manual is not a work-for-hire.

In short, when an employer hires someone to work on a potentially patentable invention or a copyrightable work, the employer needs greater protection than federal law provides. The solution is to have the employee sign an agreement that all inventions and works created during employment, and for some reasonable period after the employment ends, are considered made for hire and belong to the employer. Such agreements usually contain an express assignment of all rights to the employer.

Consideration

As a matter of basic contract law, in order for a contractual promise to be enforceable, it must be supported by consideration.

In the case of a newly hired employee, the consideration for a noncompete agreement is the offer of employment itself. Even an offer of employment at will is generally sufficient consideration to support a noncompete agreement.

In the case of existing employees, continuing employment *may* provides the consideration. Employers should be aware, however, that not all states reach that conclusion. Some states require fresh consideration to support an existing employee's promise not to compete, in the form of a raise, a bonus payment, or some other benefit or item of value.

Departing employees are often asked to sign non-compete, non-solicitation, and confidentiality agreements. In that case, the employer definitely will have to offer fresh consideration, such as a severance payment or salary continuation. The law would not enforce a noncompete from a departing employee absent fresh consideration. The departing employee is also unlikely to sign the agreement in the first place without some new consideration. For these reasons, it makes sense to get noncompetes at initial hire or at least at a time when employment is likely to continue for some substantial period.

EMPLOYER TIP

Threatening to withhold a departing employee's final paycheck until he or she signs a noncompete agreement will definitely not solve the consideration problem, since the employer has no right to withhold pay that is clearly due. (see Chapter 5.)

EMPLOYER TIP

A liquidated damages clause, specifying the amount of damages recoverable in case of breach, could overcome the problem of proving damages, so long as the amount specified is a reasonable estimate of actual damages and not merely punitive.

REMEDIES FOR BREACH OF AGREEMENT

The typical remedy sought by an employer when a former employee breaches a noncompete, nonsolicitation, confidentiality, or work-for-hire agreement is an *injunction*. An injunction is a court order prohibiting specified conduct, violation of which could result in fines or jail time. The alternative remedy would be a suit against the employee for money damages, but the employer may have difficulty proving the dollar value of the injury suffered or proving that a decline in sales was caused by this particular employee's disloyalty and not by some other event.

When an employer learns that a former employee is now working for the competition in violation of a noncompete agreement, the first step should be to write to the former employee a *cease and desist letter*. Whether the employer should also write to the new employer depends on how confident the employer is that the noncompete agreement is valid and enforceable.

A letter to the new employer, informing it about the agreement and insisting it not participate in the employee's breach of the agreement, can often be the simplest and cheapest means of enforcing the agreement.

EMPLOYER TIP

Arbitration agreements that require employment disputes to be resolved by binding arbitration instead of by lawsuits, should contain an exception permitting the employer to go to court for an injunction against violation of restrictive covenants. (Arbitration agreements are discussed in Chapter 1.)

This works because the new employer, once on notice of the agreement, can be sued for *tortious interference with contract* if it ignores the agreement and continues to enjoy the benefits of the former employee's misconduct. (see Chapter 23.)

On the other hand, if the noncompete agreement has been poorly drafted so as not to apply in this particular circumstance or if it is unreasonably broad or otherwise unenforceable, the employer may have liability for interfering with the new employment relationship.

EMPLOYEE DISHONESTY

Employee theft is a recurring, and some say, growing, problem. It covers a wide range of activities—from personal long-distance phone calls, to the misappropriation of goods held for sale, to embezzlement of hundreds of thousands of dollars—all of which are costly to the employer.

While no employer can be fully protected, safeguards exist that should help reduce the risk.

- Obtain background checks on prospective employees, particularly those who will have access to company financial records.
- Consider instituting a drug testing program.
- Be sure company financial records are secure. Electronic records should be passworded and passwords should be changed frequently.
- Separate financial functions. For example, the employee who draws company checks should not be the same person who signs them. Bank and other financial institution statements should be reconciled by yet a third person.
- Insist on seeing *original* vendor invoices before signing checks. Once a check is signed, the invoice should be marked *paid* and the date and check number should be written on the invoice.
- Compare invoices against a current list of vendors to guard against fictitious bills. Invoices should also be checked against contractual arrangements to prevent an over-billing/kickback scheme.
- Except in emergencies, limit check-signing responsibility to one person, whose familiarity with billing cycles will help spot unusual invoices.
- Require a second signature for checks over a specified limit.
- Review payroll records periodically to weed out phantom employees.
- Cancel a departing employee's password and signature authority over bank accounts.
- Distribute company credit cards sparingly and have a supervisor who is familiar with specific employee assignments review the employee's monthly account statement.

- Require employees with financial responsibilities to take periodic vacations so they are not able to continue a coverup of improper activities.
- Adopt, publicize, and enforce a company code of ethics for all employees.
- Obtain employee dishonesty insurance coverage.

If employee dishonesty is discovered, the employee involved will likely be terminated or at least be removed from the duties that enabled him or her to commit the dishonesty. If termination is appropriate, the exit interview procedures listed in Chapter 4 should be followed. The employer will also want to give prompt notice of any loss to the insurance carrier.

The decision whether to report employee theft to law enforcement is a delicate one. Some companies are reluctant to go public with internal problems for fear their clients or customers will lose confidence in them. On the other hand, the company's insurance carrier may require a police report as a condition to covering the loss. One thing the company cannot do is threaten the employee with criminal charges unless he or she repays the loss. Doing so constitutes the crime of blackmail.

If the terminated employee applies for unemployment insurance benefits, the company's decision about going public may have to be made quite quickly. Misconduct usually disqualifies an employee from benefits, either permanently or for a specified period depending on the *degree of misconduct.* (see Chapter 3.) *Gross misconduct* also disqualifies a fired employee from COBRA benefits (see Chapter 10.)

EMPLOYER TIP

Business insurance policies often do not cover employment-related claims, such as discrimination, abusive discharge, etc. For these types of claims, *Employment Practices Liability* (EPL) coverage is needed.

–20–
NONPROFIT ORGANIZATIONS

A typical business corporation is formed by *shareholders* who invest their capital in the business with the expectation of earning a profit in the form of dividends or on the later sale of their stock. Shareholders hold ultimate power over the corporation by electing directors and by deciding issues that are fundamental to the corporation's existence, such as whether to change the company's capital structure or to merge with another company. The directors, in turn, manage the company by appointing and overseeing corporate officers.

A *nonprofit organization*, on the other hand, is not formed to make a profit. Typically, it is a corporation organized under special provisions of state law that prohibit issuance of shares or the payment of dividends. Nonprofit organizations therefore have no shareholders and they do not distribute earnings to owners. (Nonprofit organizations may have *members* who elect directors or trustees, but the members do not *own* the organization. In fact, nobody *owns* a nonprofit.)

Although not organized to make a profit, nonprofit organizations are not required to operate at a loss. Any surplus of revenues over expenses must be retained or applied to nonprofit purposes and cannot be distributed to individual members.

The term *nonprofit* is often used synonymously with *tax-exempt*. The two concepts, though related, are distinct. Nonprofit refers to the organization's purposes as expressed in its articles of incorporation and as governed by state law. Tax-exempt on the other hand means that the organization's net earnings are not subject to income tax. All tax-exempt organizations must be nonprofit, but just because an organization is nonprofit does not necessarily mean it qualifies for tax exemption.

Of course, the reason an entity organizes as a nonprofit is usually to obtain tax-exempt status. For purposes of this chapter, the terms will be used interchangeably.

Section 501(c) of the Internal Revenue Code contains a long list of organizations that qualify for tax-exempt status, including:

- corporations organized and operated exclusively for religious, charitable, scientific, testing for public safety, literary, or educational purposes, or for the prevention of cruelty to children or animals, no part of the net earnings of which inures to the benefit of any private shareholder or individual—so-called *501(c)(3) organizations*;
- civic leagues organized and operated exclusively for the promotion of social welfare;
- labor, agricultural, or horticultural organizations;
- business leagues, chambers of commerce, real estate boards, and boards of trade; and,
- recreational clubs.

To achieve tax-exempt status, a nonprofit organization must submit an application to the IRS. If the IRS is satisfied that the organization is organized and is being operated for one of the exempt purposes listed in the statute, it issues a determination letter to that effect. Exemption from state income taxes can usually be obtained on the basis of the IRS determination letter.

Another distinction that is often blurred has to do with the deductibility of contributions. While tax-exempt organizations pay no income tax, it does not necessarily follow that contributions to that organization qualify for a deduction. Deductibility of contributions to Section 501(c)(3) organizations are governed by Section 170 of the Internal Revenue Code. Payments to other types of nonprofit organizations, such as business leagues, may qualify as trade or business expenses under Section 162 of the Internal Revenue Code.

Although tax-exempt nonprofits get special treatment for some purposes, with few exceptions federal and state employment laws apply to nonprofits to the same extent as they apply to for-profit businesses. For example, nonprofits must withhold taxes from employee salaries; must provide workers' compensation; cannot discriminate (except in limited circumstances involving religious organizations); and, must provide safe workplaces.

This chapter discusses the exceptions applicable to nonprofit organizations.

TAX CONSIDERATIONS

Section 162 of the Internal Revenue Code allows for-profit corporations to deduct from gross income all ordinary and necessary expenses including a reasonable allowance for salaries or other compensation for personal services actually rendered.

As a result of this provision, every dollar a *for-profit business* corporation pays out in salaries or employee benefits reduces the corporation's federal and state tax liability. In effect, the government pays almost half of a business corporation's employment-related costs.

Because of its tax-exempt status, the same is not true for a nonprofit organization. Salaries and benefits are borne 100 percent by the organization itself and reduce the amounts available for its nonprofit purposes on a dollar-for-dollar basis. The employees themselves pay tax on their incomes just like employees of for-profit companies.

EXECUTIVE COMPENSATION

Tax-exempt organizations, such as charitable, religious, or educational organizations exempt under Section 501(c)(3) of the Internal Revenue Code, must be operated *exclusively* for the charitable, religious or educational purposes for which they were organized. If they abuse their exempt status by engaging in nonexempt activities, the IRS has the power to revoke their tax exemption.

Revocation is a drastic remedy. It would often mean the end of the organization. So historically, minor abuses either went unpunished or they got punished in a disproportionately severe way. Now the IRS has a less deadly weapon—an excise tax to punish abusers.

A 1996 amendment to the tax code, coupled with more recently issued IRS regulations, prohibit *disqualified persons* from receiving *excess benefits* from a tax-exempt organization. A disqualified person includes any person who is in a position to exercise substantial influence over the affairs of the organization. This would cover high-level employees, board members, and officers. Family members of those persons are also covered. An excess benefit is any economic benefit provided to a disqualified person in excess of the consideration received by the organization. For example, the board of a charitable organization cannot vote itself exorbitant directors' fees, nor can senior managers pull down salaries far above the norm for comparable positions.

A disqualified person who receives an excess benefit is subject to an initial 25% excise tax on the amount of the excess. The management of the organization is also subject to a 10% tax. If the excess benefit transaction is not promptly corrected, then the disqualified person is subject to an additional *200%* excise tax.

BENEFIT PLANS

With limited exceptions, the same array of benefit plans that are available to for-profit companies are also available to tax-exempt organizations. Tax-exempt organizations may even have a profit-sharing plan, although they don't have profits in the normal sense.

In addition to the usual array of plans, organizations that are exempt under Section 501(c)(3) of the Internal Revenue Code may adopt a special type of pension plan available only to them, called a *tax-sheltered annuity* or *403(b) annuity*. Although called annuity plans, the funding vehicle for these plans is not limited to annuity contracts issued by insurance companies. Other vehicles, such as bank custodial accounts, are also available.

Tax-sheltered annuities conform in many respects to other types of pension plans. However, one of their more attractive features is their portability. When the funding vehicle is an individual annuity contract owned by the employee, the employee can leave one tax-exempt organization, go to work for another, and simply have the new employer make contributions to the existing plan.

Church Plans

A *church plan* is a plan established and maintained for employees of a tax-exempt church or a convention or association of churches. Unless a church plan voluntarily elects to be subject to *Employee Retirement Income Security Act* (ERISA), it is exempt from most of ERISA's requirements, including requirements relating to coverage, vesting, benefit accrual and funding. (ERISA is discussed in Chapter 9.)

Since nonelecting church plans are generally exempt from ERISA, they do not have to provide health insurance continuation benefits under the amendment to ERISA known as COBRA. On the other hand, HIPAA does apply to church plans. (see Chapter 10.)

UNEMPLOYMENT INSURANCE

Some states allow tax-exempt organizations described in Section 501(c)(3) of the Internal Revenue Code the option of either contributing state unemployment tax just like other employers, or reimbursing the state dollar-for-dollar for actual claims charged to their accounts. Electing to reimburse may improve a charity's current cash flow, but it could prove highly expensive in the event several employees are terminated at the same time.

RELIGIOUS ORGANIZATIONS

The First Amendment to the Constitution provides that *Congress shall make no law respecting an establishment of religion, or prohibiting the free exercise thereof.* Countless federal statutes have the potential

---

EMPLOYER TIP

While being exempt from ERISA is generally considered beneficial from the employer's viewpoint, one downside is that ERISA's preemption provision does not apply. This makes nonelecting church plans subject to state laws, rather than uniform federal law. As a result, church plans and their sponsors can be sued in state court, can be subjected to jury trials; and, can have compensatory and punitive damages awarded against them if permitted under state law.

for interfering with religious practices, but they either contain express exemptions, or they have been held inapplicable or unconstitutional when applied to religious organizations.

One such federal statute is *Title VII* of the federal *Civil Rights Act* that prohibits discrimination in employment based on race, color, religion, sex, or national origin. (*Title VII* is discussed in Chapter 14.) Under a literal reading of *Title VII*, a Congregational church in Boston might be required to hire a Baptist minister from Atlanta as its next preacher. Or a Catholic church could be forced to ordain women priests, contrary to Catholic religious doctrine. Most federal courts that have considered these questions recognize a so-called *ministerial exception* that prevents such odd results.

The ministerial exception to *Title VII* is based on the constitutional right of a church to manage its own affairs free from governmental interference. Under the ministerial exception, religious institutions are exempt from civil suits in connection with the selection and employment of clergy.

The ministerial exception is not limited just to members of the clergy. It also covers lay employees of religious institutions whose primary duties consist of teaching, spreading the faith, church governance, supervision of a religious order, or participation in religious ritual and worship. As one court said, "We do not look to ordination but instead to the function of the position."

Even for employees who are not covered by the ministerial exception, religious organizations may discriminate on *religious* grounds. *Title VII*, by its express terms, does not apply to an employer with respect to a religious corporation, association, educational institution, or society with respect to the employment of individuals of a particular religion to perform work connected with its activities.

Federal labor law offers another good example of potential interference with First Amendment rights to religious freedom. By statute, an employee in a union shop who is a member of a bona fide religion that forbids union membership or union financial support may pay his or her dues to charity instead of to the union. Religious organizations may also be exempt from National Labor Relations Board jurisdiction.

–21–
UNIONS AND LABOR RELATIONS

An in-depth exposition on labor relations law would go well beyond the scope of this book. Employers need experienced labor law counsel when faced with union organizing activity, when engaged in collective bargaining, or when responding to a strike threat. What follows is a discussion of the basic issues that arise under the *National Labor Relations Act* (NLRA).

NATIONAL LABOR RELATIONS ACT

According to the NLRA, inequality of bargaining power between employees and employers prevents the stabilization of competitive wage rates and working conditions. To remedy this inequality, the NLRA:

- ◆ protects *concerted activities* by employees;
- ◆ provides a mechanism for *union representation elections*;
- ◆ promotes *collective bargaining* between employers and unions; and,
- ◆ prohibits *unfair labor practices* by employers and unions.

The principal enforcer of the NLRA is the *National Labor Relations Board*. The Board has primary jurisdiction over labor disputes and union elections. When it is not clear whether an activity is governed by the NLRA, the Board—not the state or federal courts—gets to decide whether the NLRA applies.

Despite having primary jurisdiction, the Board will often defer to arbitration procedures in a *collective bargaining agreement* for resolving grievances, even where the grievance involves an unfair labor practice.

The NLRA, and hence the Board's enforcement power, extends to any employer whose activities affect interstate commerce. This means virtually any employer. However, the Board has chosen not to exercise its jurisdiction over employers in a variety of industries that fall below specified revenue levels.

In general, the Board will not exercise jurisdiction over non-retail establishments whose gross cash flow across state lines is less than $50,000. As to retail establishments, at least $500,000 in revenue is required for the Board to exercise its jurisdiction. Separate revenue tests also apply to office buildings, hotels and motels, private colleges and universities, symphony orchestras, and certain health care institutions, among others.

The NLRA protects *employee* rights. The term employee, however, is defined in an unhelpful, circular way. The NLRA does, however, exclude from the definition various specific groups, including independent contractors and supervisors.

Independent Contractors

Historically, the Board drew the employee/independent contractor distinction based on whether the employer exercised, or had the right to exercise, control over the means and manner by which the worker did the job. Recently, the Board adopted a new test for independent contractors.

The new test asks whether the worker has a *significant entrepreneurial opportunity for gain or loss*. Stated another way, who takes the economic risk connected with the worker's job—the company or the worker? If the risk is with the company, then the worker should be classified as an employee. If the worker bears the risk, then he or she is an independent contractor.

Supervisors

The NLRA defines *supervisor* as—any individual having authority, in the interest of the employer, to hire, transfer, suspend, lay off, recall, promote, discharge, assign, reward, or discipline other employees, or responsibly to direct them, or to adjust their grievances, or effectively to recommend such action, if in connection with the foregoing, the exercise of such authority is not of a merely routine or clerical nature, but requires the use of independent judgment.

By statute, supervisors have no right to *organize* or to require employers to bargain with them. Employers may, if they wish, agree to treat supervisors as employees for bargaining purposes. Absent employer consent, however, the inclusion of supervisors in a bargaining unit is not permitted and employers cannot be forced to bargain with such a unit.

Professionals

In contrast to the exclusion of supervisors from NLRA protection, *professional employees* are entitled to unionize. (Professionals cannot be forced into a bargaining unit with nonprofessionals unless a majority of the professionals approve the arrangement.) While professionals necessarily exercise independent judgment in the course of supervising others, they still do not qualify as supervisors if their supervisory duties are *merely routine or clerical and not independent*. This tension between exclusion of supervisors but inclusion of professionals can be problematic.

In trying to resolve the tension, the Supreme Court ruled that the test for determining supervisory status applies no differently to professionals than to other employees.

CONCERTED ACTIVITIES

Employers are prohibited from interfering with employees' concerted activities—efforts to better wages, hours, and working conditions. This includes, among other things, the right to self-organize—to form or join a union.

Union organizing efforts have engendered bitter disputes and a multitude of decided cases. One recurring issue is the extent to which employees and outside organizers may solicit at the workplace and may distribute pro-union literature. As the Supreme Court has said, the right to unionize necessarily encompasses the right effectively to *communicate* with one another regarding *self-organization at the jobsite*. Employee rights at the jobsite are not unlimited, however, since those rights can conflict with the employer's own property rights and managerial interests. In short, some balance must be struck between the competing interests of employers and employees.

In general, an employer *may* ban solicitation by employees of other employees during working time and *may* ban distribution by employees during working hours and in working areas. Conversely, an employer generally *may not* restrict employee solicitation during nonworking time, and *may not* ban employee distribution during nonworking time and in nonworking areas, such as employee lounges, parking lots, etc. The only exception is if the employer can show special circumstances that would make a ban necessary to maintain production or discipline.

When it comes to outside organizers, the employer has greater rights. So long as the employer acts in a nondiscriminatory fashion, it may impose a blanket ban on solicitation and distribution by non-employees on employer property, unless the union can demonstrate that employees are not otherwise accessible to union organizers.

Selective (discriminatory) enforcement of non-solicitation and nondistribution rules can be an *unfair labor practice*. By way of example, suppose a company completely bans employee use of the company's bulletin board—a perfectly legal rule under the NLRA if the employer is not unionized or if the rule is the result of good-faith bargaining. If the company then allows employees to post personal notices, such as items for sale, church raffle notices, or cartoons, the company's attempt to enforce its ban against pro-union material amounts to an unfair labor practice.

Although the right to engage in concerted activities covers self-organization, it also protects employees who are not unionized and it protects activities that have nothing to do with the formation of a union. Examples of protected concerted activity, whether in a union or nonunion context, include:

◆ *discussing wages and working conditions*. Since the right of employees to self-organize and bargain collectively necessarily encompasses the right to communicate with one another, an employer cannot adopt a rule prohibiting employees from discussing wages or other working conditions among themselves.

- *discussing employee sexual harassment complaints.* The Board has ruled that a company confidentiality requirement prohibiting discussion of a pending sexual harassment investigation is an unfair labor practice.
- *inquiring about benefits.* Employees can be persistent in pursuing benefit claims so long as their conduct is not so flagrant or egregious as to interfere with company business practices.
- *complaining about working conditions.* An employee cannot be disciplined for complaining to management about matters of common concern to all employees. Although the employee may initially be acting alone, his or her actions will be considered *concerted* so long as they are intended to initiate or induce group action. The intent to initiate or induce group action will be assumed if, for example, the complaint is voiced at a group meeting called to discuss working conditions.
- *wearing pro-union buttons and insignia.* Wearing buttons and insignia is protected activity unless there are special considerations relating to employee efficiency and plant discipline.
- *having a witness at a disciplinary hearing.* Although the NLRB has flip-flopped on this issue, its most recent position is that when an employer seeks to interview an employee in connection with a matter that could reasonably lead to discipline of the employee, and the employee requests the presence of a coworker, the employer must either grant the employee's request and allow a coworker to be present, or cancel the interview.

> ## EMPLOYER TIP
>
> Restrictions on soliciting and distribution—even those that are consistent with the rules stated here—should have a reasonable business justification other than anti-union animus. Employers who base restrictions on safety concerns can usually expect to have them upheld.

EMPLOYER TIP

Concerted activity by union members or groups of employees to better wages and working conditions is exempt from antitrust laws, even though the activity may amount to a restraint of trade. (see Chapter 5.)

REPRESENTATION ELECTIONS

The Board has adopted detailed rules for initiating and conducting representation elections. The process usually starts with a union organizer obtaining signatures on union cards authorizing a particular labor organization to represent the employees. When a *substantial number of employees* (at least 30%) have signed such cards, the labor organization then files a petition with the Board requesting recognition as the exclusive bargaining representative.

The Board then determines:

- whether the employer's operations *affect commerce* within the meaning of the NLRA;
- the *appropriateness* of the bargaining unit;
- whether the election would *further the policies* of the NLRA and *reflect the free choice* of employees in the bargaining unit; or,
- whether there is a *sufficient probability*, based on the evidence of representation, that the employees have selected the union to represent them.

If the Board is satisfied on these points, it orders a representation election to take place by secret ballot and supervises the actual conduct of the election. If a majority of employees in the bargaining unit vote in favor of the union, the union is then certified as the bargaining representative of all employees in the unit.

The elections themselves must be conducted in *laboratory conditions*, free from threats, coercion, promises, or other misconduct that reasonably tends to interfere with the voters' free choice. An election can be set aside even if the misconduct does not arise to the level of an unfair labor practice.

Management need not, of course, muzzle itself during an organizing campaign. Management is free, for example, to express the company's views, arguments, and opinions about unionization. But management **cannot**:

- threaten employees with retaliation for voting pro-union;
- make promises conditioned on rejection of the union;
- interrogate employees about their organizing activity; or,
- conduct surveillance to determine who is supporting the union.

DUTY TO BARGAIN

Federal labor law makes it an unfair labor practice for a unionized employer to refuse to bargain collectively with its unions. The term *bargain collectively* is defined as the performance of the mutual obligation of the employer and the representative of the employees to meet at reasonable times and confer in good faith with respect to wages, hours, and other terms and conditions of employment.

Closely connected with an employer's duty to bargain is its duty to provide the union with all requested information relevant to the union's duties as representative of union members. The courts apply a broad definition of *relevant* in this context, so that there need only be a *probability* that the information will be useful to the union.

Project Labor Agreements

Special provisions of the NLRA apply to employers in the building and construction industry. An employer in that industry is allowed to enter into a *project labor agreement* (PLA) with a union, even though the union has not yet been established as the representative of a majority of the employees to be covered by the PLA. Typically, a PLA requires all contractors and subcontractors who will work on a project to agree in advance to a *master collective bargaining agreement* under which wages, hours, and other conditions of employment are standardized for all employees at the project. The PLA requirement is incorporated into bid specifications, so any company that is awarded a contract is bound to join in the PLA.

Bargaining Subjects

Bargaining over some subjects is *mandatory*, because those subjects involve *wages, hours, and other terms and conditions of employment.* Other subjects are *permissive*, in that employers and unions are free to bargain over them if they wish, but neither side can insist, to the point of impasse, on inclusion of a mere permissive subject in a collective bargaining agreement.

The mandatory subjects over which employers *must* bargain if requested to do so by their unions are subjects that are *directly germane to the working environment.* However, a company has a right to run its business without interference. So a company need not bargain over *managerial decisions which lie at the core of entrepreneurial control,* such as decisions concerning the commitment of investment capital and the basic scope and direction of the enterprise.

In addition to wages, hours, and benefits, examples of mandatory bargaining subjects include:

- company decisions that directly affect job security, such as a decision to contract out work previously done by union employees (but decisions that only *indirectly* affect job security, such as a decision to discontinue a particular product line, are not subject to mandatory bargaining);
- changes in working conditions;
- union security clauses, where such clauses are not forbidden under state right-to-work laws;
- seniority rights;
- management rights clauses, reserving, for example, the company's right to sell its business free of liabilities under the collective bargaining agreement, to discontinue operations, to determine the number of hours per day and per week that operations should be carried on, and to suspend, discharge or otherwise discipline employees;
- prices and availability of services at in-plant cafeterias and vending machines;
- hiring practices;
- tardiness policies;

- use of company bulletin board;
- drug and alcohol testing; and,
- installation of security cameras to deter employee theft.

Conflicting Duties

Sometimes an employer's duty to bargain will conflict with, or appear to conflict with, other legal duties imposed on the employer. Take, for example, a disabled employee who requests reassignment to a vacant position as an accommodation for a disability. (The duty of reasonable accommodation under the *Americans with Disabilities Act* is discussed in Chapter 17.) While ADA principles might well require the reassignment, doing so may, at the same time, violate established seniority practices. In that circumstance, the Supreme Court has ruled that, generally, seniority will trump ADA requirements. If the employer's seniority practice is one in name only, then the employer will have a difficult time defending a refusal to accommodate based on seniority.

The ADA-NLRA conflict is heightened when the union objects to reassignment on seniority grounds and asks to see the disabled employee's medical records supporting the need for accommodation. Although the records are normally confidential (see Chapter 17), both the *Equal Employment Opportunity Commission (EEOC)* and the Board have ruled that the employer must bargain in good faith over disclosure of the records—even where the disabled employee objects to disclosure.

It is important to remember that even though a subject of negotiation falls in the mandatory category, the employer's only duty is to *discuss* the subject with an open mind. The duty to bargain does not mean that the employer is obligated, after good faith negotiations, to agree with the union's position.

In fact, there are times when agreeing with the union's position would be perilous. Take, for example, a *collective bargaining agreement* (CBA) that restricts an employer's ability to investigate and address a complaint of sexual harassment. Since the employer has a duty under federal anti-discrimination laws to respond promptly and effectively to such complaints, the employer cannot hide behind the provisions of a CBA. As one court pointed out, a CBA is not *imposed* on an employer. Rather, a CBA is an agreement every provision of which has been consented to by the employer. The employer alone must bear the consequences of its labor-relations decisions.

Ending the Duty to Bargain

The employer's duty to bargain ends if a majority of employees in the bargaining unit no longer support the union. For the first three years while a collective bargaining agreement (CBA) is in place, a conclusive presumption exists that the union enjoys majority support. However, after three years or when a CBA expires, the presumption of majority support is no longer conclusive. The employer may then attempt to rebut the presumption by showing that, in fact, the union no longer represents a majority of workers.

ADDITIONAL UNFAIR LABOR PRACTICES

Unfair labor practices (ULPs) come in many forms. A number of them have been discussed above, such as refusal to bargain, selective enforcement of nonsolicitation rules, and adoption of workplace policies that interfere with concerted activities. The NLRA itself lists the following as employer unfair labor practices:

- ◆ interfering with, restraining, or coercing employees in the exercise of the rights guaranteed by the NLRA;
- ◆ dominating or interfering with the formation or administration of a labor organization or contributing financial or other support to it;
- ◆ discriminating in regard to hiring or tenure of employment or any term or condition of employment to encourage or discourage membership in any labor organization;
- ◆ discharging or otherwise discriminating against an employee because he or she has filed charges or given testimony under the NLRA; and,
- ◆ refusing to bargain collectively with the employees' representative.

A few of these merit further discussion.

Company-Dominated Employee Committee

Historically, a favorite way for employers to keep out, or at least keep control of, unions was to form an organization for its employees that appeared to, but in reality did not, give employees a voice in their conditions of employment. By making it illegal for an employer to dominate or interfere with a *labor organization* (defined as any organization of employees that exists to *deal with* the employer concerning grievances, wages, hours, or working conditions), the law effectively stops this practice.

Not all employee committees are illegal. In one case, committees composed of both employees and management made decisions by consensus on a wide variety of workplace issues, such as production, quality, training, attendance, safety, maintenance, and even discipline (short of suspension or discharge). The court ruled that these committees did not exist to *deal with* management; the committees *were* management.

Discrimination against Salts

In an attempt to unionize a nonunion shop, a union may *salt* the shop by sending union organizers as applicants for job openings. When an employer refuses to hire, or even consider such applicants, and the employer is motivated, at least in part, by anti-union animus, the employer commits an unfair labor practice.

Collusion with Union

In a recent case, an employee ran for union office against an incumbent Teamsters official. Despite a hard-fought campaign, the employee failed to defeat the incumbent. During later re-negotiations of the labor contract between the Teamsters and the company, the union offered to concede on a point important to the company if the company would fire the employee. The company had an excuse for doing so, because the employee had been involved in a preventable, although extremely minor, accident while driving a company truck.

The employee's supervisor at first refused to fire him. The supervisor also refused to report the accident, fearing that it would be used as a pretext to discharge the employee. When a higher company official insisted that the employee be fired, the supervisor finally did so. The supervisor himself was then fired, supposedly for failing to report the accident.

Both the employee and the supervisor filed unfair labor practice charges with the Board, which ruled in their favor. On appeal, the court agreed with the Board, pointing out that the NLRA prohibits the discharge of an employee for engaging in protected activity such as running for a union election. It also prohibits the discharge of an employee, including a supervisory-level employee, for refusing to engage in activity that is unlawful under the NLRA. The Court went on to say that unions themselves cannot cause an employee to be fired for engaging in protected activity, nor can unions act in a manner contrary to the interests of their members, as the Teamsters did here by putting the personal gain of incumbent union officers ahead of the interests of union members.

UNION SECURITY AND THE RIGHT TO WORK

Union security clauses are designed to protect union membership or at least union revenue. For example, under a *union shop* arrangement, all eligible employees must join the union upon being hired and must maintain membership as a condition of continued employment. In an *agency shop*, employees need not be union members but they must pay the same union dues that members pay.

Federal labor law permits union shop and agency shop agreements between employers and unions. However, since 1947 when the *National Labor Relations Act* was amended by the *Taft-Hartley Act*, federal labor law has also permitted individual states to enact so-called *right-to-work laws* making union security agreements illegal in those states.

For a current listing of the states that have right-to-work provisions in their state constitutions or statutes, go to **www.dol.gov/esa/ programs/whd/state/righttowork.htm**.

Religions Convictions

If an employee in a union or agency shop holds religious or moral convictions against union participation, federal law provides a limited escape clause. Any employee who is a member of and adheres to a bona fide religion that has historically held conscientious objections to joining or financially supporting labor organizations may, instead of paying union dues, pay an equal amount to a designated charity.

Government Contractors

Special rules apply to government contractors. In February 2001, President Bush signed Executive Order 13201, requiring all federal government contracts to contain a provision that the contractor will post a notice informing employees of their rights not to join a union and to limit their dues payments only to specified union functions. The notice must include the following provision:

> *Under federal law, employees cannot be required to join a union or maintain membership in a union in order to retain their jobs. Under certain conditions, the law permits a union and an employer to enter into a union-security agreement requiring employees to pay uniform periodic dues and initiation fees. However, employees who are not union members can object to the use of their payments for certain purposes and can only be required to pay their share of union costs relating to collective bargaining, contract administration, or grievance adjustment.*

STRIKES AND LOCKOUTS

The NLRA says that, except as otherwise expressly stated in the Act, nothing in the Act shall be construed so as either to interfere with or impede or diminish in any way the *right to strike*. The courts have characterized the right to strike as a legitimate economic tool that implements and supports the principles of the collective bargaining system and that labor unions may use as they see fit.

At the same time, once an employer has exhausted its duty to bargain in good faith and reached an impasse, it is free to use the economic weapons at its disposal. An employer's use of a *lockout* solely in support of a legitimate bargaining position is not in any way inconsistent with the duty to bargain collectively or with the right to strike.

The right to strike includes the *right to picket*. In general, picketing must relate to a primary dispute (a labor dispute between the picketing workers and the employer who is being picketed). Secondary pickets, like secondary strikes (see below), are not protected by the NLRA. The right to strike also includes the right to refuse to cross a picket line in connection with a primary dispute. The right to strike does not include slowdowns, unannounced walkouts, sitdown strikes, violence or threats of violence, or defamation of the employer's goods.

> **EMPLOYER TIP**
>
> A worker who is out on strike is generally ineligible for unemployment insurance benefits. However, a non-striking, unemployed worker will not become ineligible for benefits by turning down a job offer that would involve replacing a striking worker.

When workers are out on strike, they remain employees, since the statutory definition of *employee* includes any individual whose work has ceased as a consequence of, or in connection with, any current labor dispute or because of any unfair labor practice, and who has not obtained any other regular and substantially equivalent employment. This means that an employer cannot retaliate against strikers for their union activity.

An employer's right to hire *permanent replacements* for striking workers depends on the nature of the strike. If the strike is economically motivated (to improve wages, hours, or other terms and conditions of employment), the employer may hire permanent replacements. However, if the strike is to protest an unfair labor practice, the strikers are entitled to reinstatement with backpay upon making an unconditional offer to return to work.

Even for economic strikes, the employer faces certain limitations. For example, it cannot pick and choose who it will replace based on the extent of involvement in union activities. The employer also cannot offer *super seniority* to replacements. Doing so is an unfair labor practice because it discriminates between strikers and nonstrikers, both during and after the strike.

An employee's good faith refusal to work under abnormally dangerous conditions is not a strike under the NLRA. So unlike workers who are on strike for economic reasons, employees who are absent for safety reasons cannot be permanently replaced. (see Chapter 13.)

> **EMPLOYER TIP**
>
> Government contractors who permanently replace lawful strikers are subject to debarment under *Executive Order 12954*.

Limitations

Although the NLRA preserves workers' right to strike, the right is subject to a number of limitations.

Duty to bargain. Perhaps the most important exception to the right to strike arises from the union's duty to bargain in good faith over matters that are considered mandatory subjects of bargaining. Until the employer and the union have bargained to impasse, the union may not strike and the employer may not lock out.

No-strike clause. Employees can bargain away their right to strike by agreeing to a no-strike clause in their collective bargaining agreement.

Secondary strikes. The NLRA expressly prohibits labor unions from engaging in strikes or boycotts for the purpose of forcing a *different* employer to recognize or bargain with a labor union.

Taft-Hartley injunctions. When a strike or lockout affects an entire industry (or a substantial part of an entire industry) and, if permitted to occur or continue, *would imperil the national health or safety*, the President of the United States may appoint a board of inquiry to investigate the issues in dispute and make a report to the President. With the board of inquiry's report in hand, the President may direct the Attorney General to go to court and request an 80-day injunction against the strike or lockout.

Health care institutions. The NLRA requires labor organizations whose employees work at health care institutions to give at least ten days' prior notice, both to the institution itself and the Federal Mediation and Conciliation Service, of its intent to strike, picket, or engage in some other concerted refusal to work. If the Service believes a strike would *substantially interrupt the delivery of health care in the locality concerned*, the Service may appoint a board of inquiry. Pending the board's report and for fifteen days thereafter, the pre-impasse status quo must be maintained.

–22–
ALTERNATIVE WORK ARRANGEMENTS

Employees, especially those in two wage-earner households, are becoming less interested in money and more interested in lifestyle issues, such as time with their families and opportunities for leisure activities. In a tight labor market, employers have to recognize these trends to compete for quality employees.

Employers who are willing to be creative and to consider alternative working arrangements can reap huge rewards in terms of worker satisfaction, leading to greater productivity and less turnover. A number of options are suggested below.

TELECOMMUTING

Telecommuting means working at a remote location that is connected with the office by high-tech communications equipment. By some estimates, as many as 15 million employees now telecommute for at least some portion of the workweek. That number is likely to grow as our economy shifts from goods-based to service-and information-based.

There is no *technical* reason why a computer programmer, for example, or a customer service representative, cannot work just as effectively at home in the suburbs as in a cubicle in the central business district. An employer, however, needs to determine if the arrangement will work for its circumstances.

Establishing a virtual office for selected employees may well be in the employer's best interests. Consider that:

◆ many quality employees find the idea of telecommuting attractive. Implementing a telecommuting program should therefore help to attract and retain just such employees;

◆ so long as care is taken in selecting participants for a telecommuting program, productivity should not suffer. With fewer distractions, productivity may even increase;

◆ telecommuting encourages employees to work independently and to problem-solve on their own (again, careful selection is critical); and,

◆ office space (and rent) can be reduced.

Bills have even been introduced in Congress to give incentives to companies that have telecommuting programs.

Employers who are considering a telecommuting program often worry about the trust issue. They are concerned whether an employee who spends most of his or her time out of the employer's presence will work as diligently as in the office. This concern is probably overstated, given that good candidates for telecommuting are the very employees who should be encouraged to work independently and whose productivity is not measured by hours logged. The programmer, for example, is evaluated less on the time put in, or even on the shear volume of code produced, and more on the quality and timeliness of the product. If his or her programs work as required and are delivered by deadline, it makes little difference that he or she attends to personal matters during *normal* working hours.

Telecommuting is not risk-free. When considering a telecommuting program, the employer should keep in mind that any cost savings at the office may be outweighed by the added expense of installing and maintaining equipment and phone lines at remote sites. The employer also has less direct control over participating employees, over office supplies and equipment, and over confidentiality of business information.

Telecommuting also raises additional legal issues in many areas of employment law.

FLSA

Under the *Fair Labor Standards Act*, nonexempt employees must be paid minimum wage and time-and-a-half for overtime. As with other nonexempt employees, a telecommuter must keep accurate time records so that wage and hour laws can be complied with. It may be more difficult to assure compliance for telecommuters.

OSHA

The *Occupational Safety and Health Administration* initially took the position that the federal safety and health law applies to all work-sites, including home worksites. OSHA withdrew its ruling in the face of widespread objections, but the issue is sure to surface again. OSHA continues to take the position that the federal act does apply to hazardous or dangerous work assigned to telecommuters. (Workplace safety is covered in Chapter 17.)

Workers' Compensation

An *accidental personal injury that arises out of and in the course of employment* is covered by workers' compensation. (see Chapter 11.) For traditional employees who work 9-to-5 at the employer's regular worksite, an injury that occurs offsite and after normal working hours would generally not be covered. But with an injury to a telecommuter, chances are there were no witnesses, so neither the employer nor the workers' compensation carrier can verify the employee's version of how the injury occurred. In other words, in the telecommuting situation, the employer is much more at the mercy of the employee in terms of coverage for injuries.

ADA

The *Americans with Disabilities Act* requires employers to make reasonable accommodations for persons with physical or mental disabilities. If a disabled worker requests telecommuting as an accommodation, the employer should at least consider such an arrangement.

Title VII

Discrimination laws apply to all employment policies and practices, including telecommuting. The opportunity to telecommute must be made available, without discrimination, to both genders.

Ownership of Work Product

Unless you have a contract with your employees as to ownership of *intellectual property* (see Chapter 19), employees may have a claim to any copyrightable works or patentable devices they create. Their claims may be particularly difficult to defeat if they are telecommuters and spend most of their time at home.

Starting a Telecommuting Program

If you make the decision to try telecommuting, consider the suggestions below.

- ◆ Start the program on an experimental basis. For example, limit the program to a particular department, start it on a one- or two-day per week basis, and set a trial period of no more than six months.
- ◆ Establish eligibility requirements for participation. For example, limit the program to particular job categories and to persons who have been with the company for some minimum period, say two years.
- ◆ Choose as participants no more than half of those eligible. That way a control group is retained in order to compare such things as productivity, turnover, and job satisfaction.
- ◆ Select participants carefully. Those who require close supervision and constant feedback, who do not enjoy working alone, or who do not have appropriate work space at home, are obviously not good candidates.
- ◆ Select only those who want to try telecommuting. And allow them to opt out if they find their work quality or job satisfaction deteriorating.
- ◆ Insist that telecommuters designate an appropriate space at home that is dedicated to work. (Some employers actually

inspect the work area before allowing an employee to begin telecommuting.)

- Stress that telecommuting is not intended to resolve day care problems, nor is it a fringe benefit or perk. It is simply a different job assignment. (Some employers require evidence that the employee has made appropriate day care arrangements, although those inquiries can come dangerously close to gender discrimination.)

- Be sure that telecommuters understand they must be willing to come to the office for face-to-face meetings as needed.

- Remind participating employees that they, not the employer, are responsible for any tax consequences of maintaining a home office and for complying with zoning laws.

- Require nonexempt employees (that is, employees who are subject to the minimum wage and overtime requirements of the *Fair Labor Standards Act*) to maintain an accurate log of hours worked for FLSA purposes. An employee who was non-exempt before he or she began telecommuting continues to be non-exempt *while* telecommuting.

- Do not consider a switch to telecommuting as an opportunity to reclassify your employees as independent contractors.

- Do not consider a switch to telecommuting as an opportunity to reduce employee pay, on the theory that employees incur fewer expenses by staying home. This may give rise to equal pay violations.

FLEXTIME

Flextime is an arrangement by which an employee works a normal 40-hour week, but does not work the normal five, eight-hour days. Instead, employee and employer agree on some alternative that yields 40 hours. If, for example, an employee's long-term, trusted babysitter is only available Mondays through Thursdays, the employee could work four, 10-hour days and take Fridays off. Another employee might have a much easier commute working 10-to-6 rather than 9-to-5. If you can accommodate these needs without significant disruption or loss of productivity, then it may be to the employer's benefit to do so.

These suggestions should help make a flextime policy work smoothly.

- *Flextime* means only that the employer is flexible in setting an alternative schedule. It does not mean that the employee can constantly reshuffle his or her workweek to suit the employee's day-by-day whim or convenience.
- As with all other employment decisions, the decision to permit or deny flextime must be made on a nondiscriminatory basis.
- Flextime may not work for all positions. Identify in advance which positions are likely candidates and which positions are not.
- Granting flextime may be a reasonable (and therefore a required) accommodation under the ADA where, for example, a disabled employee needs regularly scheduled medical treatment.
- Remember that whatever arrangements are made, the total number of hours a nonexempt employee can work in any given workweek without triggering overtime pay obligations is 40.

CONTINGENT WORKERS

The term *contingent worker* is loosely defined as any worker who is outside the employer's core workforce of full-time, long-term employees. As used here, the term refers to independent contractors, part-time employees, job-sharing employees, temporary employees, leased employees, and joint employees.

Independent Contractors

Classifying workers as *independent contractors* is fraught with peril. Nevertheless, in a few, carefully designed situations, an independent contractor arrangement can be both safe and effective.

Suppose a key employee, with years of experience and a wealth of institutional knowledge, is approaching minimum retirement age. With the employee's stock options, retirement plan, and independent savings, the employee no longer needs to work, and is looking forward to the free time retirement offers. Yet the employee is not quite ready for a clean break from the company.

The solution? A consultant agreement for a fixed, time period, say two years, renewable year-by-year thereafter if both parties agree. The employee retires and then signs on to be available whenever needed to advise on strategic planning, special projects and the like. Of course, with the employee's experience he or she may also be called upon occasionally to help solve the day-to-day problems routinely addressed as a full-time employee. In consideration for agreeing to hold him or herself available, he or she is paid a monthly retainer by the company, perhaps in the neighborhood of one-half or two-thirds of the former salary. However, the employee is not expected to work any particular hours, no longer has his or her own office or support staff at the company, receives none of the fringe benefits provided regular employees, and is free to consult with other companies. The employee is, therefore, an independent contractor.

An independent contractor relationship also arises when a company contracts out certain functions, without retaining control over who specifically performs those functions or how they are performed. Examples might include janitorial services, landscaping, operating a company cafeteria, and processing payroll. Legal and accounting services are examples of functions that could be performed by in-house employees or by outside independent contractors.

Part-time Employees

A valued employee or well-qualified candidate for employment is only available on a part-time basis. In the past, the company took an all-or-nothing approach—an employee worked either full-time or not at all. By abandoning this rigid approach, the company can benefit from the services of a valued worker, and the worker can remain productive without being tied to the daily 9-to-5 or 8-to-6 grind. Many companies report that their part-timers are so appreciative of the opportunity that their briefcases are always filled with homework and they end up working close to full-time. If you are uncertain whether a part-time arrangement will work, it is best to try it on an experimental basis.

If you decide to try a part-time arrangement, be sure that you and the employee are clear about what benefits the employee will and will not qualify for. While it is theoretically permissible to provide the same benefits to part-timers as to full-timers—medical expense insurance, retirement—your plan documents may limit eligibility to employees who work some minimum number or hours, such as 1000 or 1500 hours per year. Other benefits, such as vacation and sick leave, need to be considered as well.

Finally, keep in mind that discrimination laws apply to part-time as well as full-time employees. For example, the opportunity to go part-time should be made available without regard to sex, race, etc. Allowing a disabled employee or candidate to work part-time may also be a required reasonable accommodation under the ADA, so long as the employee can still perform the essential functions of his or her job.

Job-sharing

A variation on part-time employment is an arrangement by which two part-time employees share the same job, either long-term or for a temporary period. The difference is that, from an organizational viewpoint, the job is still considered a single position.

Frequently, although not always, a proposal to job-share will be initiated by the employee whose changed circumstances limit him or her to part-time work. Before

---

EMPLOYER TIP

Job-sharing can reduce an employer's overtime pay obligations. Even though the job is considered a single position for organizational purposes, if two, part-time, nonexempt employees together work more than 40 hours per week, but neither employee individually works more than 40 hours, the employer will not have to pay time-and-a-half for the excess hours.

making the proposal, the employee should first choose a compatible partner. The employer and employee also need to think through issues such as those below.

- How will the time be shared? Will the employees work half days? Alternate days? Half weeks? Alternate weeks?
- How will the work be allocated? Will each employee perform all functions or will one do only certain tasks?
- How will the employees communicate with each other to keep current?
- Will they overlap on a scheduled or as-needed basis?
- When travel is necessary, will they both go?
- Will the nonworking employee be available, if necessary, to provide continuity in resolving an on-going problem or working on a long-term project?
- What impact will job-sharing have on the cost of employer-provided benefits?
- Will the employees be evaluated individually or as a team?
- What will the effect be on the remaining employee if one of the job-sharers quits or is fired?

Temporary Employees

The term *temporary employee* is used here to mean a full-time or part-time employee whose salary or wages are paid by the employer in the usual way, but whose job is expected to last for only a limited period of time. It does not refer here to a *temp* who is provided by an agency and who remains on the agency's payroll. When an employer hires a temporary employee, say to perform

> **EMPLOYER TIP**
>
> If the temporary employee is kept on past the expected termination date, the employer should consider the need to enroll him or her in benefit plans provided to regular employees. Failure to enroll a so-called perma-temp in plans for which he or she is eligible could violate plan documents and cause loss of favorable tax treatment for the plan.

some specific, non-recurring job, the employer will usually indicate that the employment is expected to terminate by a certain date. In doing so, the employer should also make clear that, despite the stated duration of the employment, the employee is still at-will and can be terminated at any time. (see Chapter 1.) The employer should also make clear what benefits will or will not be provided.

Leased Employees

Leasing arrangements may take several forms. In the familiar temp situation, a temp agency provides a worker for a short period of time, typically to fill in for an employee on leave or to help finish a large project. The employer describes the position to be filled, but does not identify any particular employee to fill it. Although the temp is subject to the employer's control while actually at the employer's worksite, the agency hires, compensates, and fires the employee.

Another leasing arrangement involves shifting a company's existing employees from the company's payroll to a leasing agency's payroll, although the company, not the agency, continues to make all hiring and firing decisions. The purpose is simply to free the employer from payroll and related duties while retaining operational control over the employee.

Under leasing arrangements, the question arises of who the actual employer is for discrimination law purposes. The *Equal Employment Opportunity Commission (EEOC)* has issued guidelines addressing the question under the various scenarios. For example, the true temp is generally considered the employee of the temp agency only, whereas the leased employee is generally considered an employee of both the leasing agency and the company that has retained operational control. In the final analysis, these distinctions do not really matter. The company that operates the worksite will be guilty of illegal discrimination if it discriminates against temps or leased employees at its worksite, if it encourages a temp agency to discriminate with regard to the selection and treatment of temps, or even if it simply knows that the temp agency discriminates.

Joint Employees

A joint employee is a person who, for legal purposes, is an employee of both the company that operates the worksite and a *professional employer organization* (PEO). While the arrangement is similar to leasing, a PEO typically provides a wider range of employment-related services than just payroll. For example, a PEO provides workers' compensation and unemployment insurance, it might assist in hiring, evaluations, discipline, and firing (with the worksite company retaining ultimate control over those decisions), it might provide qualified benefits (medical expense insurance, disability, pension, etc.), and it could handle discrimination and other employment-related claims. PEOs advertise themselves as being in the *business of employment*, enabling the PEO's client to focus on the *business of business*. Through economies of scale, PEOs may well be more cost-effective and efficient in providing employment-related services than some smaller, individual employers.

The relationship between a PEO and the worksite company is based on a lengthy written contract that spells out in detail the parties' responsibilities and their respective liabilities. Any employer considering the PEO option will want to review the contract with great care and arrive at a thorough understanding of just how the relationship works. The PEO should also be able to provide a comparative cost analysis showing whether the arrangement will, in fact, be a financial benefit. Finally, the employer should be satisfied as to the PEO's integrity, experience, and financial standing before signing on.

–23–
EMPLOYER LIABILITY TO THIRD PARTIES

Most of this book deals with the rights and obligations that exist directly between employers and employees, as developed by the common-law or as imposed by government statute or regulation. This chapter considers the liability employers have to third parties arising out of the employment relationship. (The term *third party* as used here means someone outside the employment relationship, such as a customer, another employer, a stockholder, or an innocent bystander.)

VICARIOUS LIABILITY

As a matter of social policy, the law has long held employers liable to pay damages suffered by third parties due to an employee's negligent conduct that occurs within the scope of the employee's employment. This type of indirect or *vicarious liability* to third parties is based on the legal doctrine known as *respondeat superior*—let the employer respond (by paying damages). It does not matter that the employer is guiltless or even that the employee acted contrary to the express instructions of the employer when the negligent conduct occurred.

The policy of imposing vicarious liability is based in part on the notion that, as between the employer (who has the right to control the employee's conduct) and an innocent third party, the employer should bear the cost of the third party's injuries. The policy also recognizes that, for the most part, the employer is in better position to pay damages, or, at least, to assess the risks involved in a business and carry appropriate insurance.

An essential requirement to the imposition of vicarious liability is that the employee be *acting within the scope of employment*. The acting-within-the-scope requirement depends on a number of factors, such as:

- ◆ was the conduct that caused the injury the kind of conduct the employee was hired to perform;
- ◆ did the conduct occur during a period and in a locality reasonably connected with the employee's duties; and,
- ◆ was the conduct motivated, at least in part, by a purpose to serve the employer.

Examples of vicarious employer liability abound—from the trucking company whose driver carelessly runs a red light and strikes a pedestrian, to the local supermarket whose produce manager fails to mop a wet floor resulting in a slip-and-fall injury, to the restaurant whose waiter spills hot coffee on a customer.

INTENTIONAL MISCONDUCT

While vicarious liability is usually based on negligent (that is, careless but unintentional) employee misconduct, intentional acts by an employee can sometimes give rise to employer liability as well. As with negligence, the critical question is whether the employee was acting within the scope of his employment.

Example: An argument develops between the clerk at a retail store and a customer of the store. The customer claims that certain merchandise is on sale, but the clerk insists the sale ended the previous day and the regular price must be paid. As voices rise, the clerk grabs the merchandise from the customer's hand and, in the process, knocks her to the floor and injures her.

Most courts in this situation would impose vicarious liability on the store, even though the clerk's acts were intentional and even though the clerk had been explicitly instructed never to use force with a customer. The reason is that the clerk's conduct occurred within the scope of employment and it was motivated, at least in part, by a purpose to serve the employer.

Sexual Assaults

A surprising number of cases involve sexual assaults. Most courts tend to view sexual assaults as outside the course and scope of employment, since the employee's motivation has nothing to do with serving the employer.

However, some courts have ruled otherwise. In one situation where a furniture store delivery driver sexually assaulted a customer, the court ruled that deliverymen, endeavoring to serve their masters, are likely to be in situations of friction with customers, and that when they secure entry into a customer's premises by means of a badge of employment, these foreseeable altercations may precipitate violence for which recovery may be had, even though the particular type of violence was not in itself anticipated or foreseeable.

> **EMPLOYER TIP**
>
> When a supervisory employee sexually assaults or otherwise harasses a subordinate employee (as opposed to a third party), the employer can be held liable for sex discrimination. (see Chapter 15.)

ALCOHOL-RELATED LIABILITY

Some states have so-called *dramshop laws* that make a tavern owner liable for injuries caused by an intoxicated patron who was served alcohol while obviously intoxicated. These laws also apply to the sale of alcohol to underage persons. If the inebriated patron or minor causes an auto accident while driving home, the tavern owner can be held liable for resulting injuries or death.

> **EMPLOYER TIP**
>
> If the event is mandatory for employees or even if attendance is merely expected, time spent at the event may count as work time. The employer might then be obligated to pay hourly workers and to pay overtime to nonexempt employees.

While most dramshop laws are limited to commercially operated facilities, some laws have been held applicable to social hosts, including employers. If the employer is *selling* the alcohol, dramshop liability is more likely to be imposed.

The following checklist should help limit alcohol-related liability at social functions.

❏ Before the function, review the company's liability insurance policy to be sure the function is covered and that any special policy requirements have been satisfied.

❏ Before the function, remind employees of the company's alcohol abuse policy and its sexual harassment policy.

❏ Schedule the function during nonworking hours at an off-site location.

❏ Obtain any required liquor licenses.

❏ Make clear that attendance is optional.

❏ Open the function to employees' families.

❏ Do not charge for alcoholic beverages.

❏ Be sure that plenty of food and nonalcoholic beverages are available.

❏ Hire professional bartenders. Instruct them not to serve minors or obviously intoxicated guests.

❏ Require that a ticket be turned in for each alcoholic beverage, and issue the tickets at a location removed from the bar.

❏ Close the bar well before the function is scheduled to end.

❏ Provide alternate means of transportation for guests who are unable to drive home safely.

NEGLIGENT EMPLOYMENT

Just because an employer is not *vicariously* liable, does not mean it necessarily escapes liability. Employers can be held *directly* liable under the doctrine of *negligent employment* (sometimes called *negligent hiring, negligent supervision, or negligent retention*, depending on the circumstances) based on the employer's hiring or retaining an employee who had a known or discoverable propensity for violence or other criminal conduct. These types of claims will succeed if it is shown that the employee did, in fact, have a dangerous propensity, that the employer knew about or could easily have discovered that propensity, and that the employer nevertheless placed the employee in a position in which he or she could do harm.

Example: Suppose that your company owns and operates several apartment buildings. In each of those buildings, it has a resident manager who has a passkey to all the units. One day a newly hired resident manager uses the passkey to gain entrance to a unit, where the manager assaults the tenant.

The manager has obviously committed a crime that is answerable in criminal court. The tenant can also sue the manager in civil court for damages. Chances are, however, that the manager has limited financial means, so that the tenant would like to be able to sue your company on a theory of vicarious liability. As pointed out above, most courts take the view that the manager's assault was outside the scope of his employment, so the company has no vicarious liability.

But suppose the manager had a history of similar assaults and the company either knew about that history or it could easily have found out had it called the manager's references or done a criminal convictions check. In that case, the company will likely have *direct* liability, on the theory that the company owed a special duty to its tenants not to employ a person as resident manager who had a history of assaults.

In short, when the work involves serious risk of harm to others if the employee is unfit, the employer may not just assume that the employee is competent. Instead, the employer must conduct an appropriate investigation, such as checking references, inquiring about gaps in employment, and doing a criminal convictions check.

No list of what work qualifies as involving a serious risk of harm to others could be exhaustive. Examples might include:

- resident managers;
- airline pilots;

- train, bus, and subway drivers;
- heavy equipment operators;
- toxic waste handlers;
- armed security guards; and,
- health care workers who have close physical or psychological contact with patients.

The best approach is to consider the risks a particular employment position—any position—could present, and then make inquiries that are reasonable under the circumstances to ferret out any dangerous propensities in an applicant for the position. Always make a written record of your inquiries and place it in the applicant's or employee's personnel file.

Direct employer liability can also arise when an employer allows an employee to use the employer's premises for purely personal reasons, but the employer knows the employee's behavior is likely to be dangerous. To illustrate, say that workers routinely engage in horseplay during their lunch hour, putting customers or passersby at risk. Courts have said that an employer's failure to police its own premises in this circumstance will subject the employer to suit.

> **EMPLOYER TIP**
>
> You should retain records of pre-employment investigations on rejected applicants, as well as persons whom you actually hire, as evidence in the event of a later discrimination claim.

Negligent entrustment is another basis for employer liability. This could arise, for example, where the employer allows an employee to use a company vehicle or some other dangerous instrument, knowing that the employee is unable or unlikely to use the instrument safely.

REFERENCES

Employers face an obvious dilemma in giving references. If they give what they believe to be an accurate reference, they may get sued for defamation by the former employee. (see Chapter 4.) If they withhold information, they are subject to possible suit by a subsequent employer or by the victims of subsequent misconduct. One solution is to adopt a *no-reference policy* under which the employer will only confirm the dates of prior employment. This protects the employer, but at a substantial social cost. Another solution is to require a *written release* from the former employee before giving a substantive reference. Whatever course you take, make sure that any recommendation letter does not contain any affirmative misrepresentation regarding the former employee.

TORTIOUS INTERFERENCE

When a successor employer hires an employee who has previously worked for the competition, or for a company in a related or similar field, the successor employer needs to be concerned about its own potential liability. For example, the new employer can be sued under the *Uniform Trade Secrets Act* if it encourages or participates in the theft of trade secrets from the former employer. (see Chapter 19.) An employer can also be sued on a cause of action known as *tortious interference with contract* if it knows that the new employee is bound by a noncompete or confidentiality agreement and, despite that knowledge, encourages the employee to breach the agreement or enjoys the benefits of a breach. (Noncompete agreements are also covered in Chapter 19.)

Because the validity of noncompete agreements depends on the unique circumstances of each case, it is not always easy to tell in advance whether a judge will enforce a particular agreement as written, will enforce it with modifications, or will reject it entirely as unenforceable. One thing an employer does know, however, is that litigation over a non-compete agreement or a trade secrets claim will be costly, time-consuming, and disruptive.

When hiring a new employee, follow these guidelines to reduce the risk of suit by the employee's former employer.

- ◆ Insist on a clean break. Require your new employee to resign completely from his or her old job and cease all work for the former employer before starting a new job with you.
- ◆ Insist on reviewing any *personal files* your new employee brings with him or her (or have a third party do it for you) for possi-

ble trade secrets. Return any improperly removed materials without studying or copying them.

◆ Ask candidates for employment whether they are covered by noncompete or similar agreements or by any court orders or injunctions relating to employment. If they say *no*, get them to certify that to you in writing as part of the application process. If they say *yes*, get a copy of the agreement or order.

◆ If a candidate is covered by a noncompete, nonsolicitation, or confidentiality agreement, review it carefully, and have it reviewed by counsel if there is any question as to its scope or enforceability.

◆ If you decide to hire an employee who is covered by a noncompete agreement, make sure you can assign him or her work that does not violate the agreement and that you can separate him or her from any involvement—even casual lunch-time involvement—with your existing employees who are engaged in competing work.

◆ Do not overlook the possibility of negotiating a three-way settlement among you, an attractive candidate for employment, and the candidate's former employer. A lump-sum payment to the former employer or a short-term arrangement that isolates the employee from direct competition may well be an acceptable compromise.

RACKETEER INFLUENCED AND CORRUPT ORGANIZATIONS ACT

All employees must, at time of hire, prove their eligibility to work in the U.S. by completing Form I-9 and exhibiting appropriate documentation to the employer. (see Chapter 2.) It may come as a surprise that employers who hire undocumented workers may be classed as *racketeers* under the federal *Racketeer Influenced and Corrupt Organizations Act* (RICO).

RICO was passed in 1970 to combat organized crime. It provides both criminal penalties and civil liability for persons who engage in a *pattern of racketeering activity* through an *enterprise*. Racketeering activity is the commission of one of the numerous federal or state crimes listed in RICO, and a pattern of racketeering activity is committing two or more of those crimes. Among the listed crimes is any act that is indictable under the *Immigration and Nationality Act*. An enterprise is basically any form of association.

While RICO does not really change an employer's obligations when it comes to hiring undocumented workers, it does raise the stakes substantially. RICO provides for *treble* (triple) damages, just as antitrust laws do, and RICO permits a successful plaintiff to recover attorneys' fees.

INDEMNITY AND SUBROGATION

Employees themselves are personally liable to third parties for their actions, even when they are acting in the course of their employment and even though the employer may be vicariously liable as well. This would certainly be true, for example, in the case of an employee who, while driving a company vehicle, negligently runs a red light and injures a pedestrian.

An employee's personal liability can also occur in more subtle circumstances. Take, for example, the chief financial officer of a company whose duties include serving as a trustee of the company's profit-sharing plan. If the CFO misreads a provision of the plan and mistakenly reduces benefits to a plan participant, he or she might be held personally liable. The same applies to the human resources director who gives a reference for a former employee and inadvertently includes a false, highly damaging statement.

Absent an indemnity arrangement, the company usually has no legal obligation to offer protection. In fact, the company could, if it wished, even demand reimbursement from the CFO or HR director for whatever loss the company suffers through the company's own vicarious liability. However, so long as the employee acted in good faith—that is, did not knowingly or intentionally shortchange the participant or maliciously write the defamatory reference letter— most companies will usually offer full protection from claims of third parties (called *indemnity*), by defending any lawsuits and paying any damage awards.

As senior-level employees become aware of the personal liability risks they face, they often bargain with their employers for protection. This protection may take the form of an indemnity clause in their employment contracts, or an indemnity provision in the company's corporate bylaws.

The decision to provide indemnity should not be made lightly or without professional advice. The following should be considered before implementing any plan.

- ◆ Many states have statutory provisions governing the extent to which corporations may, or must, indemnify corporate officials. The indemnity clause needs to be coordinated with those statutory provisions.
- ◆ For tax purposes, indemnity payments may not be fully deductible by the employer if they are unreasonable or excessive, or if they cover fines or penalties.
- ◆ Indemnity payments made in connection with a highly publicized event could prove embarrassing to the company or could anger shareholders.
- ◆ Indemnity provisions should be reviewed for consistency with the company's Directors and Officers (D&O) insurance coverage. The company does not want to make indemnity promises that its own insurance company will not cover.

INSIDER TRADING

Insider trading—buying or selling publicly-traded securities using information that is generally not available to the public—is illegal under federal and state laws. Senior company officials should know that. Lower-level employees may not.

Example: Suppose a company whose stock is thinly traded on a regional stock exchange is approached by a Fortune 1000 company concerning a possible merger. Negotiations progress to the point at which deal papers are drawn, press releases are drafted, and appropriate regulatory filings are prepared. At just that point, a mid-level manager for the smaller company, who has never previously owned any stock in his company, places an order with his broker for 10,000 shares of company stock. The unusual trading activity is flagged by the regional stock exchange, which notifies the Securities and Exchange Commission. An SEC investigator telephones the smaller company for information and is told about the possible merger. When the Fortune 1000 company learns of the phone call, it immediately cancels merger negotiations and threatens suit against the smaller company. A disaster, to say the least.

An insider trade can prove highly embarrassing. It may trigger an SEC or stock exchange investigation. It can result in criminal charges or civil fines. It may prompt a class-action suit, and it can kill a stock offering, a merger negotiation, or some other pending transaction. In short, it is in the company's interest to prevent insider trading.

A company should take the following steps to prevent insider trading in its own stock or in stock of companies with which it has business relationships. The best way to do this would be to:

- ◆ adopt, publicize, and enforce a strict policy against insider trading;
- ◆ educate employees at all levels about the risks involved, and;
- ◆ safeguard sensitive information.

CONCLUSION

The rules of modern workplace law defy capture in a single volume. And even if capture were possible, it would only serve to frame a scene in a movie that is still being filmed.

This book has accomplished much if it has provided you with a broad understanding of the employment relationship and alerted you to the hazards you face as an employer. The next time you hear a racial epithet on the factory floor or see a sexist cartoon on the company bulletin board, you will know that trouble lurks. And when rumors start flying that a handful of employees have been talking about unions, you will consult competent labor counsel instead of firing the *troublemakers*.

Equipped with this new knowledge, and no longer bewildered by the complexities of the employment relationship, you are now free to devote your energies where they belong—making your business a success!

GLOSSARY

360-degree evaluation. An evaluation system that has employees not only rated by supervisors, but by peers, direct reports, and sometimes clients and customers.

401(k) plan. A type of qualified retirement plan authorized by Section 401(k) of the Internal Revenue Code.

A

abusive discharge. Sometimes called *wrongful discharge*, the termination of an at-will employee for engaging in protected activity or for refusing to commit an illegal act.

affirmative action. Action, required of most government contractors and subcontractors, to assure equal employment of minorities, women, persons with disabilities, and certain veterans.

Age Discrimination in Employment Act (ADEA). The ADEA prohibits discrimination because of age against persons forty or more years old.

agent. A person who acts on behalf of another (called the principal), who has the power to bind the other person in contract. Employees and independent contractors can each be, but are not necessarily, agents of their employers.

agency shop. A type of union security arrangement where union membership is optional, but as a condition of continued employment, nonunion members pay to the union amounts equal to initiation fees and periodic dues paid by union members.

alternative dispute resolution (ADR). A procedure for resolving disputes other than by a lawsuit. Arbitration and mediation are forms of ADR.

alternate payee. An employee's spouse, child, or other dependent who, pursuant to a Qualified Domestic Relations Order (QDRO), is awarded an interest in the employee's pension plan. Also, an employee's child who, pursuant to a Qualified Medical Child Support Order (QMCSO), becomes entitled to health insurance coverage under the plan in which the employee participates.

Americans with Disabilities Act (ADA). The ADA prohibits discrimination against a qualified person with a disability and requires reasonable accommodation of disabled applicants and employees.

arbitration. One of several forms of dispute resolution that are alternatives to litigation in court.

at-will employment. Employment that is not for any fixed or definite term. In an at-will employment relationship, the employee can quit at any time and the employer can fire the employee at any time with or without cause.

B

backpay. Pay awarded to an employee or applicant for employment that, but for discrimination, an unfair labor practice, or other wrongful conduct by the employer, would have been earned between the time of the wrongful conduct and the time the award is made.

base period. For unemployment insurance purposes, the most recent four out of five completed calendar quarters (quarters in which the employee worked) preceding the filing of a benefit claim.

base period employer. Any employer for whom an unemployment insurance claimant worked during his or her base period.

belo plan. An exception to the *Fair Labor Standards Act's* general overtime rules that allows an employer to pay a fixed salary to nonexempt employees who work an irregular number of hours from week to week because of the nature of the job.

blacklisting. The practice of circulating the names of former employees who should not be hired because of their history of union organizing efforts or other protected activity.

bona fide occupational qualification (BFOQ). BFOQs are exceptions to certain forms of discrimination.

borrowed servant. An employee who is transferred from his or her regular employer to another employer on a temporary basis.

Bureau of Citizenship and Immigration Services (BCIS). Part of the U.S. Department of Homeland Security. The BCIS is the successor agency to the Immigration and Naturalization Service of the Department of Justice.

C

cafeteria plan. *See section 125 plan.*

cash balance plan. A pension plan that has characteristics of both a defined contribution plan and a defined benefit plan. In a cash balance plan, the ultimate benefit is defined in terms of periodic contributions to a separate hypothetical account for each employee and an assumed interest rate earned on those contributions.

cash or deferral arrangement (CODA). A feature of some deferred compensation plans under which the employee can elect to take taxable cash or a nontaxable contribution to the plan.

casual employee. An employee who is not covered by workers' compensation because he or she works irregularly, for a brief period only, doing work not normally performed by employees of the employer.

cause. A reason that is legally sufficient to discharge an employee who has an employment contract.

Chapter 13. A provision of the U.S. Bankruptcy Code that allows an individual with a regular income to spread out repayment of his or her debts for up to three years.

child labor. Labor by a person under 18 years of age.

Circular E. An IRS publication for employers, also known as Publication 15, containing instructions and tables for federal income tax withholding and payroll tax obligations.

Civil Rights Act. The Act that was significantly amended in 1991, is the principal federal statute prohibiting discrimination in employment and public accommodations. *Title VII* is the portion of the Civil Rights Act dealing with employment discrimination.

closed shop. A type of union security agreement where employees must be union members in order to be hired.

COBRA (Consolidated Omnibus Budget Reconciliation Act). COBRA requires continuation of group health insurance coverage under certain circumstances when coverage would otherwise end.

collective bargaining agreement (CBA). An agreement between an employer and a union dealing with employee pay, benefits, disciplinary and grievance procedures, and other conditions of employment.

commerce clause. A clause in Article I of the U.S. Constitution empowering Congress to regulate commerce with foreign nations, among the several States, and with the Indian tribes.

common-law. The body of legal principles developed by court decisions in England and this country that are not based on legislative enactments.

comp time (compensatory time). Leave taken in lieu of overtime pay. Use of comp time to compensate a nonexempt employee who works more than 40 hours in one workweek generally violates wage and hour laws.

concerted activity. Union organizing activity or other activity by employees for the purpose of bettering wages, hours, or working conditions. Concerted activity is protected by the *National Labor Relations Act*.

consideration. In contract law, the inducements, rights, or things of value that the parties to a contract agree to exchange.

constructive discharge. A termination where the employee is forced to quit, either directly or as a result of intolerable working conditions.

consumer report. A credit report and/or an investigative report about a person. The obtaining and use of consumer reports by employers are regulated by the Fair Credit Reporting Act and by some state laws.

consumer reporting agency (CRA). A person or entity which, for a fee, regularly assembles or evaluates credit information or other information on consumers for the purpose of furnishing consumer reports to third parties. The obtaining and use of consumer reports from a CRA is regulated by the Fair Credit Reporting Act and by some state laws.

contingent worker. A worker who is outside an employer's core workforce of full-time, long-term employees. Contingent workers include independent contractors, part-time employees, job sharers, temporary employees, leased employees, and joint employees.

D

D & O insurance (directors and officers insurance). Coverage that protects company officials from personal liability for good faith actions taken in the course of their employment.

defamation. A false written (libel) or spoken (slander) statement that injures a person's reputation.

deferred compensation. Compensation set aside for an employee but not currently taxable to the employee because the employee's receipt and enjoyment of the compensation is deferred.

defined benefit plan. *See defined contribution plan.*

defined contribution plan. A type of retirement plan in which the amount contributed to the plan is fixed by a predetermined formula and the benefit amount depends on the value of each participant's separate account within the plan.

dilution. Reduction in the value of a company's outstanding stock caused by issuance of additional stock.

direct liability. Liability for an employer's own negligence in hiring, retaining, or failing to supervise an employee who presents an unreasonable risk of injury or damage to the public.

direct threat defense. A provision of the *Americans with Disabilities Act* that allows employers to exclude disabled employees from certain jobs where the disabled person would pose a direct threat to his or her own health or safety or to the health or safety of others in the workplace.

disability. For *Americans with Disabilities Act* purposes, a physical or mental impairment that substantially limits one or more major life activities.

discovery. The formal process by which parties to court proceedings obtain information and documents from opposing parties and question opposing parties and nonparty witnesses under oath.

discrimination. Treating an applicant, an employee, or a group of applicants or employees differently for a reason that is prohibited by law, such as race, color, religion, gender, national origin, age, disability, etc.

disparate impact. *See disparate treatment.*

disparate treatment. In discrimination law, intentional adverse treatment of an applicant or employee because of his or her race, religion, gender, etc.

domestic partners. Persons other than spouses and relatives who live together and have a voluntary, committed relationship with each other.

due process clause. A clause in the Fifth Amendment to the U.S. Constitution that provides that no person shall be deprived of life, liberty, or property, without due process of law. The Fourteenth Amendment also prohibits states from depriving any person of life, liberty, or property, without due process of law.

E

earned rate. For unemployment insurance purposes, the rate used to compute an employer's contribution obligation based upon the employer's actual claims experience.

Electronic Communications Privacy Act (ECPA). The federal law that regulates the interception of wire, electronic, and oral communications.

Electronic Federal Tax Payment System (EFTPS). The system for paying employment taxes and other federal taxes electronically.

employee. A person whose manner of work the employer has a right to control.

employee assistance plan (EAP). A fringe benefit some employers offer, that may include short-term counseling, alcohol or drug abuse treatment, and similar services.

employee handbook. A handbook of rules, policies, procedures, etc., issued by the employer for the guidance and information of employees.

Employee Polygraph Protection Act (EPPA). The EPPA prohibits employers from using lie detectors except in extremely limited circumstances.

Employee Retirement Income Security Act (ERISA). ERISA is the principal federal law regulating retirement plans and other employee benefit plans.

employee stock ownership plan (ESOP). An ESOP is a form of retirement plan in which the retirement fund holds stock of the employer company.

employee stock purchase plan. A plan for granting stock options to an employer's general workforce in proportion to their compensation.

Employer Identification Number (EIN). The number employers obtain from the IRS to use in filing tax returns and reports.

Employer Information Report (EEO-1). The form filed annually with the *Equal Employment Opportunity Commission* by employers who have 100 or more employees, and, by certain government contractors, to provide the EEOC with a breakdown of the workforce by sex, race, and national origin.

employment contract. An agreement that employment will last for a specific term and/or that the employment will only be terminated for cause or in accordance with specified procedures.

employment practices liability insurance (EPL insurance). A relatively new form of coverage that protects employers from employment-related claims.

Equal Employment Opportunity Commission (EEOC). The EEOC is the principal enforcer of Title VII of the federal *Civil Rights Act*, the *Age Discrimination in Employment Act*, and the employment provisions of the *Americans with Disabilities Act*.

Equal Pay Act. *See Fair Labor Stamdards Act.*

ergonomics. The science that studies the relationship between workers and their work environment.

excess benefit plan. An unfunded plan maintained by an employer solely to avoid the contribution and benefit limitations imposed on qualified plans by Section 415 of the Internal Revenue Code. Excess benefit plans are exempt from most provisions of the Employee Retirement Income Security Act.

exempt employee. An employee who is not covered by minimum wage and overtime requirements of the federal *Fair Labor Standards Act* (and the parallel provisions of state law) because he or she is employed in an executive, administrative, or professional capacity or falls within some other statutory exemption.

Executive Order 11246. An executive order issued by President Lyndon Johnson in 1965 which, as amended, prohibits employment discrimination and requires affirmative action plans by most federal contractors and subcontractors.

exit interview. A meeting between an employee and management immediately prior to termination of the employee's employment.

F

Fair Credit Reporting Act (FCRA). The FCRA regulates the obtaining and use of consumer reports.

fair employment practice agency (FEPA). FEPAs, also known as deferral agencies, are state or local agencies that enforce equal employment laws comparable to federal law.

Fair Labor Standards Act (FLSA). The FLSA establishes minimum wages and overtime requirements and prohibits oppressive child labor. As amended by the *Equal Pay Act*, the FLSA also prohibits employers from paying different wages to males and females who do the same work.

False Claims Act. A federal law that permits a whistleblower to file suit in the name of the U.S. Government against companies that have allegedly defrauded the Government.

Family and Medical Leave Act (FMLA). The FMLA requires employers who have fifty or more employees to grant extended leave to employees with serious medical conditions, for the birth or adoption of a child, and when a family member has a serious medical condition.

Federal Arbitration Act (FAA). The FAA provides for enforcement of arbitration agreements.

Federal Insurance Contribution Act (FICA). FICA imposes a tax on employers and an identical tax on employees to fund the social security system.

federal per diem rates method. A method for reimbursing employees for business travel based on daily rates established by the federal government. The rates are divided into two groups, known as CONUS (continental U.S.) and OCONUS (outside continental U.S.).

Federal Unemployment Tax Act (FUTA). FUTA imposes a tax on employers to finance the federal portion of the unemployment insurance program.

fiduciary. A person who holds a special position of trust with respect to another person, such as the trustee of a pension plan. Fiduciaries are required to act solely in the best interests of the persons for whom they hold the special trust position and not in their own self-interest.

flexible spending arrangement or flexible spending account (FSA). An employer-sponsored arrangement under which an employee can contribute pre-tax dollars to a special trust account and obtain reimbursement out of the account for uninsured medical expenses and/or dependent care expenses.

flextime. An arrangement under which employees may choose a work schedule different from the employer's normal work schedule, so long as the total hours worked per week meet the employer's minimum requirement.

fresh consideration. Something of value, such as a promotion or pay raise, offered to an existing employee in exchange for the employee's signing a non-competition agreement.

Friendship, Commerce, and Navigation Treaties (FCN Treaties). FCN treaties permit foreign companies doing business in the U.S. to engage, at their choice, high-level personnel essential to the functioning of the enterprise, effectively permitting them to discriminate in favor of their own nationals.

front pay. *See backpay.*

full faith and credit clause. A provision of the U.S. Constitution that requires each state to recognize the laws of every other state.

G

garnishment. A wage attachment. A court order requiring the employer to pay a percentage of the wages of an employee (garnishee) to someone (garnishor) who has obtained a money judgment against the employee.

general duty clause. The *Occupational Safety and Health Act* requirement that every employer furnish its employees with employment and a place of employment free from recognized hazards that cause or are likely to cause death or serious physical harm.

general employer. An employer who transfers an employee to another employer (called the *special employer*) for a limited period of time. While the transfer is in effect, the special employer has temporary responsibility and control over the employee's work.

glass ceiling. The invisible barrier to advancement faced by women and minorities.

golden parachute. Payments promised to key personnel in the event of a change in ownership or control of a company.

H

half-time plan. Sometimes called a fluctuating workweek plan, an exception to the *Fair Labor Standards Act's* general overtime rules that allows an employer to pay only half-time, instead of time-and-a-half, for overtime worked by nonexempt employees. The exception only applies where the employee's workweek fluctuates and where the employer has entered into an agreement to pay a fixed salary to cover the straight time component of all time worked in a workweek.

harassment. A form of discrimination involving conduct that has the purpose or effect of unreasonably interfering with a person's work performance or that creates an intimidating, hostile, or offensive work environment.

Health Insurance Portability and Accountability Act (HIPAA). HIPAA imposes requirements on group health plans to make it easier for employees who change jobs to be eligible for full coverage under their new employer's plan.

health reimbursement arrangement (HRA). An employer-funded health insurance plan, often paired with a high-deductible group health insurance policy, used to reimburse employees for uninsured medical expenses.

hostile environment. A work environment made offensive by harassment.

human resources (HR). Formerly called *personnel.*

I

I-9. The form employers must complete and maintain for each employee as a record that the employee is eligible to work in the U.S.

Immigration Reform and Control Act of 1986 (IRCA). An amendment to the *Immigration and Nationality Act,* IRCA prohibits employers from hiring aliens who are ineligible to work in the U.S. IRCA also prohibits discrimination against noncitizens.

indemnity plan. *See managed care plan.*

independent contractor. A person whose work methods the employer does not have a right to control.

inevitable disclosure. A legal doctrine, adopted in a few states, permitting a court to enjoin a former employee from working for a competitor when the former employee has confidential information and when the old and new jobs are so similar that disclosure of the confidential information is inevitable.

inside build-up. The accumulation of tax-exempt income within a deferred compensation plan.

insider trading. Buying or selling publicly-traded securities using information that is generally not available to the public. Insider trading is illegal under federal and state laws.

Internal Revenue Code (IRC). The set of laws passed by Congress regarding tax related matters.

involuntary servitude. Slavery or other forms of compulsory work, prohibited by the Thirteenth Amendment to the Constitution and federal law.

L

last chance contract. An agreement between an employer and an employee that gives the employee a final opportunity to conform to company requirements or else be fired.

liquidated damages. In contract law, an amount specified by the parties in advance that a party would be entitled to receive if the other party breaches the contract. While a liquidated damage provision eliminates the need to prove a party's actual damages, the amount of damages specified must be reasonable and cannot be so high as to amount to a penalty that the courts will not enforce.

living wage. A wage rate higher than the federal minimum wage that some local jurisdictions require government contractors to pay their employees.

love contract. A contract required by some employers that sets out certain ground rules for an office romance, especially one between a supervisor and a lower-level employee. By having the parties acknowledge that the relationship is consensual and can be terminated by either party at any time, the employer hopes to avoid later claims of discrimination based on sexual harassment.

M

managed care plan. A type of health insurance plan in which the participant is limited in his or her choice of health insurance providers but pays either nothing or only a small amount for services.

managers only manual. A manual of policies and procedures distributed only to management-level employees.

mass layoff. A layoff of at least fifty employees at a single site that amounts to at least 33% of the workforce at that site.

master-servant relationship. An outdated reference to an employer-employee relationship.

Material Safety Data Sheet (MSDS). An *Occupational Safety and Health Administration* form used to communicate information about hazardous chemicals.

minimum wage. The minimum hourly amount that employers must pay employees pursuant to the *Fair Labor Standards Act* (or the parallel provisions of state law).

ministerial exception. An exception to laws prohibiting discrimination on the basis of religion. Under the ministerial exception, religious organizations may discriminate in the selection of their clergy.

N

negligent employment. *See direct liability.*

nepotism. The practice of hiring relatives or favoring them in workplace decisions.

no-match letter. A letter issued by the Social Security Administration to an employer stating that an employee's name and Social Security Number as reported on a W-2 form do not match the Administration's records.

noncompete agreement. An agreement that an employee will not compete with his former employer after the employment terminates.

nonexempt employee. An employee who is covered by minimum wage and overtime requirements of the *Fair Labor Standards Act* (or the parallel provisions of state law).

North American Industry Classification System (NAICS). A system of six-digit numbers used to classify industries. NAICS is replacing the SIC system.

O

Occupational Safety and Health Act (OSHA). An act that requires employers to comply with a variety of safety and health standards for the protection of thier employees.

Office of Federal Contract Compliance Programs (OFCCP). An office within the U.S. Department of Labor's Employment Standards Administration that administers government contractors' compliance with Executive Order 11246, the *Rehabilitation Act*, and the *Vietnam Era Veterans' Readjustment Assistance Act*.

Older Workers Benefit Protection Act (OWBPA). An amendment to the *Age Discrimination in Employment Act*, OWBPA imposes special requirements for releases of ADEA claims in connection with exit incentive programs offered to groups of employees.

open shop. A workplace that employs both union and nonunion employees.

oppressive child labor. With certain exceptions, employment of any child who is under the age of 16, regardless of the occupation, and employment of a child who is between the ages of 16 and 18 in mining, manufacturing, or other hazardous industries.

P

paid time off (PTO). PTO plans replace various forms of leave traditionally offered to employees.

perma-temp. Slang for a worker who, despite long tenure on the job, is still classified as temporary for benefit or other purposes.

personnel manual. *See employee handbook.*

personal protective equipment (PPE). Equipment required by various *Occupational Safety and Health Administration* standards to be worn to reduce excessive exposure to workplace conditions that could cause personal injury.

polygraph. A lie detector. Polygraph tests in connection with employment are generally prohibited.

predatory hiring. A campaign to hire workers away from a particular company in order to harm that company's ability to compete. Predatory hiring may violate antitrust laws.

Pregnancy Discrimination Act (PDA). An amendment to *Title VII* of the federal *Civil Rights Act* that defines sex discrimination to include discrimination because of pregnancy, childbirth, or related medical conditions.

prevailing wage. The wage paid for a particular job category. An employer must obtain a prevailing wage determination as part of the process of applying for an H-1B visa. State and local government contracts sometimes contain provisions requiring contractors to pay their employees prevailing wages.

principal. The person on whose behalf an agent acts.

professional employment organization (PEO). An organization that, for a fee, jointly employs a company's employees in order to provide HR-related functions, such as benefit plan administration, payroll services, and workers' compensation coverage.

progressive discipline. A policy of imposing increasingly severe discipline for repetitive misconduct.

project labor agreement (PLA). A multi-employer pre-hire agreement used on construction projects, that requires all contractors and subcontractors who will work on the project to agree in advance to a master collective bargaining agreement.

protected health information (PHI). Information about employees and others that is subject to privacy regulations of the *Health Insurance Portability and Accountability Act.*

Q

Qualified Domestic Relations Order (QDRO). An order entered by a domestic relations court in compliance with the *Employee Retirement Income Security Act* that awards an interest in a pension plan to an alternate payee.

qualifying event. An event that triggers an opportunity to elect COBRA coverage.

Qualified Medical Child Support Order (QMCSO). Under a QMCSO, an employer with a group health insurance plan can be ordered to enroll an employee's child (the alternate payee) if the employer's plan includes a family coverage feature.

qualified plan. *See excess benefit plan.*

quid pro quo. A type of sex discrimination involving sexual favors in exchange for tangible job benefits.

R

rabbi trust. A deferred compensation arrangement for select management or highly compensated employees. Employer contributions to a rabbi trust are not currently deductible by the employer or includible in the employer's income because the trust assets remain subject to claims by creditors of the employer.

Racketeer Influenced and Corrupt Organizations Act (RICO). A 1970 federal statute, primarily aimed at organized crime, that has been applied to employers who repeatedly violate immigration or other laws.

reasonable accommodation. A requirement under the *Americans with Disabilities Act* to protect persons with disabilities. A requirement under *Title VII* of the federal *Civil Rights Act* to allow for employee religious practices.

Rehabilitation Act. Federal law that prohibits most federal contractors and subcontractors from discriminating against persons with disabilities and requires affirmative action to ensure equal employment opportunity.

restrictive covenant. A noncompete agreement. An agreement that an employee will not compete with a former employer after the employment terminates.

respondeat superior. The legal doctrine that imposes vicarious liability on an employer for the negligence of its employees.

retaliation. Taking adverse action against an employee for exercising rights protected by law.

reverse discrimination. Discrimination against members of an historically advantaged group which results from treating members of an historically disadvantaged group more favorably. Quota systems and some affirmative action plans can amount to reverse discrimination.

right-to-work law. A state law that prohibits collective bargaining agreements from containing union security clauses.

S

salt. A person who applies for a job in order to unionize the workplace once hired.

second injury fund. A special fund established under state workers' compensation laws. Second (or *subsequent*) injury funds share responsibility for benefits due employees who have pre-existing, nondisabling conditions and who become disabled through the combined effects of the pre-existing condition and a subsequent injury.

Section 125 plan. A benefit plan that offers cash, or a variety of benefits in lieu of cash from which the employee may choose. Cash payments are taxable to the employee, but qualified benefits are not.

seniority system. A system followed by management, either by custom or pursuant to a collective bargaining agreement with its unions, under which an employee with greater longevity will be favored for promotion or reassignment over otherwise equally qualified candidates.

special employer. An employer who has borrowed an employee from another employer (called the *general employer*) for a limited time period and has temporary responsibility and control over the employee's work.

Standard Industrial Classification system (SIC). A system of four-digit numbers used to classify industries. The SIC system is being replaced by NAICS.

statute of frauds. A provision in state law requiring certain contracts to be in writing to be enforceable in court.

statute of limitations. A provision in law that bars lawsuits that are not filed within a specified time period.

statutory employee. A person who, by law, is classified as an employee for income tax, workers' compensation, or other purposes, even though he or she might otherwise qualify as an independent contractor.

subrogation. The right of a person who pays a claim to seek reimbursement from the wrongdoer. (When an employee is injured on the job by the negligence of a third party and receives workers' compensation benefits from his or her employer, the employer is subrogated to the employee's rights and may sue the third party.)

Summary Plan Description (SPD). A written description, required by the *Employee Retirement Income Security Act*, of the provisions of a benefit plan provided by the employer.

supremacy clause. The provision in Article VI of the U.S. Constitution stating that the Constitution, the laws of the United States, and treaties "shall be the supreme Law of the Land" binding in every state.

T

tax deferral. A feature of some employee benefit plans, such as qualified pension plans, that permits the employee to exclude plan contributions from gross income for income tax purposes until a later time, such as retirement.

telecommuting. Working at home or at a facility other than the employer's office, that is connected with the office by high tech communications equipment.

teleworking. The *Equal Employment Opportunity Commission's* name for telecommuting.

tester. A person who applies for a job for the sole purpose of testing the employer's hiring practices for discrimination.

third party administrator (TPA). A company that administers a health insurance plan but does not provide any insurance against the risk involved.

time off plan. An exception to the *Fair Labor Standards Act's* general overtime rules that allows an employer under certain narrow circumstances to award compensatory time to nonexempt employees in lieu of time-and-one-half for overtime.

Tip Rate Alternative Commitment (TRAC). An agreement between the IRS and an employer in the food and beverage industry under which the employer agrees to establish an educational program and reporting procedures designed to promote accurate tip reporting by employees, and the IRS agrees to assess payroll taxes based on tips as reported by employees.

Tip Rate Determination Agreement (TRDA). An agreement between the IRS and an employer under which the IRS and the employer determine and agree in advance on the rate of tips to be reported by employees. TRDAs require at least 75 percent of the affected employees to join in the agreement.

Title VII. The sections of the *Civil Rights Act* that prohibit discrimination in employment.

top hat plan. *See excess benefit plan.*

trade secret. Business information, such as a customer list, formula or process, that has value because it is not widely known and its confidentiality is protected.

U

unemployment insurance. A federal/state system funded by employers, under which employees who have involuntarily lost their jobs receive temporary benefits.

unfair labor practice (ULP). Conduct by an employer or a union that violates the *National Labor Relations Act*.

Uniformed Services Employment and Reemployment Rights Act (USERRA). USERRA requires service members on military leave to continue to be carried as employees for certain benefit and seniority purposes and to be reemployed when they return from military leave.

union security clause. A provision in a collective bargaining agreement that protects union membership or revenue. A union security clause may require that employees be union members in order to be hired (closed shop), that they join a union after being hired (union shop), or that, in the case of nonunion employees, they pay dues as if they were members (agency shop).

union shop. A type of union security arrangement under which employees are required to join a union within a specified time after hire.

V

variable pay. Pay, such as bonuses or commissions, that may vary in amount depending on productivity, company profitability, or other factors.

vested. Nonforfeitable. When pension plan benefits are vested, they belong to the employee even if employment ends or the plan is terminated.

vicarious liability. *See direct liability.*

Vietnam Era Veterans' Readjustment Assistance Act (VEVRAA). VEVRAA prohibits most federal contractors from discriminating against Vietnam-era and disabled veterans and requires affirmative action to ensure equal employment opportunity.

W

W-2. The federal tax form employers issue to employees and also send to the IRS to report wages.

weekly benefit amount (WBA). For unemployment insurance purposes, the amount a claimant is entitled to (but for any disqualification) as determined from his or her base period wages.

Welfare-to-Work tax credit. A federal tax credit allowed to employers who hire long-term family assistance recipients.

whistleblower. An employee who discloses fraud or other wrongdoing by an employer.

white collar exemptions. Exemptions from the *Fair Labor Standards Act's* overtime requirements for persons employed in bona fide executive, administrative, or professional capacities and as outside salespersons.

withholding order. A court order in a domestic relations case, similar to a garnishment, requiring an employer to withhold and turn over a portion of an employee's earnings to cover the employee's family support obligations.

Worker Adjustment and Retraining Notification Act (WARN). A federal law that requires employers with 100 or more employees to give 60 days' advance notice of a mass layoff or plant closing.

workers' compensation. A state statutory arrangement funded by employers, under which employees who suffer work-related injuries or occupational illnesses receive benefits while out of work or while limited in their ability to work. Death benefits are provided to dependents of employees who are killed. The statutes also typically provide for payment of medical expenses, funeral benefits, and vocational rehabilitation.

work-for-hire. A product created or invented by an employee for his or her employer, the copyright or patent rights of which belong to the employer.

work-sharing agreement. An agreement between the *Equal Employment Opportunity Commission* and a state or local *Fair Employment Practice Agency* that allocates responsibility for processing charges of employment discrimination. Work-sharing agreements usually provide that a filing with one agency constitutes a filing with the other agency as well.

Work Opportunity Tax Credit (WOTC). A federal tax credit allowed to employers who hire persons in targeted groups–recipients of assistance under TANF, veterans, ex-felons, summer youths, food stamp recipients, and SSI recipients.

wrongful discharge. *See abusive discharge.*

–Appendix A–
REQUIRED FEDERAL POSTINGS

A number of federal, state, and local employment laws require covered employers to post notices at the workplace informing employees of their rights under those laws. Failure to post exposes the employer to civil and criminal penalties. It may also affect rights under the particular law involved, such as extending the employee's time to file a claim. Posters are generally available from the government agency charged with enforcement. (Private publishers also sell sets of posters.)

Listed below are the various *federal* posting requirements, followed by citations to the statute or regulation that imposes the requirement. The website where the poster may be downloaded is also listed. Employers should check with *state* and *local* agencies to determine whether additional posting requirements apply.

Discrimination
29 C.F.R. Sec. 1601.30(a)
www.dol.gov/esa/regs/compliance/posters/eeo.htm

Discrimination/Affirmative Action by
Federal Contractors and Subcontractors
EO 11246
41 C.F.R. Sec. 60-1.4(a)(1)
41 C.F.R. Sec. 60-250.5(a)(9)
41 C.F.R. Sec. 60-741.5(a)(4)
www.dol.gov/esa/regs/compliance/posters/eeo.htm

Family and Medical Leave
29 C.F.R. Sec. 825.300(a)
www.dol.gov/esa/regs/compliance/posters/fmla.htm

Migrant and Seasonal Workers
29 U.S.C. Sec.1821(b)
29 C.F.R. Sec. 500.75(c)
www.dol.gov/esa/regs/compliance/posters/mspaensp.htm

Occupational Safety and Health
29 U.S.C. Sec. 657 (c)(1)
29 C.F.R. Sec. 1903.2(a)(1)
www.osha-slc.gov/Publications/poster.html

Polygraph Protection
29 C.F.R. Sec. 801.6
www.dol.gov/esa/regs/compliance/posters/eppa.htm

Wages-and-Hour Requirements
29 C.F.R. Sec. 516.4
www.dol.gov/esa/regs/compliance/posters/flsa.htm

–Appendix B–
FEDERAL STATUTORY THRESHOLDS

Many, but not all, federal laws relating to employment only apply if the employer has a specified, minimum number of employees. *Title VII* of the federal *Civil Rights Act*, for example, applies to employers with fifteen or more employees. The thresholds of most of the federal statutes discussed in this book are listed below.

Author's Caution: *There are two notes of caution. First, counting employees to determine whether a federal statute is applicable is not as straightforward as it may seem. See Chapter 14 for a discussion of the issues involved. Second, states and local jurisdictions have passed their own laws, often with lower thresholds, addressing many of the same matters covered by federal statutes. So just because a federal statute is inapplicable does not mean that the conduct in question is unregulated.*

ADA (Americans with Disabilities Act)—*15 or more employees*
ADEA (Age Discrimination in Employment Act)—*20 or more employees*
COBRA (health insurance continuation)—*20 or more employees*
DFWA (Drug-Free Workplace Act)—*federal contractors and grant recipients*
ECPA (Electronic Communications Privacy Act)—*all employers*
EPPA (Electronic Privacy Protection Act)—*all employers*
ERISA (Employee Retirement Income Security Act)—*all employers*

FCRA (Fair Credit Reporting Act)—*all employers*

FLSA (Fair Labor Standards Act)—*most employers with annual sales volumes of $250,000 or more, and construction companies, laundries, cleaners, tailors, hospitals, nursing homes, schools, and other institutions regardless of sales volume*

FMLA (Family and Medical Leave Act)—*50 or more employees*

HIPAA (Health Insurance Portability and Accountability Act)—*all employers*

IRCA (Immigration Reform and Control Act)—*all employers as to eligibility to work and I-9 requirements; 4 or more employees as to non-discrimination provisions*

OSHA (Occupational Safety and Health Act)—*all employers as to compliance with health and safety standards; 11 or more employees as to record-keeping, posting, and reporting requirements*

Section 1981—*all employers*

Title VII—*15 or more employees*

WARN—(Worker Adjustment and Retraining Notification Act)—*100 or more employees*

–Appendix C–
EMPLOYER'S FEDERAL TAX CALENDAR

Listed below are some of the typical *federal* tax reporting and related deadlines faced by calendar-year employer and calendar-year employee benefit plans. For deadlines that fall on a weekend or holiday, the actual due date is usually the following business day. Deadlines for transmitting withheld income taxes are shown for quarterly filers only. As with other employment-related laws and regulations, these deadlines are subject to change and to exceptions.

For more information, see IRS Publication 509, available at **www.irs.gov**.

Date	Form	Description
Jan 15	1040ES	For individuals, 4th installment of prior year's estimated income tax due to IRS
Jan 31	W-2	Statements of prior year's compensation and withholdings due to employees
	1099-MISC	Statements of prior year's compensation due to independent contractors
	940	Return of prior year's unemployment tax due to IRS
	941	Return of withheld income tax and FICA for 4th quarter of prior year due to IRS

Feb 28	W-2 & W-3	Copy A of W-2s for prior year, with transmittal form W-3, due to Social Security Administration
	1099-MISC	Copy of 1099-MISC for prior year due to IRS
Mar 15	1120 or 1120-A	For C corporations and for partnerships and LLCs that have elected taxation as corporations, income tax return for prior year due to IRS
	1120S	For S corporations, income tax return for prior year due to IRS
	K-1	For S corporations, partnerships, and LLCs that have elected taxation as partnerships, statement of distributions due to shareholders/partners/members
Apr 15	1040	For individuals, income tax return for prior year due to IRS
	1065	For partnerships and LLCs that have elected taxation as partnerships, income tax return for prior year due to IRS
	1040ES	For individuals, 1st installment of current year's estimated income tax due to IRS
	8109	For C corporations, 1st installment of current year's estimated income tax due to IRS
Apr 30	941	Return of withheld income tax and FICA for 1st quarter of current year due to IRS
May 15	990	For exempt organizations, information return for prior year due to IRS

Jun 15	1040ES	For individuals, 2nd installment of estimated income tax for current year due to IRS
	8109	For C corporations, 2nd installment of current year's estimated income tax due to IRS
Jul 31	941	Return of withheld income tax and FICA for 2nd quarter of current year due to IRS
	5500 or 5500-EZ	For employee benefit plans, 5500 series of forms due to IRS
Sep 15	1040ES	For individuals, 3rd installment of estimated income tax for current year due to IRS
	8109	For C corporations, 3rd installment of estimated income tax for current year due to IRS
Oct 31	941	Return of withheld income tax and FICA for 3rd quarter of current year due to IRS
Dec 15	8109	For C corporations, 4th installment of estimated income tax for current year due to IRS

–Appendix D–
LEGAL HOLIDAYS

The federal government prescribes *legal* holidays. (5 U.S.C. Secs. 6103, 6104 and Executive Order 11582.) However, the only *legal* effect is on government employees, mail delivery, and, in some cases, banks. Other employers are not required to be closed unless they have signed collective bargaining agreements or individual employment contracts obligating them to honor legal holidays. When a holiday falls on a weekend, the following Monday (or in some cases the preceding Friday) is the day of observance.

Please see the following page for the legal holiday list.

New Year's Day—January 1

Inauguration Day—January 20 of each fourth year (2005, 2009, etc.) for District of Columbia employees and for federal employees employed in the District of Columbia; Montgomery and Prince George's Counties; Maryland, Arlington, and Fairfax Counties; and Alexandria and Falls Church Cities, Virginia

Martin Luther King Day—third Monday in January

Washington's Birthday—third Monday in February

Memorial Day—last Monday in May

Independence Day—July 4

Labor Day—first Monday in September

Columbus Day—second Monday in October

Veterans Day—November 11

Thanksgiving Day—fourth Thursday in November

Christmas Day—December 25

–Appendix E–
INTERNET RESOURCES

The Internet has become a ubiquitous source of information—some useful, some not. The U.S. Government has been a leader in providing information, opening to the world its vast collection of laws, regulations, forms, policies, and guidelines. For those readers who want more information on an employment issue, who have a question not explicitly answered in the book, or who need primary source material, this appendix lists the websites of most of the federal agencies whose activities touch upon the employment relationship, as well as nongovernment organizations that have proved helpful in the past.

U.S. GOVERNMENT OFFICES

ADMINISTRATIVE OFFICE OF U.S. COURTS
Homepage
www.uscourts.gov
Links to federal circuit, district court, and bankruptcy court opinions
www.uscourts.gov/links.html

CITIZENSHIP AND IMMIGRATION SERVICES, BUREAU OF
Homepage
www.immigration.gov/graphics/aboutus/index.htm

EQUAL EMPLOYMENT OPPORTUNITY COMMISSION

Text of laws enforced by EEOC; EEOC regulations, guidelines, and policies

www.eeoc.gov

FEDERAL TRADE COMMISSION

Fair Credit Reporting Act information

www.ftc.gov/os/statutes/fcrajump.htm

Prescribed form of notice of rights that employers must give to employees in connection with use of a consumer report under the Fair Credit Reporting Act

www.ftc.gov/os/statutes/2summary.htm

GENERAL SERVICES ADMINISTRATION

Federal Consumer Information Center

www.info.gov

Links to federal government agencies and information

http://firstgov.gov

Federal forms

www.fedforms.gov

GOVERNMENT PRINTING OFFICE

Access or links to U.S. Code, Code of Federal Regulations, and Federal Register

www.access.gpo.gov

Government Information Locator Service (GILS); locates publicly available federal information resources, including electronic information resources

www.access.gpo.gov/su_docs/gils/whatgils.html

Code of Federal Regulations

www.access.gpo.gov/nara/cfr/cfr-table-search.html

HEALTH & HUMAN SERVICES, DEPARTMENT OF
New hire report forms and information for multistate employers
www.acf.dhhs.gov/programs/cse/newhire/employ/emult.htm

HOUSE OF REPRESENTATIVES
Homepage
www.house.gov

U.S. Code
http://uscode.house.gov

JUSTICE, DEPARTMENT OF
Homepage
www.usdoj.gov

Americans with Disabilities Act technical assistance manuals and information
www.usdoj.gov/crt/ada/publicat.htm

LABOR, DEPARTMENT OF
Homepage
www.dol.gov

Employment law guide
www.dol.gov/asp/programs/guide

Statistical information about employment provided by the Bureau of Labor Statistics (BLS)
www.bls.gov

Information about programs under the jurisdiction of the Wage-and-Hour Division (WHD) of the Employment Standards Administration (ESA), including minimum wage, overtime pay, record keeping, and child labor requirements of the Fair Labor Standards Act, Employee Polygraph Protection Act, Family and Medical Leave Act, and the wage garnishment provisions of Consumer Credit Protection Act

www.dol.gov/esa/aboutesa/main.htm

Information about programs under the jurisdiction of the Office of Federal Contract Compliance Programs (OFCCP), including EO 11246, Rehabilitation Act and Vietnam Era Veterans' Readjustment Assistance Act.

www.dol.gov/esa/ofcp_org.htm

General information for employers provided by the Employment and Training Administration (ETA)

www.doleta.gov

Information about pension plans governed by ERISA

www.dol.gov/ebsa

Information about programs under the jurisdiction of the Office of Small Business Programs (OSMB), including procurement opportunities for small, disadvantaged, and women-owned small businesses and small business regulatory compliance

www.dol.gov/osbp/welcome.html

Information about programs under the jurisdiction of the Veterans' Employment and Training Services (VETS), including securing employment and rights and benefits of veterans, reservists, and National Guard members

www.dol.gov/vets

Information about programs under the jurisdiction of the Women's Bureau (WB)
www.dol.gov/wb

Occupational Safety and Health Administration (OSHA) homepage
www.osha.gov

LIBRARY OF CONGRESS

Homepage
www.loc.gov/homepage/lchp.html

Copyright information and forms
www.loc.gov/copyright

Information about Congress, including pending bills and scheduled hearings; Congressional Record
http://thomas.loc.gov

NATIONAL ARCHIVES

Homepage
www.nara.gov

Executive Orders
www.nara.gov/fedreg/eo.html-top

Presidential Documents
www.archives.gov/federal_register/presidential_documents /website_guide

NATIONAL LABOR RELATIONS BOARD

Homepage
www.nlrb.gov

NLRB rules and regulations
www.nlrb.gov/rr.html

NLRB decisions
www.nlrb.gov/decision.html

NLRB manuals
www.nlrb.gov/manuals.html

PATENT & TRADEMARK OFFICE

Patent and trademark information, including searchable databases
www.uspto.gov

PENSION BENEFIT GUARANTY CORPORATION

Regulations, information, and forms relating to pension plans
www.pbgc.gov

SENATE

Homepage
www.senate.gov

SECURITIES & EXCHANGE COMMISSION

Homepage
www.sec.gov

Electronic Data Gathering, Analysis, and Retrieval system (EDGAR); searchable database of submissions by companies and others who are required by law to file forms with the SEC
www.sec.gov/edgarhp.htm

SMALL BUSINESS ADMINISTRATION

Homepage
www.sba.gov

Forms and information for small businesses
www.sba.gov/lib/library.html

Links to state government homepages
www.sbaonline.sba.gov/world/states.html

SOCIAL SECURITY ADMINISTRATION

Homepage
www.ssa.gov

Business Services Online (BSO)
www.ssa.gov/employer/bsohbnew.htm

SUPREME COURT

Homepage
www.supremecourtus.gov

TAX COURT, U.S.

Homepage
www.ustaxcourt.gov

TREASURY, DEPARTMENT OF

Homepage
www.treas.gov

IRS homepage, including forms and publications
www.irs.gov

Office of Small and Disadvantaged Business Utilization (OSDBU)
www.treas.gov/sba

WHITE HOUSE

Homepage
www.whitehouse.gov

ORGANIZATIONS

ADA INFORMATION CENTER
Training, information, and technical assistance on ADA to businesses, consumers, and state and local governments
www.adainfo.org

ALEXANDER HAMILTON INSTITUTE
Employment law resources
www.ahipubs.com

AMERICAN ARBITRATION ASSOCIATION
Homepage
www.adr.org/index2.1.jsp

AMERICAN BAR ASSOCIATION
List of ABA publications of general interest, including several on employment-related issues
www.abanet.org

AMERICAN LEGAL PUBLISHING
Municipal codes
http://amlegal.com/online_library.htm

AMERICAN MANAGEMENT ASSOCIATION
Homepage
www.amanet.org

CHERRY ENGINEERING SUPPORT SERVICES INC.
Technical information for complying with the ADA
www.adata.org

FEDERATION OF TAX ADMINISTRATORS
Links to state tax forms
www.taxadmin.org/fta/link/forms.html

FINDLAW

Homepage
www.findlaw.com

Labor and employment law topics
www.findlaw.com/01topics/27labor/index.html

U.S. Constitution, U.S. Code, Code of Federal Regulations, Supreme Court opinions, and federal circuit court opinions
www.findlaw.com/casecode

State legal resources
www.findlaw.com/11stategov

GENERAL CODE PUBLISHERS

Municipal codes
www.generalcode.com/webcode2.html

HIEROS GAMOS

Law-related information and links
www.hg.org

HR COMPLY

Internet-based reference tools and compliance training
www.hrcomply.com

JAMS

Homepage
www.jamsadr.com/home.asp

Employment dispute rules and procedures
www.jamsadr.com/employment_guide-2003.asp

LAW MEMO

Law-related information and links
www.lawmemo.com

LEXIS-NEXIS
Homepage
www.lexis-nexis.com

Municipal codes
www.bpcnet.com/codes.htm

MARTINDALE-HUBBELL
Lawyer and law firm locator
www.martindale.com

MICHIE
State codes
www.michie.com

NATIONAL CENTER FOR STATE COURTS
Homepage
www.ncsconline.org

NATIONAL ASSOCIATION OF SECRETARIES OF STATE
Homepage
www.nass.org

PIPER RESOURCES
Links to state and local government websites
www.piperinfo.com/state/index.cfm

PRAIRIENET
Links to state statutes
www.prairienet.org/~scruffy/f.htm

RESIDENT AGENTS
Corporate resident agent information for U.S. and Canada
www.residentagentinfo.com

SOCIETY FOR HUMAN RESOURCE MANAGEMENT
Homepage
www.shrm.org

SPHINX PUBLISHING
Homepage
www.sphinxlegal.com

U.S. CHAMBER OF COMMERCE
Homepage
www.uschamber.org

WESTLAW
Lawyer locator
www.wld.com

–Appendix F–
TABLE OF FEDERAL STATUTES AND REGULATIONS

The following appendix contains various federal statutes and regulations that are applicable to the employment setting. The material is presented by *subject matter* and followed by its *coverage* and a *summary description*. The *statutory citation* (United States Code, or Public Law) and/or the *regulation or rule citation* (Code of Federal Regulation or Executive Order) follows. The abbreviation or common name of the law follows the citation.

Age Discrimination
Employers with 20 or more employees. Prohibits discrimination in employment against employees 40 years of age or more because of age; imposes special procedural requirements for releases of ADEA claims by individual employees and for groups who are offered exit incentives.
    29 U.S.C. Sec. 621(*ADEA*) and (*OWBPA*)
    29 C.F.R. Sec. 625

Arbitration
Employers engaged in interstate commerce (except in transportation industries). Provides for enforcement of arbitration agreements.
    9 U.S.C. Sec. 1 (*FAA*)

Benefit Plans

All employers. Regulates employee benefit plans.

29 U.S.C. Sec. 1001

26 U.S.C. Sec. 401 (*ERISA*)

29 C.F.R. Sec. 2509

26 C.F.R. Sec. 1.401

Child Labor

All employers. Prohibits *oppressive child labor*, defined generally as employing any child under age 16 regardless of occupation (with certain exceptions) and employing a child between the ages 16-18 in mining, manufacturing, or other hazardous industries.

29 U.S.C. Sec. 212 (*FLSA*)

29 C.F.R. Sec. 570

All employers. Prohibits employment of children in the production of child pornography for distribution in interstate commerce.

18 U.S.C. Sec. 2251

Child Support

States. Requires states to implement a *state plan* for enforcement of child support, including enforcement of medical expense obligations through enrollment of children in group health insurance available through employment.

42 U.S.C. Sec. 654

45 C.F.R. Sec. 302

Civil/Human Rights, generally

Employers with 15 or more employees. Prohibits discrimination in employment because of race, color, religion, sex, or national origin.

42 U.S.C. Sec. 2000e (*Title VII*)

29 C.F.R. Sec. 1601

All employers. Extends to all persons within the U.S. the same right to make and enforce contracts as is enjoyed by white citizens.

42 U.S.C. Sec. 1981 (*Section 1981*)

Government contractors with contracts over $10,000 as to non-discrimination requirements; government contractors with 50 or more employees and with contracts of $50,000 or more as to affirmative action requirements. Prohibits discrimination in employment because of race, color, religion, sex, or national origin; requires affirmative action plans.

> EO 11246
> 41 C.F.R. Sec. 60-1

Consumer/Credit Reports

All employers. Regulates obtaining and use of consumer reports.

> 15 U.S.C. Sec. 1681a (*FCRA*)
> 16 C.F.R. Sec. 600

Court Appearance Leave

All employers. Prohibits docking salary of employees who are exempt under FLSA for absences caused by court attendances; permits offset to extent employee is paid as witness.

> 29 C.F.R. Sec. 541.118

Disability Discrimination

Employers with 15 or more employees. Prohibits discrimination in employment against qualified persons with disabilities; requires reasonable accommodation of disabled persons.

> 42 U.S.C. Sec. 12102 (*ADA*)
> 29 C.F.R. Sec. 1630

Government contractors with contracts over $10,000 as to nondiscrimination requirements; government contractors with 50 or more employees and with contracts of $50,000 or more as to affirmative action requirements. Prohibits discrimination in employment against qualified persons with disabilities; requires reasonable accommodation of disabled persons.

> 29 U.S.C. Sec. 793 (*Rehabilitation Act*)
> 41 C.F.R. Sec. 60-741

Domestic Partners
All employers. Defines *spouse* as a person of the opposite sex for purposes of pension benefits; gives states choice not to recognize another state's same-sex marriages.

    1 U.S.C. Sec. 7

    28 U.S.C. Sec. 1738C (*DOMA*)

Driving Records
States. Regulates release of personal information obtained by states in connection with driving records.

    18 U.S.C. 2721

Drug and Alcohol Testing
Federal grant recipients and most federal contractors. Requires employers to establish and administer policies to ensure workplace free of controlled substances.

    41 U.S.C. Sec. 701 (*Drug-Free Workplace Act*)

Electronic Monitoring
All employers. Prohibits interception of wire communications without consent of at least one party.

    18 U.S.C. Sec. 2510 (*ECPA*)

Equal Pay
All employers. Prohibits wage discrimination on basis of sex.

    29 U.S.C. Sec. 206 (*FLSA*)

    29 C.F.R. Sec. 1620

Family & Medical Leave
Employers with 50 or more employees. Requires employers to provide up to 12 weeks' unpaid leave per year for employees with serious health conditions; to care for spouse, child or parent with serious health condition; or birth or adoption of a child; requires employers to continue health insurance coverage during leave.

    29 U.S.C. Sec. 2601 (*FMLA*)

    29 C.F.R. Sec. 825

Foreign Employers

Foreign states. Immunizes foreign states from suit by any court in U.S. except for claims arising out of commercial activities.

28 U.S.C. Sec. 1602 (*FSIA*)

Garnishments

All employers. Regulates garnishments; prohibits employers from firing employees for single garnishments.

15 U.S.C. Sec. 1671
29 C.F.R. Sec. 870
Federal Rule of Civil Procedure Rule 69

Government Contractors

Employers with 50 or more employees and with U.S. government contracts of $50,000 or more as to all requirements; employers with U.S. government contracts of more than $10,000 as to nondiscrimination requirements. Requires inclusion of disability nondiscrimination provisions in contract; prohibits discrimination on account of disability and requires reasonable accommodation; requires affirmative action plan and periodic compliance reports.

29 U.S.C. Sec. 793 (*Rehabilitation Act*)
41 C.F.R. Sec. 60-1

Employers with 50 or more employees and with U.S. government contracts of $50,000 or more as to all requirements; employers with U.S. government contracts of more than $10,000 as to nondiscrimination requirements. Prohibits discrimination against Vietnam-era veterans; requires affirmative action plan and periodic compliance reports.

38 U.S.C. Sec. 4212 (*VEVRAA*)
41 C.F.R. Sec. 60-1

Employers with 50 or more employees and with U.S. government contracts of $50,000 or more as to all requirements; employers with U.S. government contracts of more than $10,000 as to nondiscrimination requirements. Requires inclusion of Title VII-type nondiscrimination provisions in contract; prohibits discrimination on basis of race, color, religion, sex, or national origin; requires affirmative action plan and periodic compliance reports.

EO 11246

41 C.F.R. Sec. 60-1

U.S. government agencies. Prohibits agencies from contracting with employers that permanently replace lawfully striking employees.

EO 12954

Government contractors. Subjects government contractors who employ illegal aliens to debarment.

EO 12989

Government contractors. Requires government contractors to post notices informing employees of right-to-work provisions of federal labor laws.

EO 13201

Health Insurance Continuation

Employers with group health plans and with 20 or more employees. Requires employers to provide continuing coverage to participating employee or family member, at cost of participant, after *qualifying event* such as death of employee, termination of employment (except for gross misconduct), divorce, or child ceasing to be dependent.

26 U.S.C. Sec. 4980B

29 U.S.C. Sec. 1161 (*COBRA*)

Health Insurance Portability

All employers with group health insurance plans. Requires plans to limit preexisting condition exclusions based on prior coverage with another employer; requires special enrollment periods and requires the furnishing of certificates of prior coverage.

29 U.S.C. Sec. 1181 (*HIPAA*)

29 C.F.R. Sec. 2590

All employers with group health insurance plans. Implements the privacy requirements of Administrative Simplification subtitle of HIPAA by regulating use and disclosure of *protected health information*.
45 C.F.R. Sec. 160.101

Holidays
U.S. and D.C. governments and certain banks. Establishes legal holidays.
5 U.S.C. Sec. 6103
EO 11582

Immigration
All employers as to eligibility to work and I-9 requirements; employers with 4 or more employees as to non-discrimination provisions. Requires employers to obtain proof of eligibility to work from all applicants; requires employers to complete and retain Form I-9; prohibits employers from discriminating because of citizenship status or national origin.
8 U.S.C. Sec. 1324a (*IRCA*)
8 C.F.R. Sec. 1

Government contractors. Subjects government contractors who knowingly employ illegal aliens to debarment.
EO 12989

Insider Trading
Publicly-traded companies. Requires principal executive and financial officers to certify periodic financial reports; requires chief executive and chief financial officers to forfeit incentive compensation received after violation of securities laws; prohibits insider trading during "blackout" periods; prohibits most personal loans to executives and directors.
P.L. 107-204 (*Sarbanes-Oxley Act*)

Involuntary Servitude

All employers. Prohibits slavery or involuntary servitude.
   U.S. Const., Amend. 13
   18 U.S.C. Secs. 1584, 1859

Income Tax (generally)

All employers. Imposes tax on taxable income of for-profit employers; allows deductions for various expenses, including employee wages and benefits; imposes tax withholding obligations on employers.
   26 U.S.C. Sec. 1 (*I.R.C.*)
   26 C.F.R. Sec. 1

Jury Duty

All employers. Prohibits docking salary of employees who are exempt under FLSA for absences caused by jury duty; permits offset to extent employee is paid as juror.
   29 C.F.R. Sec. 541.118

Labor Relations

All employers. Prohibits employers from interfering with employee unionizing efforts and other concerted activities for betterment of wages, working conditions.
   29 U.S.C. Sec. 151 (*NLRA*)
   29 C.F.R. Sec. 101

All employers. Requires employers who have financial dealings with unions, union officers or labor relations consultants to file Form LM-10 with Office of Labor-Management Standards; prohibits threats or use of force or violence to interfere with a union member's exercise of his rights.
   29 U.S.C. Sec. 401 (*LMRDA*)
   29 C.F.R. Sec. 401

Government contractors. Subjects government contractors to debarment for permanently replacing lawfully striking employees.
    EO 12954

Layoffs & Plant Closings
Employers with 100 or more employees. Requires employers to give 60 days' advance notice of mass layoffs or plant closings.
    29 U.S.C. Sec. 2101 (*WARN*)
    20 C.F.R. Sec. 639

Mail Privacy
All employers. Prohibits obstruction of mail correspondence.
    18 U.S.C. Sec. 1702

Medical Examinations
Employers with 15 or more employees. Prohibits most pre-employment medical examinations.
    42 U.S.C. Sec. 12102 (*ADA*)
    29 C.F.R. Sec. 1601

Migrant/Seasonal Workers
Farm labor contractors, agricultural employers, agricultural associations, and providers of migrant housing. Requires farm labor contractors to register withe the Dept. of Labor; requires all covered employers to furnish written terms of employment to migrant and seasonal workers, to post notice of statutory rights, and to comply with various wage-payment, safety and record-keeping provisions.
    29 U.S.C. Sec. 1801 (*MSPA*)
    29 C.F.R. Sec. 500

Military Service
All employers. Prohibits employers from discriminating against persons on the basis of U.S. military service (including National Guard); requires employers to re-employ persons who have left employment

for military service for 5 years or less, unless re-employment would be impossible, unreasonable or an undue hardship.

   38 U.S.C. Sec. 4301 (*USERRA*)

All employers. Prohibits docking salary of employees who are exempt under FLSA for absences caused by temporary military leave; permits offset to extent employee is paid for military service.

   29 C.F.R. Sec. 541.118

Government contractors with contracts over $10,000 as to non-discrimination requirements; government contractors with 50 or more employees and with contracts of $50,000 or more as to affirmative action requirements. Prohibits discrimination against Vietnam-era veterans; requires affirmative action plan and periodic compliance reports.

   38 U.S.C. Sec. 4212 (*VEVRAA*)
   41 C.F.R. Sec. 60-1

Occupational Safety & Health

All employers. Requires employers to provide employment free from recognized hazards; requires employers to comply with occupational and health standards promulgated by Secretary of Labor; imposes record-keeping, posting and reporting requirements on employers, with limited exceptions for employers with 10 or fewer employees and employers in certain industries; authorizes Secretary to review and approve state plans.

   29 U.S.C. Sec. 651 (*OSHA*)

Polygraph Protection

All employers. Generally prohibits employers from using lie detector tests on employees.

   29 U.S.C. Sec. 2001
   29 C.F.R. Sec. 801

Report of New Hires

States and all employers. Requires states to establish Directory of New Hires; requires employers to report new hires to state within 20 days after hiring; allows multistate employers to file all reports electronically with one state where they have employees.

   42 U.S.C. Sec. 653a

Right to Work

States. Authorizes states to prohibit union security clauses in collective bargaining agreements.

   29 U.S.C. Sec. 151

Substance Abuse Treatment

All employers. Imposes strict confidentiality requirements on substance abuse treatment records, such as those maintained in connection with employee assistance programs.

   42 U.S.C. Sec. 290dd-2
   42 C.F.R. Sec. 2.1

Tax Credits

All employers. Allows tax credit for wages paid to AFDC and TANF recipients.

   26 U.S.C. Sec. 51

Trade Secrets

All employers. Criminalizes unauthorized access to computers.

   18 U.S.C. Sec. 1830 (*CFAA*)

All employers. Criminalizes the theft of trade secrets relating to a product in interstate commerce.

   18 U.S.C. Sec. 1831 (*Economic Espionage Act*)

Unemployment Insurance
All employers except tax-exempt charities. Requires employers to pay FUTA tax to IRS to cover cost of administering unemployment insurance program.

26 U.S.C. Sec. 3301 (*FUTA*)

Wage-and-Hour Law
All employers. Prescribes minimum wage and overtime requirements for most employees except executives, administrators and professionals.

29 U.S.C. Sec. 201 (*FLSA*)

29 C.F.R. Sec. 500

Employers in bankruptcy. Gives priority treatment, subject to limitations, to employee claims against employers in bankruptcy for 90 days of past-due wages and 180 days of past-due benefit plan contributions.

11 U.S.C. Sec. 507

Whistleblower Protection
All employers. Prohibits retaliation against whistleblowers who bring claim under False Claims Act for employer fraud against the U.S. Government.

31 U.S.C. Sec. 3730 (*False Claims Act*)

Publicly-traded companies. Prohibits retaliation against employees for providing information or testifying in connection with an investigation of securities fraud.

P.L. 107-204 (*Sarbanes-Oxley Act*)

INDEX

ABOUT THE AUTHOR

Charles H. Fleischer has an undergraduate degree in political science from the University of Rochester in New York and a law degree (with honors) from the George Washington University in Washington, D.C. He is admitted to practice in Maryland and the District of Columbia and is a member of the law firm of Oppenheimer, Fleischer & Quiggle, P.C., Bethesda, Maryland. The firm's website is **www.OFQLaw.com**.

Fleischer was the principal author of the employer's petition for writ of certiorari and of the merits briefs in *Meritor Savings Bank v. Vinson*, the first Supreme Court case dealing with sexual harassment. He served as pro bono counsel in a suit against Montgomery County, Maryland, involving the Americans with Disabilities Act. He has advised numerous businesses and associations on employment law issues and he writes and speaks extensively on the topic.

Fleischer lives with his wife in Potomac, Maryland.